PRECISION BIDDING IN ACOL

Eric Crowhurst

PRECISION BIDDING IN ACOL

——————— ♠♠ ———————

PELHAM BOOKS
LONDON

First published in Great Britain by
Pelham Books Ltd
52 Bedford Square
London WC1B 3EF
OCTOBER 1974
SECOND IMPRESSION NOVEMBER 1976

ISBN 0 7207 0765 X

Printed in Great Britain by
Hollen Street Press Ltd at Slough
and bound by Dorstel Press at Harlow, Essex

CONTENTS

FOREWORD

Fashions change. This applies to bidding in bridge just as much as to women's clothes. The current trend in bidding is towards artificial club systems, but this is, of course, nothing new. Earlier generations of bridge players toyed with Vienna, Nottingham Club and Vanderbilt Club before returning to so-called 'natural' methods. The current best-sellers are the Blue Club and the Precision Club, and several bridge writers are attempting to cash in on the popular market by prescribing the artificial club system as the panacea for all our bidding troubles. However, there is little to suggest that this fashion trend will last any longer than the previous ones. It is, in fact, possible to draw a fairly close parallel between the Vienna system, with its weak one club, strong one no trump and asking bids, and the current favourite Precision system, with its weak one no trump, strong one club and asking bids. And very few partnerships use Vienna today.

One of the principal reasons for this particular swing to the artificial club is the phenomenal string of successes achieved by the famous Italian Blue Team in recent years. Fourteen world championships in the last seventeen years is a record which is unlikely ever to be equalled and, since the Italians have employed a series of club systems throughout this period, the doubtful conclusion has been drawn that therein lies the key to their success. This entirely overlooks the elementary fact that the Italian team has developed such good partnership understanding, such excellent judgement in competitive situations, and such first-rate card play technique that they would undoubtedly have won a good many tournaments playing the strong no trump, Stayman and Blackwood. Moreover, there is no evidence to suggest that they would not have won all their fourteen world championships if they had adopted a natural bidding system like Acol and developed and analysed it with their customary thoroughness.

This is neither the time nor the place for a diatribe against the various club systems. Suffice it to say that there is little evidence to indicate that any artificial club system can bid a random collection of bridge hands any more efficiently than a more natural system; in fact, it is possible to formulate an extremely powerful argument to suggest that, in a tough competitive game in which the opponents will attempt to disrupt your bidding communications as much as they possibly can, a bidding system which revolves around a strength-showing opening bid of one club is likely to be considerably less effective.

This is all hypothetical. However, one point is completely certain. Any experienced Acol player who is anxious to improve his bidding need not adopt a complex new system in order to do so: he can do just as well, and arguably considerably better, by putting in just a little more work on his existing bidding methods. He undoubtedly has at his disposal the framework of an extremely efficient bidding system, and sufficient additional accuracy for all practical purposes can be achieved by building on that framework. This is, in fact, the underlying theme of this book.

The Acol system has been favoured over the years by having a number of excellent writers among its supporters. Skid Simon, Iain Macleod, Terence Reese and Albert Dormer have all written convincing books on the subject, but the unfortunate fact remains that none of these works really goes far enough. They all explain the philosophy of the system, and they all deal in reasonable detail with the opening bid, the first response and, to a lesser extent, the opener's rebid. Subsequent bids are rarely covered, however, and, in my view, much of the apparent superiority which the artificial club systems can claim on certain hands arises from the fact that Acol has never been adequately developed and analysed. Even the most ardent supporter of the system is forced to admit that certain Acol sequences are distinctly hazy. For example:

North	South
1◇	1♠
2♣	3♣

Are you competely certain that you know what 3♣ means in this sequence? It is clearly a try for game, but is South showing a club guard and looking for 3NT, or is he making a trial bid for game in spades?

North	South
1♠	2♡
2♠	2NT
3◇	

What do you think North is trying to convey with his 3◇ bid in this sequence? Is it forcing, showing a feature in diamonds and continuing the search for the correct game contract? Or is it a weak bid, attempting to sign off in the safest part score? And if it is an attempted sign-off, does 3◇ show four or five diamonds?

One final example.

North	South
2NT	3♣
3♠	4♣

Most players agree that 3♣ over 2NT is a Baron response, asking the opener to bid his four-card suits in ascending order. But what about South's 4♣ bid? Is it a cue bid agreeing spades? Or a natural bid showing a four-card club suit and seeking a 4-4 club fit for slam purposes? Or does 4♣ show a five-card club suit?

To my mind, if all the ambiguous sequences of this kind can be resolved and if a number of hitherto idle sequences can be harnessed and given a useful meaning, Acol will take its rightful place alongside the most accurate and effective bidding systems of all time; what is more, it will do so without necessitating prodigious feats of memory on the part of anyone who uses it.

This book on Acol is designed to carry on where the earlier ones left off. Its aim is to discuss in some detail every sequence of bidding which is likely to occur in an uncontested auction. The emphasis is on the basic structure and framework of the system and, while you will find one or two specialised conventions suggested to fill obvious gaps in certain areas of bidding, this book is not merely a collection of gadgets and gimmicks: once you have a firm grasp of the fundamentals of the system, you will be in a good position to graft on your own particular favourite pieces of bidding gadgetry.

You will notice that this book only deals with uncontested auctions. The unrealistic assumption throughout these pages is that the opponents remain obligingly silent and that you and your partner have the stage to yourselves. This is unfortunate, but I found it completely impossible to cover the many various situations which arise when the opponents intervene without expanding the book to unmanageable proportions. If my publishers agree, I hope to produce a second volume to cover the contested auctions in due course; in the meantime, I am certain that you will be better prepared to hold your own in competitive auctions if you have a thorough understanding of the meaning of your selected sequence in a clear run.

The book is divided into five parts: The Opening Bid, The First Response, The Opener's Second Bid, The Responder's Second Bid, and The Development of the Auction. Finally, there is a unique index which attempts to list in a logical order all the uncontested bidding sequences likely to occur at the table and which tells you where you can find a detailed discussion of each sequence within the main body of the book.

My sincere thanks are due to my good friend and bridge partner, Alan Wardman, who spent many hours checking through my first draft of the book and making many helpful suggestions.

ERIC CROWHURST
1974

Part One

THE OPENING BID

♠♠

James Thurber once suggested that the principal merit of his writing was that he appeared always to have started from the beginning and to have reached the end by way of the middle. Since this would be an equally good testimonial for a bridge book, this first section follows the recommended pattern by starting from the beginning, considering every Acol opening bid from one club to four no trumps. The fact that this section constitutes as much as one quarter of what claims to be an advanced book on bidding need not give rise to alarm and despondency: for the sake of tidiness, the chapters relating to 1NT, 2NT and opening two bids also include a detailed study of the subsequent bidding.

Part 1 is divided into five chapters.

CHAPTER 1. *One of a suit.* This includes a summary of the principles governing the choice of which suit to open, and an enquiry into the mysteries surrounding the necessary evil known as the 'prepared club'.

CHAPTER 2. *One no trump.* This chapter runs quickly through the factors which you should take into account when you are deciding the strength of your 1NT opening bid. It follows with a critical examination of the usual structure of responses to 1NT, including a brief introduction to an important new development in this field: the transfer bid.

CHAPTER 3. *Two no trumps.* The bidding after 2NT is an area of Acol which is particularly badly defined and inefficient: in fact, just the sort of area which is scheduled for redevelopment in this book. This chapter takes a critical look at the normal responses to 2NT; it then goes on to suggest an improved structure of responses which, while basically similar to existing methods, will give a sharper definition and a new clarity to the exploratory sequences after a 2NT opening bid.

CHAPTER 4. *Forcing opening bids.* After a fairly brief exposition of the bidding following a 2♣ opening bid or an Acol Two Bid, this chapter proposes a new approach to opening two bids. The prototype multi-purpose 2◇ bid is unveiled. This allows you to enjoy the advantages of weak two bids in the major suits, and also provides a simple system for dealing with Acol Twos and with the notorious blind spot of the Acol system – the powerful three-suited hand.

CHAPTER 5. *Pre-emptive opening bids.* This chapter discusses the general philosophy of pre-emptive bidding and investigates the best use for opening bids of 3NT, 4♣ and 4◇.

1. ONE OF A SUIT

WHICH SUIT TO OPEN

Other worthy text books have devoted page after page to what you should open when your hand is not suitable either for an opening bid of 1NT or for a strength-showing two bid. Nevertheless, an alarmingly large number of bidding mishaps which occur at the table can be directly attributed to a poor choice of opening bid. Although this book is not strictly designed to deal with elementary bidding situations, therefore, it will do no harm to run quickly through the basic principles governing the choice of which suit to open, occasionally adding one or two new thoughts as they come to mind.

(a) *With only one four-card or longer suit*, there is rarely any problem: the only occasion on which you do not open with your suit is where you have a 4-3-3-3 hand with 12–14 points and only three clubs.

♠ A 7 2
♥ A Q 10 4
♦ 10 7 5
♣ K 8 6

This hand is a good advertisement for the weak no trump. If your 1NT bid at the prevailing vulnerability would be strong, however, you should not follow general principles by opening with your longest suit: an opening bid of 1♥ would leave you without resource if partner chose to respond 2♣ or 2♦, for to rebid 2NT would guarantee 15 or 16 points and to raise partner's minor suit would be an appalling distortion on such a balanced hand. The only solution to the problem is to open 1♣; this is one of the few occasions on which it is correct to open with what is generally referred to as a 'prepared' club.

(b) *With two five-card suits*, the general rule is that you should open with the higher-ranking suit first.

♠ 7
♥ A Q 8 6 3
♦ J 2
♣ K Q 7 5 4

Open 1♥. There is a risk, of course, that you might never be able to show your five-card club suit, for you are not strong enough to reverse and you will have to rebid 2♥ if partner makes the awkward response of 2♦. However, this is a lesser risk than opening 1♣ for, if the auction starts 1♣–1♠–2♣, your excellent five-card heart suit might be lost forever.

A possible exception to the general rule occurs when your two suits are clubs and spades.

♠ A Q 10 7 3
♡ 8
◇ Q 4
♣ K Q 10 6 5

Many experts would recommend an opening bid of 1♣ on this hand, arguing that this will permit you to introduce your other suit at the one level and to show your exact distribution economically in sequences of this kind:

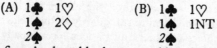

$$\begin{array}{llll} \text{(A)} & 1\clubsuit & 1\heartsuit & \qquad \text{(B)} & 1\clubsuit & 1\heartsuit \\ & 1\spadesuit & 2\diamondsuit & & 1\spadesuit & 1\text{NT} \\ & 2\spadesuit & & & 2\spadesuit & \end{array}$$

This sounds fine. At the table, however, things have an unpleasant habit of not working out according to plan and, if the opponents intervene over 1♣, the opener may find himself forced to climb to dizzy heights if he is anxious to show his distribution. Since the opponents will find it more difficult to creep into the auction over 1♠ than over 1♣, therefore, there is a strong case for temporarily concealing the club suit and opening a 5–5 hand with 1♠; partner will almost certainly be interested in learning about your five-card spade suit as soon as possible and, on a weakish hand on which you would be reluctant to make three bids if the going becomes sticky, the best practical solution is to open 1♠ and rebid 2♣ over a red-suit response by partner.

♠ A Q 10 7 3
♡ A Q
◇ 8
♣ K Q 10 6 5

On this stronger hand, the case for opening with the technically correct bid of 1♣ is more compelling. The point is that you will now be pleased to make three bids in order to show your exact distribution, even if intervention by the opponents forces the bidding up a little; furthermore, the fact that you are so much stronger makes it less likely that the opponents will stage an effective counter-attack.

(c) *With five-four distribution in two non-touching suits*, you should always open with the longer suit first, bearing in mind that you will not always be able to show the second suit unless you have the values for a reverse.

♠ A J 9 6 3   ◇ A K J 10
♡ 7 2   ♣ 6 5

Open 1♠, intending to rebid 2◇ over a response of 1NT or 2♣. If partner responds 2♡, however, you will have to conceal the excellent diamond suit and be content with a simple rebid of 2♠.

(d) *With five-four distribution in two touching suits*, you will always open with the longer suit first if it also happens to be the higher-ranking. Similarly, if the higher-ranking suit is the shorter, you should normally follow the general rule and open the five-card suit first. Indeed, some authorities suggest that you should *always* do this, but common-sense insists that there must be exceptions to the rule

♠ K 8
♡ A K J 10
◇ Q 7 5 4 2
♣ 5 4

Open 1♡. Since you are not strong enough for a reverse bid, you will have to rebid the jejune diamond suit if you open 1◇ and hear partner respond either 1♠ or 2♣. To open 1♡ will enable you to bid both your suits without misleading partner about your strength. Furthermore, if your side is outgunned and the opponents eventually play the contract, you will particularly welcome an opening heart lead from partner.

To summarise. The exception to the general rule that you should open your longer suit first when you have a 5–4 distribution occurs when the two suits are 'touching' and when the higher-ranking suit, although the shorter, is much stronger than the five-card suit. It would certainly not be wise to go to the extremes suggested by some authorities and open the higher-ranking suit on *all* 5–4 distributions in touching suits, particularly if, as is recommended in a later section of this book, false preference is part of your bidding armoury. However, it will often ease your rebid problems if you open a good four-card suit before a poor, lower-ranking five-card suit.

(e) *With three four-card suits*, the general rule is simple: open the suit below the singleton, the suit 'below' clubs for this purpose being spades. One exception to this occurs when one of your four-card suits is very weak; in that case, it is better to forget about the weak suit and treat the hand as though it were a two-suiter.

♠ 7
♡ J 9 6 4
◇ A K 10 3
♣ A Q 4 2

Open 1◇. Pure theory suggests that the correct opening bid on this hand is 1♡, the suit below the singleton. In practice, however, it will often work out poorly to open on such a feeble suit, and it is better to ignore the hearts unless partner is able to introduce them from his

side: give partner a good picture of where your strength lies by opening
1◇ and rebidding 2♣ over the likely response of 1♠.

Similarly:

    ♠ A K J 9
    ♡ K Q 10 2
    ◇ 3
    ♣ 10 8 7 5

Open 1♠. While the theoretically correct opening of 1♣ will
probably work out satisfactorily in practice, there is a strong case for
opening 1♠ and rebidding 2♡ over a response of 2◇ – thereby bidding
the two suits which contain all your high-card strength. The other
advantages of the 1♠ opening are that it will make it more difficult
for the opponents to intervene, that you will welcome a spade lead if
the opponents eventually play the hand, and that it will occasionally
unearth a 4–4 spade fit which might vanish in the fourth suit jungle
if the auction were to commence 1♣–1◇–1♡.

This last point leads us to the other exception to the rule governing
the choice of opening bid on 4–4–4–1 hands. Assuming that the three
suits are all of a reasonable quality, there is a strong argument for
opening 1♡ when your singleton is in clubs.

    ♠ K J 8 7
    ♡ A J 9 5
    ◇ K J 6 4
    ♣ 3

Open 1♡, intending to rebid 2◇ over a 2♣ response. This will
simplify the search for a 4–4 major suit fit. To open 1♠ might make
it difficult to find a 4–4 heart fit if the auction commences 1♠–2♣–2◇,
for hearts will now be the fourth suit and the situation threatens to
become obscure.

(f) *With two touching four-card suits*, the general rule is simple: open
the higher-ranking suit first. The only exception to this occurs when
you are 4–4 in the major suits and have a hand which is strong enough
for a rebid of 2NT or 3NT.

    ♠ A 10 7 2
    ♡ K 9 8 5
    ◇ A Q
    ♣ K 7 5

Open 1♡, intending to rebid 2NT if partner responds in a minor suit.
To open 1♡ will simplify the search for a fit in either major suit; to
bid 1♠ first will make things slightly awkward if partner bids 2♣ or
2◇, for to rebid 2NT will risk missing a heart fit and to rebid 2♡ will
give partner no idea of your strength or of the essentially balanced
nature of your hand.

(g) *With two non-touching four-card suits*, each case has to be considered separately; a parrot-like recitation of a set of rules will not always produce the correct answer.

With four hearts and four clubs, matters will never get out of hand if you open 1♣: if partner responds 1♢, you can rebid 1♡; and if he responds 1♠, you can either raise to 2♠ or rebid 1NT, depending on the nature of your hand. There are occasions, however, on which an opening bid of 1♡ is preferable.

    ♠ A Q
    ♡ A K 10 9
    ♢ Q 6 4
    ♣ J 9 7 5

Open 1♡. As your hand is far from minimum, there is no need to open with the feeble, ineffective club suit. If partner bids 2♢ over 1♡, you can describe your hand admirably by rebidding 2NT; and if he responds 1♠ to 1♡, you can rebid 1NT or 2♣, depending on your methods. The advantages of opening 1♡ on this hand are clear: it is always best to open with a major suit if it is at all possible, just in case the opening bid is passed out; 1♡ will indicate the correct opening lead if the opponents eventually buy the contract; you will be better placed if the opponents are able to compete vigorously in spades, in that a heart fit will come to light before it is too late; and finally, 1♡ makes it slightly more difficult for the opponents to intervene.

With four spades and four diamonds, the situation is even more difficult. To make life easy for yourself, you should open 1NT if it is at all possible. If the prevailing vulnerability means that a suit opening is imperative, however, the correct opening bid depends partly on the strength and partly on the distribution of your hand.

If the hand is suitable for a 2NT rebid, it will often be best to open 1♠.

    ♠ A Q 8 4
    ♡ 7 3
    ♢ K 10 9 3
    ♣ A Q 4

Open 1♠, intending to rebid 2♢ over 2♣ and 2NT over 2♡. To open 1♢ will leave you with an awkward decision if partner responds 2♣.

1♠ will also be the correct opening bid if the full shape of the hand is 4–3–4–2, in that precise order.

    ♠ A Q 10 4
    ♡ Q 7 2
    ♢ K Q 9 3
    ♣ 8 2

Open 1♠. You can rebid 2♢ over 2♣, and over a response of 2♡.

which guarantees a five-card suit, you will be perfectly entitled to raise to 3♡.

The really awkward problem arises when you have a weakish hand with a 4–2–4–3 distribution, and here I regret to report that there is no perfect solution.

♠ K 10 7 2
♡ 6 3
◇ A Q 4 2
♣ A 9 3

Assuming that a 1NT opening is precluded by your methods, this hand is almost unbiddable. You clearly cannot open 1♠, for a response of 2♡ would leave you completely without resource. However, to open 1◇ is by no means foolproof, for a response of 2♣ would leave you with the choice of raising to 3♣ on sketchy three-card support or of rebidding the indifferent four-card diamond suit, either of which courses of action might fatally mislead partner. My own view is that holdings of this kind are best handled by opening 1♣ on the three-card suit, but please do not ask for your money back if you are not satisfied.

THE PREPARED CLUB

While the strong no trump, particularly when vulnerable, is generally agreed to save money and, to a lesser extent, match-points, it has the unfortunate side effect of making certain hands difficult to bid without resorting to opening on a three-card club suit – the dread 'Prepared Club'. We have already come across two hands on which it is either essential or desirable to open 1♣ on a three-card holding:

♠ A 7 2	♠ K 10 7 2
♡ A Q 10 4	♡ 6 3
◇ 10 7 5	◇ A Q 4 2
♣ K 8 6	♣ A 9 3
HAND A	HAND B

Assuming that the weak no trump is not in use, it is imperative to open 1♣ on Hand A, for a 'natural' opening bid of 1♡ would find you severely embarrassed by a response of 2♣ or 2◇. Similarly, 1♣ will be the most flexible opening bid on Hand B. 1♠ is out of the question, bearing in mind the chaos which would be caused by a 2♡ response; and to open 1◇ will leave you badly placed after a response of 2♣.

There is another situation in which the Prepared Club occasionally comes to the rescue. This is where to make the theoretically correct opening bid would involve bidding an emaciated major suit. For example:

♠ 10 8 4 2	◇ 3 2
♡ A K 10 3	♣ A Q 4

Open 1♣. To open 1♠ on such a suit would be an abomination, particularly if you have to invite preference by rebidding 2♡ over a response of 2◇. Since an opening bid of 1♡ would find you embarrassed by a 2◇ response, the best solution is to open 1♣ – keeping your fingers crossed that a major suit fit will soon be revealed.

The one controversial point relating to the Prepared Club concerns the opener's rebid after opening with a three-card suit. There is a surprisingly well supported school of thought which suggests that to open 1♣ and rebid in another suit guarantees that the club suit is genuine, but this theory can be shown to be completely unsound.

♠	A Q 4 2		
♡	A 6 3	1♣	1◇
◇	7 5 3	?	
♣	K J 2		

Bid 1♠. The fact that you have opened with a three-card club suit does not make it any less important to find a 4–4 spade fit. Indeed, it would be extremely strange if this were to be so, and the authorities who recommend a 1NT rebid in this situation are guilty of muddled thinking. Suppose the full hands are as follows:

	WEST		EAST	WEST	EAST
♠	A Q 4 2	♠	K J 7 5	1♣	1◇
♡	A 6 3	♡	7 2	1♠	4♣
◇	7 5 3	◇	A K 8 4		
♣	K J 2	♣	Q 4		

Notice how important it is to search for the major suit fit on this deal. If West is forced by his beliefs to rebid 1NT just because he has only three clubs, he will find himself in serious danger of incurring a minus score in 3NT.

It is, in fact, theoretically sound to introduce your major suit on the second round if you have opened 1♣ on a 4–3–3–3 or 3–4–3–3 distribution. The worst fate that can befall you is to hear partner give preference to your first suit; in that case, however, you can always give return preference to his first suit without raising the level of the bidding. The sequence:

$$1♣–1◇–1♠–2♣–2◇$$

should not be interpreted as showing extra values; the opener is merely admitting that he has opened the bidding on a three-card club suit.

The only case in which it may be prudent to conceal a four-card major suit after starting with a Prepared Club is where your distribution is 4–2–4–3 or 2–4–4–3.

♠	Q 10 4 2		
♡	9 3	1♣	1♡
◇	A Q 8 6	?	
♣	A J 7		

Bid 1NT. No rebid is completely sound in this position. To rebid 1NT might result in a 4–4 spade fit being missed. On the other hand, to rebid 1♠ might provoke partner into giving preference to the non-existent club suit, and you can no longer give return preference to his first suit. For this reason, the slightly unsound 1NT rebid probably constitutes the lesser risk.

♠ ♠

2. ONE NO TRUMP

The range of the opening bid of 1NT is a matter of personal choice. 12–14 or 13–15 throughout is common amongst tournament players these days, particularly since the weak no trump fits conveniently into the various artificial club systems. However, there is still strong support for the variable 1NT, that is, 12–14 not vulnerable and 15–17 vulnerable; others favour the so-called 'Three Quarter No Trump', and a number of very experienced operators still prefer the strong 1NT at any vulnerability and at any form of scoring. The choice is yours, and it is not within the scope of this book to attempt to influence your decision in any way. Well, maybe just a little . . .

While its pre-emptive value provides a powerful argument for its use at match-pointed pairs, the weak 1NT vulnerable is a dangerous tool in team play or for money. The reason for this distinction is an important one. In a pairs game, it is the frequency of any gain or loss which is all-important and, if the weak 1NT vulnerable brings in three or four good results by snatching the part-score or by causing the opponents to alight in the wrong spot, these will more than compensate for the occasional bottom which you will incur when you are doubled and carried away for 800 or so. At rubber bridge, and to a lesser extent at team play, it is the size of the gain or loss which matters; you will need to collect an awful lot of part-score swings to make up for just one 800 penalty.

The other point to make in connection with the weak 1NT vulnerable is that one does not only have to worry about the occasional 800 or 1100 penalties. In my experience, it is the −200 entries on the score-card which prove so expensive, particularly at pairs, and it is this factor which makes the 'Three Quarter' 1NT an illogical compromise: to lose 200 on a part-score hand will be a poor result whether the opponents are vulnerable or not.

In view of this, I personally favour the traditional Acol variable 1NT, particularly if the 1NT rebid is sufficiently flexible to permit as many

balanced hands as possible to be played in no trumps after an opening
bid of one suit. But maybe I am growing old even faster than I think.

RESPONSES TO 1NT

(1) STAYMAN 2♣

Despite the xenophobic doubts about its ancestry, the Stayman 2♣
bid is one of the most popular bidding conventions of all time; most
systems incorporate some sort of 2♣ major suit enquiry in response to
1NT. As the convention is so well-known, it is not proposed to devote
too much valuable space to it in these pages. It will be sufficient to
run quickly through four important topics which arise in connection
with Stayman and which rarely receive any publicity.

(a) The first point concerns the opener's action if he has two four-
card majors in response to a 2♣ enquiry. A great deal of muddled
thinking occurs in this connection. Some schools of thought favour
showing spades first; others insist that you should start by bidding
the hearts; but the truth of the matter is that it could not matter less
which suit is bid first. Unless he has used Stayman either as an escape
mechanism or as a stepping-stone on the way to a game try in a long
major suit, the responder will convert to no trumps if the opener's
reply to 2♣ fails to unearth a major suit fit. Suppose that the auction
commences:

The opener can be certain that his partner has four hearts in Sequence
A and four spades in Sequence B, for his Stayman enquiry would
otherwise be completely meaningless. If the opener happens to be 4–4
in the major suits, therefore, he can introduce the other suit with
absolute confidence in these situations, and the correct denomination
will be reached no matter which suit is bid first over 2♣. For this
reason, the best practical solution is for the opener to bid his better
major when he is in the fortunate position of holding both: as we have
seen, it will not matter which he bids first if the responder has fair
values, and there will be a definite advantage in playing in the stronger
suit if the responder is effecting an escape operation and is planning to
pass the reply to 2♣.

One more important point arises in connection with Sequence A
above.

    1NT   2♣
    2♠   2NT

If the opener is 4–4 in the majors, he must remember to limit his hand
at the same time as showing his heart suit: 3♡ at this point would
show a minimum hand on which the opener would have passed after the

sequence 1NT–2♣–2♡–3♡; the opener must therefore jump to 4♡ over 2NT if he has the values for game.

(b) *Game Tries after Stayman*

(A)	1NT	2♣	(B)	1NT	2♣
	2◊	2♠		2♡	2♠
(C)	1NT	2♣	(D)	1NT	2♣
	2◊	3♠		2♠	3♡

An important point for regular partnerships to discuss is the meaning of the introduction of a major suit by the original Stayman bidder. Sequence A above is best interpreted as a sign-off, for this will enable the responder to search for the correct part-score contract when he is at least 5–4 in the majors and has a weak hand. Sequence B, on the other hand, cannot logically be construed as weak. Since the responder was clearly not interested in hearing about hearts, he cannot now be showing a weak hand with a long spade suit: on such a hand, he would have bid a simple 2♠ on the first round. The only sensible interpretation of his actions is that he is making a try for game based on a five-card or longer spade suit, and this is, in fact, another purpose for which the ubiquitous Stayman convention can be employed.

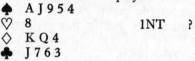

♠ A J 9 5 4
♡ 8   1NT   ?
◊ K Q 4
♣ J 7 6 3

While this hand has chances of game opposite 1NT and is clearly too strong for a weakness take-out into 2♠, it is not quite strong enough for a game-forcing jump to 3♠. The solution is to set the ball rolling with a Stayman 2♣ enquiry. If partner makes the unlikely response of 2♠, he must have excellent chances of making game; if he bids 2♡, you can express your interest in a game by bidding 2♠; and if he bids 2◊, you will have to jump to 3♠ (see Sequence C above) to show that your hand is better than minimum – 2♠ at this point would be a belated weakness take-out, implying a four-card heart suit in addition to five spades.

Sequence D above has the same invitational, non-forcing meaning, showing an intermediate hand with a five-card or longer heart suit and being exactly equivalent to Sequence C. As in all these cases, the opener will only push on to game if he has a maximum hand or a particularly good fit.

(c) *SID – 'Stayman In Doubt'*

        1NT   2♣
        2♡   3◊

The responder's bid of 3◊ in this sequence is of little value in a

natural sense. He can scarcely have a weak hand with diamonds, or
he would have bid 2◊ in the first place; neither can he have a game-
going hand with five or more diamonds and four spades, or he would
either have started with a game-forcing jump to 3◊ or settle for 3NT
at this point. The only conceivable natural interpretation of the 3◊
bid is that the responder has an indifferent hand containing six diamonds
and four spades, and that his plan was to make an ambitious try for
game if he could locate a spade fit and to settle for a diamond part-score
otherwise. While this treatment might work well from time to time,
opportunities for its use would clearly be extremely rare. For this
reason, modern theorists have suggested an alternative conventional
use for the 3◊ rebid by the responder after his Stayman enquiry has
elicited a major suit from the opener. Consider the following hand:

♠ A 7 5
♡ K Q 9 3   1NT   ?
◊ J 7 2
♣ K 8 4

Many experts would probably not bother with Stayman in this
situation, assuming from the balanced nature of the hand that it will
play just as well in 3NT even if there is a 4-4 heart fit available. This is a
slightly dangerous assumption, however, and it is possible to show that
it is actually more important to play in a 4-4 fit when the responder is
completely balanced than when he has a 4-4-3-2 distribution. For the
sake of argument, let us suppose that there is a 4-4 major suit fit between
the two hands and that the opener's shape is 4-4-3-2. If the responder
is also 4-4-3-2, the chances are that each player's doubleton will
coincide with his partner's second four-card suit, thereby considerably
reducing the dangers involved in playing the hand in no trumps. If
the responder's distribution is 4-3-3-3, on the other hand, the opener's
doubleton is certain to be opposite a three-card holding, and it will be
more prone to attack in a no trump contract.

Returning to the responder's hand shown above, therefore, he must
realise that it will probably play better in a 4-4 heart fit if the opening
hand contains a doubleton. If the opener is also precisely 3-4-3-3,
however, there will be little advantage in playing in a suit fit and it
will be preferable to contract for a mere nine tricks in no trumps. It is
here that the so-called SID convention comes into operation. The
responder bids 2♣ and, if the opener is able to reply 2♡, rebids 3◊
to show four-card heart support and a completely balanced hand; this
precise information should enable the opener to judge the correct
denomination in which to play the hand.

Furthermore, if the opener decides to play in the 4-4 heart fit, he
can show the strength of his hand by simply rebidding 3♡ or by
jumping to 4♡ over 3◊. While the responding hand is known to have

sufficient high-card strength to play in 3NT, it is also known to be completely balanced and therefore rather unsuitable for a suit contract; if the opener shows a minimum hand by rebidding 3♡, therefore, the responder may occasionally elect to play in a safe part-score, particularly in a match-pointed pairs competition. For example:

WEST	EAST	WEST	EAST
♠ K 10 8	♠ A 7 5	1NT	2♣
♡ A J 7 4	♡ K Q 9 3	2♡	3◇
◇ Q 5	◇ J 7 2	3♡	No
♣ Q 9 6 2	♣ K 8 4		

Notice that, despite the combined holding of 25 high-card points, no game contract stands any real chance of success. Even 3♡ might be defeated by careful defence, and East-West will be assured of an extremely good result if they can collect +140 on this deal.

Another application of SID occurs on hands on which the responder receives a favourable reply to his Stayman enquiry and now has interest in a slam contract. This extension of the convention was suggested by my regular partner, Alan Wardman, who is normally so loth to clutter his mind with gadgets and gimmicks that his occasional contributions to the theory of bidding should always be taken seriously.

Consider the following hand:

♠ A Q 7 3		
♡ K 5	1NT	2♣
◇ Q 10 5	2♠	?
♣ A Q J 4		

Now that your Stayman enquiry has succeeded in locating a 4–4 spade fit, you must have hopes of a slam, even opposite a 12–14 1NT. The problem is how to convey your enthusiasm to your partner, for there are very few bids available for use at this point. 3♣ would show a weak hand with a long club suit; 3♡, as we saw a little earlier, would be a game try based on a long heart suit; 3♠ and 4♠ would be non-forcing limit bids; 4♣ and 4◇, as we shall see shortly, are usually reserved for the Sharples convention, seeking a minor suit fit for slam purposes; and 4NT, even assuming that partner interpreted it as conventional, would not tell you all you want to know.

The suggested solution is to temporise by bidding 3◇. Partner will clearly assume that this is SID. If he jumps to 4♠, suggesting a maximum hand with a bit of shape, the chances of a slam are even better and you can proceed by way of a 5♣ cue bid. And if partner attempts to retreat to 3NT or 3♠ over 3◇, you can emerge from the bushes by bidding 4♣; he will then realise that you are agreeing spades and making a slam try, and everything thereafter should be quite straight-forward. This extension of the SID convention does, in fact, make it

considerably easier to investigate major suit slams after the bidding
has started 1NT–2♣.

(d) *Extended Stayman*

1NT   2♣

2◇   3◇

We have already considered a rebid of 3◇ by the responder after
the opener has shown a major suit. It clearly cannot have the same
meaning after an initial 2◇ reply, and the 3◇ bid in this situation
is generally agreed to be 'Extended Stayman', inviting the opener to
bid a three-card major suit. His replies to 3◇ are as follows:

3♡   to show three hearts and two spades.

3♠   to show three spades and two hearts.

3NT   to show two spades and two hearts (just in case you had
          your hand mis-sorted and opened 1NT on a 5–4–2–2
          distribution).

4♣   to show two three-card major suits.

This simple convention makes one awkward type of hand much easier
to handle.

  ♠ A J 7 5 3

  ♡ K Q 10 4   1NT*   2♣

  ◇ K 8 2   2◇   ?

  ♣ 5   *12–14

Since an immediate response of 3♠ would risk missing a 4–4 fit in
hearts, you were clearly correct to start with a Stayman 2♣ enquiry.
If the opener had been able to bid 2♡ or 2♠, all your problems would
have been over. However, difficulties have arisen now that he has
denied a four-card major suit, for a jump to 3♠ over 2◇ would not be
forcing and a raise to 3NT would risk missing a superior game contract
in a 5–3 spade fit. The solution lies in Extended Stayman. 3◇ at this
point asks partner to bid a three-card major suit. If he bids 3♠ or
4♣, you can bid 4♠ and play in the known 5–3 fit; if he bids 3♡,
denying three spades, you will have to settle for 3NT; and if he bids
3NT, a confession that he has opened 1NT on a 5–4–2–2 distribution,
you can pass and start looking around for a new partner.

Extended Stayman can also be used to make sure you play in the best
trump suit when you are 5–5 in the majors opposite an opening bid
of 1NT.

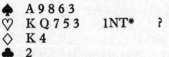

  ♠ A 9 8 6 3

  ♡ K Q 7 5 3   1NT*   ?

  ◇ K 4

  ♣ 2   *12–14

The traditional way of handling this kind of holding is to bid 3♠,
intending to convert to 4♡ if the opener rebids 3NT. The slight

disadvantage of this method is that you will alight in the inferior trump fit if the opener has three spades and four hearts and correctly raises 3♣ to 4♣. This can be avoided if you are armed with the Extended Stayman convention. Bid 2♣, hoping that the opener will be able to show a four-card major suit; if he is forced to bid 2◇, you can still make sure of playing in a 5–3 fit by asking again with 3◇.

(2) TRANSFER BIDS

One of the most important advances made in the theory of bidding in recent years is the development of transfer bids in response to an opening bid of 1NT. Basically, the scheme is that any suit response (apart from 2♣, which is Stayman as before) is a request for the opener to convert to the next highest suit. This simple idea leads to a number of significant advantages:

(a) Transfer bids enable an eventual suit contract to be played by the 1NT opener, so that the opening lead comes into, rather than through, his presumed tenace holdings in the other suits. This point applies particularly, of course, if the opening 1NT is strong or if the responder has a weak hand on which he decides that the final contract should be 2♡ or 2♠.

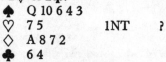

    ♠ Q 10 6 4 3
    ♡ 7 5   1NT   ?
    ◇ A 8 7 2
    ♣ 6 4

Playing transfers, bid 2♡ and pass the compulsory conversion to 2♠. It is clear that the final contract should be 2♠, and it is also clear that it will be better if partner plays the hand. This is not only a tribute to the quality of his card-play; he may well benefit from the opening lead, and the fact that the stronger hand remains concealed may make the subsequent defence more difficult.

(b) Transfer bids provide an ideal solution to an awkward problem which arises all too often at the table.

    ♠ 9 6
    ♡ A J 7 5 3   1NT*   ?
    ◇ K 9 4
    ♣ Q J 2   *12–14

This kind of holding is difficult to handle under normal methods. The two equally unattractive approaches are to make a quantitative raise to 2NT, concealing the five-card heart suit, or to make a try for game in hearts by bidding 1NT–2♣–2◇–3♡, which misrepresents the essentially balanced nature of the hand and which makes it impossible to rest in the comparative safety of 2NT if partner has a minimum hand containing a doubleton heart. Playing transfer bids, this hand is duck soup. The auction commences

1NT   2◇
2♡   2NT

and you have described your hand exactly: a raise to 2NT containing a five-card heart suit.

Similarly, game tries based on a six-card major suit can be expressed with perfect clarity by way of transfers.

♠ 9 6
♡ A J 7 5 3 2   1NT*   ?
◇ K 9 4
♣ Q 2   *12–14

Under normal methods, this type of hand has to be shown by the overworked 1NT–2♣–2◇–3♡ routine, and partner cannot be certain about the exact nature of your holding. Once again, transfer bids remove the ambiguity.

1NT   2◇
2♡   3♡

This sequence can be used to show a game try based on a six-card heart suit.

(c) Transfer bids add a new dimension to the bidding after 1NT. For example, certain 5–4 hands which are impossible to describe under normal methods can be bid with complete accuracy.

♠ A Q J 6 5
♡ J 8 4   1NT*   ?
◇ 7
♣ A Q 10 5   *12–14

Traditional Acol methods leave very little scope on a hand of this kind. All you can do is to offer partner a choice of game contract by jumping to 3♠, and you have no real chance of mentioning your club suit at all. If transfer bids are part of your armoury, on the other hand, you can complete a full description of your holding without progressing beyond the three level. After the sequence:

1NT   2♡
2♠   3♣

the opener should be in a good position to judge whether the best game contract is 3NT, 4♠ or 5♣. Moreover, if the hands are revealed to be a particularly good fit, there might even be a slam in one of your suits:

WEST	EAST	WEST	EAST
♠ K 7	♠ A Q J 6 5	1NT	2♡
♡ A K 5 3	♡ J 8 4	2♠	3♣
◇ J 10 6	◇ 7	3♡	3♠
♣ K 9 4 3	♣ A Q 10 5	4♣	4◇
		6♣	

Notice how the additional bidding space released by East's transfer response at the two level allows the partnership to discover the mutual weakness in diamonds before it is too late. East's failure to bid 3NT over 3♡, followed by his cue bid in diamonds, makes it clear to West that the hands are an excellent fit, and enables him to bid the odds-on club slam. Notice, too, that traditional methods might result in an ignominious minus score, for the auction could well proceed 1NT–3♠– 3NT–No.

Just one more illustration of the greater depth of bidding which is permitted by a transfer system over 1NT should be sufficient to convince any non-believers. Under normal methods, any game-going hand containing a five-card heart suit has to be developed by way of a response of 3♡ to 1NT; playing transfer bids, the various types of 3♡ response can be usefully distinguished by means of the following sequences:

(A)	1NT	2◇		(B)	1NT	2◇
	2♡	3♣			2♡	3NT
(C)	1NT	2♠		(D)	1NT	3◇
	2NT	3♡			3♡	3♠
(E)	1NT	3◇				
	3♡	3NT				

The omnibus 1NT–3♡ sequence is therefore replaced by five distinct sequences, and regular partnerships can amuse themselves by allocating a different shade of meaning to each one. Having passed many happy hours myself tinkering with the countless possible transfer sequences, my impression is that there are more sequences available than there are categories of hands which can be usefully described. This is a measure of the extent to which transfer bids can improve the accuracy of bidding after a 1NT opening.

(3) THE WEAKNESS TAKE-OUT

If transfer bids are not in use, a simple response of 2◇, 2♡ or 2♠ to 1NT is normally played as a weak bid, showing a long suit and a hand with no ambitions of any kind. This is the so-called 'weakness take-out', and the opener is expected to pass.

The general rule is that the responder should make a weakness take-out on any weak hand containing a five-card or longer suit – unless, of course, his suit is clubs. As always, however, there are exceptions to this rule.

(a) Whereas 5–4–3–1 and 5–4–2–2 hands will normally play better in a suit contract, balanced hands with a 5–3–3–2 distribution and fair values will probably play as well in 1NT. Each case clearly has to be considered on its merits, but my personal rule is to pass 1NT on 5–3–3–2 hands when it is certain that there are at least 20 points in the two hands.

♠ J 7
♡ 10 6 4   1NT*   ?
◇ K J 8 5 3
♣ K 6 2   *12–14

Pass. You know that partner has at least 20 points between the two
hands, and he must therefore have a good chance of making 1NT;
furthermore, even if he is unable to do so, it is by no means certain
that you will be any more successful in 2◇.

(b) It is not always prudent to make a weakness take-out, particularly
in 2◇, on a very poor hand. To do so makes it easier for the opponents
to compete, partly because you are openly announcing your weakness
and partly because you are giving your right-hand opponent, who
previously passed over 1NT, another chance to enter the auction.

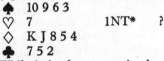

♠ 10 9 6 3
♡ 7   1NT*   ?
◇ K J 8 5 4
♣ 7 5 2   *12–14

Pass. While it is almost certain that you would make more tricks
in 2◇ than partner will in 1NT, to bid 2◇ in this situation would be
to ask for trouble. If the opponents' strength happens to be fairly
evenly divided, 1NT may be passed out; the knowledge that you would
pass 1NT on 9 or 10 points may deter your left-hand opponent from
entering the lists. If you bid 2◇, on the other hand, you are issuing
an open invitation for the opponents to take action; furthermore, you
are giving your right-hand opponent a second chance to make a
contribution.

(4) THE JUMP RESPONSE IN A MAJOR SUIT

A jump response of 4♡ or 4♠ to 1NT is intended to end the auction,
showing a six-card or longer suit and a hand on which the responder
wants to play in game, but no higher. It is worth mentioning at this
point that, even if you do not favour a complete structure of transfer
bids at all levels, it is quite possible to incorporate so-called Texas
transfers into your system. Under this scheme, an immediate response
of 4◇ asks the opener to bid 4♡ and 4♡ requests 4♠, the idea once
again being that the final contract should be played by the stronger
hand and by the hand containing the tenaces in the side suits. Alternatively, just in case there is the slightest danger of the opener making
a sleepy pass of a natural-sounding 4♡ response, it is possible to play
what is known as Minor Suit Texas, whereby 4♣ requests 4♡ and 4◇
requests 4♠. This method precludes the use of the Gerber 4♣ ace-
asking convention, but it might be favoured by those of a nervous
disposition.

The fact that major suit responses at the two level and the four

level are needed as limit bids means that the responder must jump to
3♡ or 3♠ over 1NT if he has either (a) a five-card major suit and a
game-going hand, or (b) a six-card or longer suit and a hand with slam
interest. The primary meaning of this response is to offer the opener
the choice between 3NT and four of the major. Generally speaking, the
opener will return to 3NT if he only has doubleton support for the
responder's suit and will prefer to raise to 4♡ or 4♠ if he has three- or
four-card support; however, he must not neglect the opportunity to
make an advance cue bid if he has particularly powerful support for the
responder's major suit.

♠ K 10 7 2		
♡ A 7	1NT	3♠
◇ Q 10 4 2	?	
♣ A 9 8		

Bid 4♣. This hand is so strong in support of spades that you must
not merely make a sleepy raise to 4♠. 4♣ is an advance cue bid,
showing excellent support for spades, a maximum hand and the ace of
clubs – all in one bid. If partner has nothing to spare, of course, he will
sign off in 4♠ and you will have to respect his judgement. However,
if he is strong enough to co-operate in the search for a slam, the 4♣
bid might set the wheels in motion for a smooth sequence.

WEST	EAST	WEST	EAST
♠ K 10 7 2	♠ A J 9 6 5	1NT	3♠
♡ A 7	♡ K 10 8	4♣	4◇
◇ Q 10 4 2	◇ A J	4♡	6♠
♣ A 9 8	♣ K 3 2		

West's 4♣ cue bid is the key bid in this sequence; East is unlikely
to make a slam try if his 3♠ response is raised merely to 4♠.

If the responder bids 3♡ or 3♠ over 1NT and then perseveres with
four of the major over the opener's conversion to 3NT, he is showing
slam interest and a hand which was too good for an immediate jump to
game.

♠ A Q 10 9 5 2		
♡ 7	1NT*	?
◇ Q 10 4		
♣ A K 5		*12–14

Bid 3♠. If partner raises to 4♠, you can test the market with a
cue bid of 5♣. If he attempts to settle in 3NT over 3♠, you can show
your interest in greater things by reverting to 4♠; if the opener has
good controls and good top cards, this course of action may tempt him
to investigate slam possibilities.

(5) THE JUMP RESPONSE OF 3♣ OR 3◇

A jump to 3♣ or 3◇ over 1NT is also natural and forcing. In this case, however, the main purpose of the bid is to investigate slam possibilities rather than to offer an alternative game contract: since 5♣ or 5♦ is such a distant prospect, the responder will probably settle for 3NT if he has a long minor suit and no real hopes of a slam.

The only doubtful point to be considered in this connection concerns the opener's rebid after 1NT–3♣ or 1NT–3♦. It is important to remember that to bid a new suit at the three level is completely natural, not conveying any inference about the quality of the opener's support for his partner's minor suit. This is because, while a jump to 3♣ or 3♦ shows a five-card or longer suit and some interest in a slam, it does not deny the possession of another four-card suit.

> ♠ A Q 7 2
> ♡ 3   1NT*   ?
> ♦ A K 10 9 5
> ♣ K 8 4   *12–14

Bid 3♦. This is the only way of showing the good diamond suit and the powerful hand, for to employ the Stayman 2♣ convention would leave you with an impossible rebid if partner fails to reply 2♠. The fact that you choose to bid 3♦ on a 5–4 distribution means, of course, that the opener must introduce a four-card major suit over 3♦, whether or not he relishes the thought of playing in diamonds at a high level.

(6) SHARPLES 4♣ AND 4♦

A useful extension to the Stayman convention has been developed by Bob and Jim Sharples. It is designed to find a 4–4 minor suit fit for slam purposes, and it operates very simply. Following a bid of 2♣ on the first round, a jump to 4♣ or 4♦ by the responder shows a four-card minor suit and strong slam interest. The opener replies as follows:

   (a) To bid 4♦ over 4♣ shows a four-card diamond suit.

   (b) To bid a major suit which he has neither shown nor denied shows a four-card suit.

   (c) To bid an 'impossible' major suit or a major suit which he has already shown is a cue bid, agreeing the responder's minor suit.

   (d) To raise the responder's minor suit shows four-card support and a hand which is unsuitable for slam purposes.

   (e) To bid 4NT is a sign-off.

	WEST		EAST	WEST	EAST
♠	A 3	♠	K 8 5	1NT	2♣
♡	K 9 8 3	♡	A 7	2♡	4♣
♦	Q 10 7 5	♦	A K 6 3	4♦	4♡
♣	K 10 2	♣	Q J 8 5	4♠	5♦
				6♦	

East's original response of 2♣ is normal Stayman, and West shows his four-card heart suit. When East follows up with a jump to 4♣, however, it becomes apparent that he is seeking a 4–4 minor suit fit for slam purposes, and West now bids his diamond suit. East's 4♡ bid is clearly a cue bid agreeing diamonds, and the partnership reaches the excellent diamond slam with little difficulty. Notice that there is almost no play at all for twelve tricks in no trumps.

One more example of the convention in action.

WEST	EAST	WEST	EAST
♠ K 4 2	♠ A Q 5	1NT	2♣
♡ A 2	♡ K Q 6 4	2◇	4◇
◇ Q 10 7 5	◇ K J 9 3	4♡	4♠
♣ A 10 8 3	♣ K 6	5♣	6◇

Once again the 4–4 minor suit fit produces an excellent slam contract, while 6NT will only succeed if the declarer can engineer a squeeze position. East's jump to 4◇ shows a four-card diamond suit and denies four clubs. Since West has already denied a heart suit by his original reply to Stayman, 4♡ is clearly a cue bid agreeing diamonds; the auction proceeds smoothly from there to the lay-down slam.

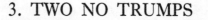

3. TWO NO TRUMPS

THE REQUIREMENTS FOR 2NT

In theory, the requirements for an opening bid of 2NT remain just as they were in the original Acol book: a balanced hand, a guard in every suit, and 20–22 points. In practice, however, it is permissible to turn a blind eye to any of these requirements in certain situations.

    ♠ A K Q 10 4
    ♡ K 7
    ◇ K 10 8 5
    ♣ A Q

This may not fall within the purist's definition of a balanced hand, but 2NT is by far the best opening bid. The disadvantage of opening with an Acol Two Bid of 2♠ is that an eventual no trump contract will be played from the wrong side of the table if partner is forced to respond 2NT.

    ♠ A K J 2
    ♡ 10 6
    ◇ K Q 8
    ♣ A K Q 4

Open 2NT. The absence of a heart guard is unfortunate, but once again there is no sensible alternative to a 2NT opening on this hand; it would be extremely dangerous to open with a mere one bid when you have 22 points.

♠ K 7
♡ A 10 4
◇ A K Q 10 6 4
♣ K 8

Open 2NT. Only 19 points, it is true, but the playing strength of this hand is far greater than that of most balanced 20-point hands and the established diamond suit is ideal for no trump purposes.

Conversely:

♠ K 7 2
♡ A Q 10 4
◇ A 5 3 2
♣ A K

Open 1♡. While this certainly ranks as a balanced hand containing 20–22 points and a guard in every suit, 2NT would be a poor opening bid. This is just the sort of hand which leads to disaster if partner passes 2NT for, even if he has slight values, you will find eight tricks an extremely tall order. I am sure you can all remember toiling hopelessly in 2NT on hands of this kind:

	WEST		EAST	WEST	EAST
♠	K 7 2	♠	8 6 5	2NT	No
♡	A Q 10 4	♡	9 5 3		
◇	A 5 3 2	◇	Q 4		
♣	A K	♣	J 9 6 4 2		

East is quite close to a sporting raise to 3NT, and yet 2NT is an absolutely hopeless contract on these hands. It is most unlikely that West will miss a game if he opens with a modest 1♡ on the above hand, and it will rarely pay to open 2NT when you have a balanced 20-point hand with no redeeming features. Notice that West would have a good chance of scrambling seven tricks in 1♡ on the above deal; and to make only six tricks will almost certainly produce a good score on the board at duplicate.

BIDDING AFTER 2NT

The bidding after an opening bid of 2NT is a department of Acol which is particularly badly defined and inefficient. Strangely enough, it is also an area of bidding which remains almost ignored by bridge writers, and even the very best text-books usually contain only an inadequate page or two on the responses to 2NT.

The two conventional responses to 2NT which are normally recommended are Baron 3♣ and Flint 3◇, and it will probably be worthwhile to examine these two bidding aids in a little more detail before we go on to consider how we might possibly improve on existing methods.

BARON 3♣

In response to an opening bid of 2NT, a bid of 3♣ is a conventional request for the opener to bid his lowest-ranking four-card suit; a rebid of 3NT by the opener shows that his only four-card suit is clubs. The partnership continues to bid its suits in ascending order in an effort to find a 4–4 fit, and this will often lead to the correct game contract.

	WEST		EAST	WEST	EAST
♠	A Q 8 5	♠	K J 7 4	2NT	3♣
♡	A 7	♡	Q 9 6 3	3♢	3♡
♢	A K Q 4	♢	7 5 3	3♠	4♠
♣	Q 9 5	♣	8 2		

Since, as in the above example, the responder might only have modest values to embark on this kind of auction, it follows that the opener must never proceed beyond 3NT in an effort to show his suits. Thus:

♠	A J 8	2NT	3♣
♡	Q 6	3♢	3♠
♢	A Q 7 4	?	
♣	A K J 10		

The opener's club suit must remain concealed at this point, for, in the absence of vigorous encouragement from partner, it is not safe for him to proceed beyond the safe haven of 3NT. Remember, too, that the responder's bid of 3♠ in this auction shows a four-card suit by definition; this means that, despite the unattractive holding in hearts, the opener must withdraw to 3NT in the above situation.

If the opener does take the bidding to the four level uninvited, there can be only one justification for such recklessness; he must be agreeing his partner's last-named suit and showing a control.

♠	A J 7 5	2NT	3♣
♡	K 8	3♢	3♠
♢	K Q J 4	?	
♣	A K 9		

Bid 4♣. This shows good four-card support for spades, a hand which is well suited for slam purposes, and first-round control of clubs – all in one bid.

So far, nothing very difficult. However, there is still a vast expanse of comparatively uncharted waters surrounding the Baron 3♣ bid, and any regular partnership would be well advised to ensure that they attempt to navigate them in the same way.

Let us suppose, for example, that it is the responder who takes the bidding beyond 3NT.

♠	A K 8 6	2NT	3♣
♡	K Q 7 4	3♡	4◇
◇	K 10	?	
♣	A Q 3		

This is fairly clear-cut. Your bid of 3♡ has already denied a four-card diamond suit, and it is therefore inconceivable that partner could wish to bid 4◇ at this point in a natural sense. The only rational explanation for his action is that he is making a slam try, agreeing hearts and showing the ace of diamonds; his hand might, in fact, be something like:

♠ 7 4
♡ A J 8 2
◇ A 7 4
♣ J 10 6 5

and this advance cue bid sequence is the only sensible way in which he can express his mild interest in a slam.

However, it may not always be as simple as that.

♠	A K 8 4	2NT	3♣
♡	K J 10	3♠	4♣
◇	A 7	?	
♣	K Q 5 3		

This sequence sounds very similar to the last one, and your first reaction might be that partner is agreeing spades and showing the ace of clubs. But are you certain? How would the responder handle a holding of the following sort?

♠	9 3		
♡	A Q 8 4	2NT	3♣
◇	8 6 2	3♠	?
♣	A J 9 4		

If you place this hand opposite the opener's hand suggested above, you will find no more than eleven tricks in no trumps and at least twelve tricks in clubs; however, it is difficult to see how the responder can search for the vital 4-4 club fit if his rebid of 4♣ is going to be interpreted as a cue bid agreeing the opener's first suit. This is clearly an important point which you should sort out with your regular partner before you find yourself faced with an insoluble problem at the table, but it is the sort of point on which text-books offer little or no guidance. My own view is that a rebid of 4♣ by the 3♣ bidder should almost always be a natural bid, showing a four-card suit and seeking a 4-4 club fit for slam purposes; without this agreement, you will find it extremely difficult to reach a number of elementary club slams.

There are, in fact, just two sequences in which a rebid of 4♣ by the responder cannot logically be natural:

(A) 2NT   3♣   (B) 2NT   3♣
       3◇   4♣   3◇   3♡
                                    3♠   4♣

The 4♣ bid in Sequence A can only be a cue bid agreeing diamonds. The responder would not have initiated a Baron sequence on a 3–3–3–4 shape and, with any other distribution, he would continue the search for a major suit fit if he had not already located a 4–4 fit in diamonds. Similarly, the opener has already shown four diamonds and four spades in Sequence B; it is therefore inconceivable that the responder could still be seeking a 4–4 fit in clubs, and the 4♣ bid must be a cue bid agreeing spades.

While we are on the subject of reaching slams by way of the Baron 3♣ convention, another particularly murky area of current bidding methods concerns the subsequent use of 4NT by the original 3♣ bidder. In at least one case, the meaning of 4NT is obvious:

♠ A K 9 3   2NT   3♣
♡ K 8 7   3◇   4NT
◇ A Q 6 4   ?
♣ A J

The 4NT bid in this sequence must be conventional, for partner's failure to continue the search for a suit fit means that he must have already located a 4–4 diamond fit. You should therefore show your controls in accordance with your normal methods.

However, suppose the situation is slightly different.

♠ A K 9 3   2NT   3♣
♡ K J 8   3♠   4NT
◇ Q 6   ?
♣ A Q J 4

Is 4NT conventional, agreeing spades and enquiring about your controls? And if it is, how should the responder handle the following kind of holding?

♠ 8 5
♡ A Q 6 4   2NT   3♣
◇ K 9 7 5   3♠   ?
♣ K 9 3

This hand will probably only come to eleven tricks in no trumps opposite the ill-fitting hand which we have just given the opener, but it will almost certainly produce at least twelve tricks in diamonds opposite the more suitable hand which we gave him in the previous example. It is therefore clearly important for the responder to search for a fit on this holding but, having done so and failed in the attempt, he still needs to be able to make a quantitative raise to 4NT. Once again it is not made clear by the authorities whether or not a delayed quantitative raise of this kind is available, and it is this sort of murky auction which makes current Acol bidding so imprecise after an opening bid of 2NT.

There are, in fact, two possible solutions to this dilemma, neither of which is completely satisfactory. The first is to agree that a delayed raise to 4NT is always quantitative unless it is obviously conventional, showing the sort of hand which would probably have produced a suit slam if a 4–4 fit could be located and which will now probably produce a no trump slam if the opener has a maximum hand for his original bid. This is the approach which I favour, but it might lead to awkward sequences if the 3♣ bid locates a fit and you are anxious to check on the opener's controls. The alternative approach to these hands is to make a direct raise to 4NT on all hands which are worth a quantitative raise, relying on the opener to show his four-card suits in ascending order if he feels that he is worth making a move towards a slam. This method is clearly inaccurate, but it at least has the merit of releasing every delayed jump to 4NT as a conventional enquiry. Some partnerships may find this simpler and therefore preferable; the really important point is that they should give the matter some thought and come to a definite decision.

Finally, let us return to earth for a short time to consider another common problem which is faced by most players but solved by very few.

♠	J 8 6 4 2		
♡	K 7 5 4	2NT	?
◇	Q 10 6		
♣	8		

What would you respond to 2NT on this everyday holding? One only has to devise three possible hands for the opener to hold opposite to understand the nature and the extent of this problem.

	HAND A		HAND B		HAND C
♠	Q 7	♠	A K 7	♠	K 5
♡	A 10 3	♡	A 10 3	♡	A Q J 3
◇	A K J 8 4	◇	A K J 4	◇	A K J 4
♣	A K 5	♣	Q 7 5	♣	Q 7 5

The correct contract with these hands is obviously 3NT, 4♠ and 4♡ respectively, but it is not clear how we are proposing to reach the best spot every time. For example, if we bid a natural 3♠ over 2NT, we shall miss the heart fit on Hand C; similarly, if we use the Baron 3♣ convention, the auction will proceed 2NT–3♣–3◇–3♡–3NT on both Hands A and B, and we shall have to guess whether or not to convert to 4♠. The whole thing is clearly far from satisfactory, and it is disturbing to find ourselves faced with an insoluble problem on a common-or-garden 6-point hand.

My suggested solution to this difficulty is a simple one and one which might be adopted by regular partnerships who have not yet devised their own mechanism: it is to use the sequence 2NT–3◇(Flint)–3♡–3NT to show game-going values and precisely five spades and four hearts, enabling the opener to select the correct final contract without difficulty. It is important to remember, of course, that no similar problem arises if the responder has a weakish hand containing five hearts and four spades, for he can simply bid 3♡ and rely on his partner to introduce a four-card spade suit if he has one.

FLINT 3◇

The Flint 3◇ convention is designed to compensate for the fact that there is no 'weakness take-out' over an opening bid of 2NT. In its simplest form, the response of 3◇ commands the opener to convert to 3♡, so that the responder can pass if he holds something like:

♠ 7 4
♡ 10 8 7 5 4 2
◇ J 8 4
♣ 9 3

If the heart and spade holdings in this example are reversed, of course, the responder rectifies to 3♠ over the mandatory 3♡, and the opener is expected to pass this.

In the original version of the Flint convention, the following sequences were also to be interpreted as weak and non-forcing:

(A) 2NT   3◇   (B) 2NT   3◇
      3♡   4♣   3♡   4◇

However, very few recognised pairs adopt this particular aspect of the system these days and, as we shall see later, these sequences are probably more useful in a forcing sense. It is, of course, extremely rare that one can judge accurately to contract for precisely ten tricks in a minor suit instead of taking a chance of eight or nine tricks in no trumps.

The efficiency of the Flint convention can be increased considerably by allowing the opener a little flexibility in his rebid over 3◇. He will, of course, normally obey instructions and bid 3♡, but there are certain hands on which the knowledge that his partner has a long major suit will give the opener visions of a game contract, even if he knows that there is a very weak hand opposite.

♠ A K 8 5
♡ A 6   2NT   3◇
◇ K Q 10 6   ?
♣ A J 3

If the responder's long suit is spades, the opener can see immediately that there must be a good chance of landing ten tricks opposite this ideally-fitting hand. However, if, as is more likely, partner's suit happens to be hearts, the opener has much less to offer and he will no doubt be well satisfied if his side can collect nine tricks. There is therefore no reason not to make the normal reply of 3♡ to 3◇; if it is your lucky day and partner converts this to 3♠, you can give him a sporting raise to four.

Now suppose that the opening hand is slightly different.

   ♠ A 6
   ♡ A K 8 5   2NT   3◇
   ◇ K Q 10 6   ?
   ♣ A J 3

Once again the opener can visualise the possibility of game if the hand happens to be a good fit. This time, however, the hope is that partner's suit is hearts, and the danger of bidding a routine 3♡ over 3◇ is that the opener may pass and collect at least ten tricks. The solution is to bid 3♠ over 3◇ on this hand; the responder will pass if spades is his suit, but he will be forced to go to the four level if he has hearts – and that is precisely where you want him to be.

Once in a blue moon, the opener will find himself in the happy position of being able to contemplate game in whichever suit his partner has.

   ♠ A K 8 5
   ♡ K Q 10 6   2NT   3◇
   ◇ A 6   ?
   ♣ A J 3

Bid 3NT. Since this hand is such an excellent fit for either major suit, it would be dangerous to bid 3♡ or 3♠, either of which partner might pass: 3NT will force him to bid game in his long suit. It is also possible to bid 4♣ over 3◇ to show this kind of hand, and this method may be preferable if it is your style to open 2NT on something like:

   ♠ Q 6
   ♡ K 8   2NT   3◇
   ◇ A Q 4   ?
   ♣ A K Q 10 7 3

As you have such a poor fit for both major suits, you may decide to take your chances in 3NT instead of compelling your partner or yourself to toil in three of his suit; you will only be able to do this if you use 4♣ as the game-forcing bid over 3◇.

THE NEW APPROACH

So much for our brief consideration of the two conventions which are widely used in response to 2NT. With certain small modifications, they will also figure in the structure of responses which I would like to recommend for regular partnerships to adopt – or at least to consider.

In actual fact, this structure is very similar to that utilised by Acol players all over the country; the only real difference is that it has fewer loose ends and, it is to be hoped, fewer of those murky, ambiguous auctions for which Acol is notorious.

The recommended responses to 2NT are as follows:

(a) A modified Baron-style 3♣ convention.
(b) The Flint 3◇ convention.
(c) A forcing 3♡ and 3♠ response.
(d) A new, natural 4♣ response.
(e) Texas responses of 4◇ and 4♡.

We must now consider each of these responses in detail.

(a) *Modified Baron 3♣: The Revised Responses*

The revised responses to 3♣ are as follows:

3◇	to show neither four hearts nor five spades.
3♡	to show a four-card heart suit.
3♠	to show a five-card spade suit.
3NT	to show a five-card heart suit.

This scheme of responses to the 3♣ enquiry has the obvious advantage of making it possible to unearth a 5–3 major suit fit when it is the opener who has the five-card suit.

♠ K 7
♡ A K Q 10 4
◇ A J 9
♣ K 8 5

Many experienced players would be loth to open 2NT on a holding of this kind, but it is by far the most descriptive and effective opening on the hand; the obvious disadvantage of opening 2♡, for example, is that it might well result in an eventual no trump contract being played from the wrong side of the table. This inborn reluctance to conceal a five-card major will vanish completely if we equip the responder with the machinery to locate it before the post mortem. If, for example, the opposite hand is:

♠ A 8 6 3
♡ J 7 2
◇ 6
♣ J 10 7 4 2

the auction will proceed 2NT–3♣–3NT–4♡ and the correct contract will be reached as a result of thorough investigation.

The absence of a single response to 3♣ to show specifically a four-card spade suit does not, of course, mean that it is no longer possible to find a 4–4 spade fit. After an initial response of 3◇ or 3♡, the responder perseveres with 3♠ to show that he has a four-card suit and that he is still interested in finding a 4–4 spade fit for game or slam purposes. If we take, for example, the illustration which we used earlier in our discussion of the Baron 3♣ convention:

WEST	EAST
♠ A Q 8 5	♠ K J 7 4
♡ A 7	♡ Q 9 6 3
◇ A K Q 4	◇ 7 5 3
♣ Q 9 5	♣ 8 2

we find that the bidding will now proceed 2NT–3♣–3◇–3♠ and the spade fit will come to light with no loss of efficiency. In fact, of course, in this particular example the opener can show his excellent spade support and his good controls by bidding 4◇ over 3♠, but it would take much more encouragement than that to persuade his partner to proceed beyond game.

Another advantage of the revised scheme of responses to 3♣ is that it solves the problem which was discussed at length earlier: that of how to handle game-going hands containing five spades and four hearts.

♠ J 8 6 4 2	
♡ K 7 5 4	2NT ?
◇ Q 10 6	
♣ 8	

We are now able to bid 3♣ with no further worries. If partner replies 3♡ or 3NT, we can convert to 4♡; if he replies 3♠, we can raise to 4♠; and if he replies 3◇, we can use a bid of 3♡, which has little value in a completely natural sense, to show this kind of holding and to ask partner to show a three-card or longer spade suit if he has one.

(i) *Minor suit slams after 3♣*: The one slight disadvantage of the suggested new responses to 3♣ is that the opener can no longer show a four-card diamond suit. This means that the responder will have to take the initiative if he is anxious to find a 4–4 minor suit fit for slam purposes, and the method he adopts is similar to that adopted to show a four-card club suit under existing methods: after first making a 3♣ enquiry, a bid of 4♣ or 4◇ by the responder is a mild slam try, showing a four-card suit.

♠ A 8	
♡ K 10 6 4	2NT 3♣
◇ K J 7 3	3◇ ?
♣ 7 5 3	

Bid 4◇. Partner's response has denied a four-card heart suit, but we must still continue the search for a diamond fit. If there is a 4–4 fit, of course, a contract of 6◇ will be a strong possibility.

Sometimes the search for a minor suit fit has to be delayed until the third round of bidding.

♠	K 8 6 3		
♡	8 5 2	2NT	3♣
◇	A 7	3◇	?
♣	K J 7 3		

Bid 3♠. Partner might still have a four-card holding in either black suit, and it is clearly important to investigate the hand fully. If the opener bids 3NT over 3♠, denying four-card support, we then test the market in the club suit with a bid of 4♣, once again showing a four-card suit.

The opener's responses to his partner's 4♣ and 4◇ probes require a little consideration. Over 4♣, of course, the opener should show a four-card diamond suit, for there is no reason why the responder should not be 4–4 in the minor suits.

	WEST		EAST	WEST	EAST
♠	A K 7	♠	8 6 4	2NT	3♣
♡	K Q 9 5	♡	A 6	3♡	4♣
◇	A Q 10 4	◇	K J 8 3	4◇	
♣	A 3	♣	K 10 7 2		

Notice the importance of locating the 4–4 fit on this deal: although the opener is completely maximum in terms of high-card points, eleven tricks are the limit in no trumps.

As regards the other responses to four of a minor, my proposal is that the constructive bidding will be simplified if 4NT is always conventional, agreeing the responder's suit and asking for his controls by whichever method you favour. This means that 4♠, which can never be needed in a natural sense, is used as the sign-off in all these sequences; it merely tells partner the bad news that there is no fit on the two hands and suggests that, unless he has extra undisclosed values, he should convert to 4NT.

♠	K Q J	2NT	3♣
♡	K Q 8 5	3♡	3♠
◇	A 6	3NT	4◇
♣	A Q 7 3	?	

Bid 4♠. Partner has four spades and four diamonds and, since we know there is no fit, we must suggest that he signs off in 4NT. 4NT at this point would, of course, be conventional, agreeing diamonds and asking for the responder's controls.

(ii) *The quantitative raise after 3♣*: Another less obvious advantage to the new 3♣ system is that, because it is no longer possible for a minor suit fit to come to light at the three level, there is almost no ambiguity over subsequent bids of 4NT by the responder. With one exception, responding hands which are worth a quantitative raise to 4NT will always proceed via 3♣ and then via 4♣ or 4◇ in an attempt to find a minor suit fit, and this means that the interpretation of sequences of this sort is now completely clear:

2NT	3♣
3♠	4NT

This must be conventional, agreeing spades for slam purposes. Without spade support, the responder's jump to 4NT would be impossible: even if he has a four-card heart suit, he must also have another four-card suit (with a 3–4–3–3 distribution he would prefer a direct raise to 4NT) and he would have looked for a minor suit fit before reverting to no trumps.

There is, in fact, only one sequence in which a rebid of 4NT by the responder is not preceded by a 4♣ or 4◇ probe and yet is quantitative:

2NT	3♣
3◇	3♠
3NT	4NT

This must be a quantitative raise and, since the responder has not investigated the possibility of a minor suit fit, the inference is that he is 4–4 in the major suits.

After seeking a minor suit fit by way of 4♣ or 4◇, of course, an unsolicited bid of 4NT by the responder is always conventional, for he can use the 4♠ sign-off which we allotted to the opener in an earlier paragraph.

♠ 7 5 4	2NT	3♣
♡ K J 9 3	3◇	4♣
◇ A 5	4◇	?
♣ K 8 6 2		

Bid 4♠. The opener has a four-card diamond suit, but he has neither four hearts nor four clubs and we must therefore suggest that he signs off in 4NT. If he has a maximum hand for his opening bid, of course, the opener can still make a further try for a slam in no trumps, for he will know from the responder's search for a minor suit fit that his hand also contains slam possibilities. 4NT by the responder over 4◇ would be conventional, agreeing diamonds and asking for the opener's controls.

(b) Flint 3◇

In our new structure of responses to 2NT, the Flint 3◇ convention takes its place in the same form as was outlined earlier; that is to say, the opener always converts to 3♡ as requested unless he bids:

(a) 3♠ to show excellent support for hearts but not for spades; or

(b) 3NT to show excellent support for both major suits.

However, the absence of a natural 3♣ or 3◇ response to an opening bid of 2NT will tend to make some minor suit orientated responding hands extremely difficult to describe, and it is proposed that an original response of 3◇ should be given more than its 'weakness take-out' meaning. The suggestion is that the sequences 2NT–3◇–3♡–4♣ and 2NT–3◇–3♡–4◇ should be given a specific meaning: the responder is making a mild slam try based on a five-card minor suit *and another four-card suit*. Without a fit for his partner's minor, the opener bids his lowest-ranking four-card suit and the partnership continues to bid suits in ascending order until a 4–4 fit is revealed or the search is proved to be abortive. Either side bids 4NT as a sign-off and can use a cue bid in an 'impossible' suit to agree the last-named suit.

♠ A Q 8 4	2NT	3◇
♡ A K 7	3♡	4♣
◇ K Q 10 3	4◇	4♠
♣ K 5	?	

Bid 5♡. The responder is showing five clubs and four spades and a hand with slam interest, and to cue bid in hearts, a suit already denied by the responder, will agree spades and show an interest in better things.

♠ Q J 7	2NT	3◇
♡ A K Q 5	3♡	4◇
◇ Q 8	4♡	4♠
♣ K Q J 4	?	

Bid 4NT. With a minimum hand containing poor support for partner's two suits, you have no alternative but to sign off in 4NT at this stage.

The other encouraging sequence after an original Flint 3◇ response is 2NT–3◇–3♡–3NT. This is a mild slam try based on a five-card or longer diamond suit. Furthermore, since the responder has not employed the new 2NT–3◇–3♡–4◇ sequence, the inference is that he does not hold another four-card suit.

(c) *The response of 3♡ or 3♠*

A response of 3♡ or 3♠ to 2NT retains its natural, forcing meaning, inviting the opener to choose between game in that suit and game in no trumps. The opener should normally opt for 4♡ or 4♠ if he has three-card support for his partner's suit for, when the vast majority of the partnership's high-card strength is concentrated in one hand, the play will generally be more flexible in the 5–3 fit.

Over a response of 3♡, the opener must always remember to show a four-card spade suit if he has one, just in case the responder has five hearts and four spades.

♠ A Q 7 4		
♡ K 9 3	2NT	3♡
◇ A K J 8	?	
♣ A 4		

Bid 3♠. If the responder converts to 3NT, denying a four-card spade suit, you can still revert to 4♡ and play in the known 5–3 fit.

If the opener has excellent support for his partner's major suit, of course, he must show some immediate signs of life by making a cue bid in a minor suit.

♠	A K 8 4		
♡	K 7	2NT	3♠
◇	K Q 10 3	?	
♣	A Q 5		

The opener must not simply bid a sleepy 4♠ in this position: bid 4♣, showing excellent spade support, mild interest in a slam, and the ace of clubs – all in one bid.

(i) *Slam bidding after 2NT–3♡ and 2NT–3♠*: An immediate response of 3♡ or 3♠ is normally merely aimed at finding the best game contract. From time to time, however, the responder will have his mind on bigger and better things, and it is when he takes the auction beyond the game level that traditional Acol methods often start to creak a little and even regular partnerships find themselves in ambiguous situations. For example, suppose the auction commences 2NT–3♡– 3NT–4♣–4NT: does the 4♣ bid show a suit or a feature? And is 4NT a sign-off or a conventional bid agreeing clubs?

In an effort to add a little more definition and clarity to this kind of exploratory auction, it is important to consider the possible sequences in detail.

If the initial response locates a fit, the subsequent auction should be fairly clear: 4NT is always conventional, and a bid of a new suit is a feature-showing bid, suggesting interest in a slam. Things become a little more difficult if the first attempt to find a fit is a failure. It is suggested that an immediate raise to 4NT should now be quantitative, inviting the opener to go on if he has a maximum hand for his opening.

♠	A K 4	2NT	3♡
♡	Q 8	3NT	4NT
◇	K Q J 7	?	
♣	K Q 9 2		

No bid. Partner's bid of 4NT is a quantitative raise and, with minimum values and a poor fit for his five-card suit, there is no justification for going any further on this hand. As we shall see a little later, if the responder has a long major suit and is anxious to ask for the opener's controls, he should start with a Texas transfer and follow with 4NT.

♠	A Q J 5	2NT	3♡
♡	Q 8	3♠	4NT
◇	K Q 9 3	?	
♣	K Q J		

This situation is a little more tricky, but the logical interpretation of the responder's second bid must be that he is again making a quantitative raise and not agreeing spades. Without this understanding, it is difficult to see how he could handle the type of hand on which he was planning to bid 2NT–3♡–3NT–4NT.

If the responder rebids his suit after a discouraging rebid by the opener, this is a mild slam try based on a good six-card or longer suit; it shows a holding of this sort:

♠	K Q 8 7 4 3		
♡	8 4	2NT	3♠
◇	K 7 2	3NT	4♠
♣	10 3		

Weaker hands with a six-card major suit are shown by making an immediate Texas transfer bid of 4◇ or 4♡; by taking the slower route to game, 2NT–3♠–3NT–4♠, the inference is that the responder has a mild interest in a slam if his partner has a reasonable fit and good top cards.

A rebid of a new suit below the game level by the responder is natural and forcing, showing at least 5–4 distribution in the two bid suits. In an effort to remove all ambiguity from this kind of sequence, it is suggested that the opener's only sign-off over 4♣ or 4◇ should be a return to his partner's major suit; this leaves 4NT available as a conventional enquiry, agreeing the responder's minor suit.

♠	A 7	2NT	3♠
♡	K Q J 4	3NT	4♣
◇	A Q J 3	?	
♣	Q J 8		

Bid 4♠, a sign-off in this sequence. Partner knows that you have no more than doubleton support and, if he feels he has done enough and intends to respect your sign-off, he can decide whether to pass 4♠ or convert to 4NT, which you will pass. 4NT by the opener in this kind of sequence would be conventional, agreeing clubs.

(d) *The response of 4♣*

Opposite such a strong opening bid as 2NT, it is obviously important for the responder to have at his disposal well-oiled, smooth-running machinery for slam bidding. To summarise what has gone before, we have provided him with a new 3♣ convention for use when he has four-card suits; if he has a five-card major suit, with or without another suit, he can set the wheels in motion with a natural response of 3♡ or 3♠; if he has a five-card minor suit and another four-card suit, he can now describe his holding by way of a Flint 3◇ response; and if he has a long diamond suit and no other suit, he can express interest in a slam by bidding 2NT–3◇–3♡–3NT.

The only type of hand which remains to be covered is that containing a five-card or longer club suit and no other four-card suit, and it is in this connection that a new interpretation of a little-used response to 2NT is suggested: one-suited hands with a club suit and mild slam interest are very difficult to express under existing methods, and, in our new structure of responses, this gap can be plugged very simply by using 4♣ to show just that kind of holding. This does mean that we can no longer have the Gerber 4♣ convention in our armoury but, quite frankly, this is not much of a loss. Hands on which the responder realises immediately that the only information he wants from his partner is the number of aces he holds are extremely rare, and he is far more likely to have 9 or 10 points with a long club suit.

♠	J 5		
♡	A 9 5	2NT	?
◇	7 4		
♣	K J 9 6 3 2		

Bid 4♣. Most partnerships will probably find this kind of hand difficult to handle under normal Acol methods, and a natural jump to 4♣ describes it well. It is suggested that a rebid of 4NT by the opener at this point should also be natural, showing a poor club fit and no interest in a slam. This leaves 4◇, 4♡ and 4♠ available as cue bids to agree clubs and to invite the responder to ask with a conventional 4NT bid; it is important to bear in mind in situations of this sort that the responder can usually benefit more than the opener from making a conventional 4NT enquiry, for only he knows the length of his long suit and only he can really assess the trick-taking potential of the two hands.

(e) *Texas transfers: 4◇ and 4♡*
Immediate responses of 4◇ and 4♡ are probably best used as Texas transfer bids, requiring the opener to convert to 4♡ and 4♠ respectively. The principal purpose of such a bid is to arrange for the final contract to be played by the stronger hand, so that the opening lead comes round to his presumed tenace holdings.

WEST		EAST		WEST	EAST
♠	A 7	♠	K 10 8 6 4 3		
♡	K 8 3	♡	7 4 2	2NT	4♡
◇	A K J 6	◇	Q 5	4♠	
♣	A Q 10 4	♣	9 5		

This hand is a good illustration of Texas in action. 4♠ played by East is in jeopardy if the opponents kick off with a heart lead; 4♠ by West will only be defeated if the cards lie very badly for the declarer.

A four-level transfer bid of this kind is normally used when the responder has a long major suit on which he has no ambitions beyond game. From time to time, however, Texas might be the vital first move in a slam venture.

♠ K J 10 7 5 4 2
♡ 8   2NT   ?
♢ 8 5 3
♣ A 9

Bid 4♡ and, when the opener obediently converts to 4♠, follow it with a Blackwood 4NT. If the opener has two aces, 6♠ is likely to be a reasonable contract on this hand. In view of the poor holding in diamonds, however, it is quite likely to be better for the slam to be played from the opener's side of the table. Let us construct two fairly typical 2NT openings opposite the above hand.

♠ Q 9 3
♡ A J 7
♢ A Q J
♣ K Q J 4
HAND A

♠ A 8 3
♡ A K Q 4
♢ K 7
♣ K Q 10 5
HAND B

In each case, twelve tricks are almost certain if the contract is played by the stronger hand; a diamond lead might be extremely embarrassing if the responder is left to toil in a high level spade contract.

CONCLUSION

That completes a brief summary of the proposed new structure of responses to 2NT. Apart from the slight modification to the Baron 3♣ convention and the introduction of a new-style 4♣ response, the methods suggested do not vary enormously from those normally adopted by Acol players. The important point is that a real attempt has at last been made to give a sharper definition to the various sequences which follow from an opening bid of 2NT, making it possible for the responder to show certain types of hands with perfect clarity and for the partnership to investigate the correct final contract along paths which are clearly sign-posted and which no longer lead to the murky areas so often visited by Acol players.

♠ ♠

4. FORCING OPENING BIDS

TWO CLUBS

Nothing new to report here. An opening bid of 2♣ retains the meaning allotted to it in the original Acol book. It covers two types of hands:

(a) Any hand containing 23 or more points.

(b) Any distributionally powerful hand which contains fewer than 23 points but which offers reasonable chances of game if the responder has thirteen cards. This kind of hand should normally contain at least 5 honour tricks.

RESPONSES TO 2♣

The positive responses to 2♣ have been steadily devalued over the years. In the early days of Acol, the requirements were so rigid and so demanding that a negative response was almost inevitable, but the modern tendency is to allow the responder to give a positive response if he has anything useful to say. This seems eminently sensible.

Generally speaking, the responder should bid a negative 2◇ on all hands containing 0–6 points. To make a positive response in a suit, he should have 7 or more points; more important, however, the responder should also have a fair suit and a useful quick-trick holding, for he cannot be certain at this early stage that his partner will be interested in hearing about a few scattered queens and knaves. To give a positive suit response at the two level, the responder should have a reasonable suit and at least 1 quick trick, that is, an ace or a king-queen; to bid a suit at the three level, which threatens to consume a complete round of bidding, the requirements are a fair suit and 1½ quick tricks.

♠	8 7 2		
♡	A Q 9 8	2♣	?
◇	7 2		
♣	J 10 5 3		

Bid 2♡. This is a minimum hand for a positive response, but the good heart suit is well worth mentioning; furthermore, 2♡ does not waste any bidding space.

If the responder has 7 or more points but has either a feeble suit or a poor honour trick holding, he should normally bid no trumps. 2NT suggests scattered values and 7–9 points; 3NT shows 10–12.

♠	Q 7 2		
♡	A 3 2	2♣	?
◇	10 4		
♣	Q 9 8 5 4		

Bid 2NT. 8 points is sufficient to warrant a positive response, but the club suit is not good enough to introduce at the three level.

OPENER'S REBIDS AFTER 2♣

With a balanced hand, the opener rebids 2NT on 23 or 24 points. The 2NT rebid is not completely forcing; in fact, 2♣–2◇–2NT is the only sequence after an opening 2♣ bid which can be dropped short of game. If the opener has 25 or 26 points, or if he simply thinks he can make game, the rebid is 3NT.

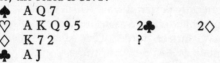

♠ A Q 7
♡ A K Q 9 5   2♣   2◇
◇ K 7 2   ?
♣ A J

Bid 2NT. Do not make the mistake of rebidding 2♡ on this hand. You are not quite strong enough to insist on game, and a rebid of 2NT describes this holding well: a balanced hand with 23 or 24 points.

To rebid in a suit after opening 2♣ suggests an unbalanced hand and is forcing to game. If the opener makes a jump suit rebid, he is showing a completely solid suit and setting the scene for an investigation of side suit controls.

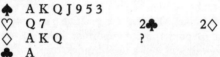

♠ A K Q J 9 5 3
♡ Q 7   2♣   2◇
◇ A K Q   ?
♣ A

Bid 3♠. Since 2♠ would be forcing to game in this situation, a jump to 3♠ shows a completely solid suit and invites partner to show his controls for slam purposes. The success of this hand will probably hinge on partner's holding in hearts, and 3♠ sets the trump suit and leaves the way clear for an exchange of cue bids. The responder shows the ace of hearts by bidding 4♡ over 3♠; if he has second-round control of the suit, he can bid 3NT over 3♠ and then bid 4♡ over your 4♣ cue bid.

RESPONDER'S SECOND BID AFTER 2♣–2◇

If the opener rebids 2NT, the responder is permitted to pass with a completely worthless hand. If he elects to push on to game, it is recommended that he should be armed with the same conventions as after an opening bid of 2NT. In any case, the one bidding aid which is absolutely essential in this situation is the Baron 3♣ convention, asking the opener to bid his four-card suits in ascending order and enabling the partnership to locate any available 4–4 fit.

If the opener rebids 3NT, it is again advisable to have a 4♣ convention at your disposal, so that you can search for a 4–4 suit fit if you are strong enough to think in terms of a slam. In principle, the responder should not bid a new suit over 3NT on a worthless hand. A sequence of this kind:

2♣   2◇
3NT   4♡

should be mildly constructive, not merely a rescue operation.

♠ Q 7 2
♡ K J 8 5 3   2♣   2◇
◇ 10 7 4   3NT   ?
♣ 8 3

Bid 4♡. This shows definite values, and the opener will know that you have a five-card heart suit and strong interest in bigger and better things.

If the opener rebids in a suit, the responder must do all he can to describe his inevitably modest values to his partner. For example, if you have adequate support for the opener's suit, you can normally distinguish the kind of hand you have by showing it in one of three basic ways. Let us suppose that the auction has commenced 2♣–2◇–2♡, and that you hold the following hands:

♠ K 7 2	♠ K 7 2	♠ 9 7 2
♡ J 9 6 4	♡ J 9 6 4	♡ J 9 6 4
◇ 10 2	◇ 10 2	◇ 10 2
♣ Q 8 5 3	♣ 9 8 5 3	♣ 9 8 5 3
HAND A	HAND B	HAND C

On Hand A, you can show your four-card trump support and goodish values by jumping to 4♡. This bid also carries the inference that you do not have an ace or a void; with a first-round control, you should prefer to bid a simple 3♡ and follow it with a cue bid on the next round.

On Hand B, you should make a non-committal raise to 3♡. However, Hand C is so weak that you should show your frailty by bidding 2NT first and converting to 4♡ later. This second-round 2NT rebid is generally known as the 'Second Negative', and it is often helpful in distinguishing between completely worthless holdings and hands which contain one or two useful assets. It also means that the responder must jump to 3NT on the second round if he has a balanced hand with reasonable values.

♠ 7 2
♡ J 10 6 4   2♣   2◇
◇ Q 8 3   2♠   ?
♣ K 9 5 2

Bid 3NT. Since you have already limited your hand to between 0 and 6 points by your initial 2◇ response, you can show fair values by jumping to 3NT at this stage. It is always important to describe your modest values as best you can in these situations; the opener will be delighted to detect any signs of life if he is looking at a really powerful collection.

Similarly, the responder can feel free to introduce any reasonable suit on the second round after limiting his hand by a 2◇ response on the first.

♠ 8 4
♡ Q 10 7 5 3   2♣   2◇
◇ 10 4 2   2♠   ?
♣ Q 9 6

Bid 3♡. You need not worry about bidding a new suit on such a poor hand: the main advantage of restricting the initial 2◇ response to hands containing 0–6 points is that the responder can describe his hand more accurately at his second turn without feeling guilty about over-stating his values.

If the responder jumps in a new suit on the second round, he is showing a suit which is solid apart from one honour card.

♠ 8 4
♡ 10 4 2   2♣   2◇
◇ K Q J 10 9 5   2♠   ?
♣ 7 2

Bid 4◇. Considered in conjunction with your original 2◇ response, this describes your hand admirably. If you are ever fortunate enough to hold a completely solid suit opposite an opening bid of 2♣, you can show it by making a jump response on the first round.

THE ACOL TWO: 2◇ 2♡ 2♠

The form of the Acol Two has changed very little over the years. It caters for the hand which is not strong enough in honour tricks to open with a game-forcing bid of 2♣, but which is too strong to open with one and follow with a jump rebid. It is normally based on a strong six-card suit and at least eight playing tricks, but it can also be used on powerful two-suited hands on which the opener would be nervous of opening with a modest one bid.

♠ A K Q 8 2
♡ A Q J 9 3
◇ 6
♣ K 7

Open 2♠. Since partner only needs to have four small hearts and nine other cards to give you a chance of success in 4♡, this hand is too strong for a 1♠ opening. It also illustrates why it is essential to play Acol Twos as 100% forcing: if partner is permitted to 'take a view' and pass 2♠ on a feeble hand with very few spades, an excellent heart game might well be missed.

The two tests to apply if you are not sure whether to open with one or two are as follows:

(a) If you open with a one bid, is there a real danger of your missing game if everyone passes?

(b) If you open with a one bid, are you going to have difficulty in describing your hand adequately on the next round?

If the answer to either, or both, of these questions is in the affirmative, the indications are that an Acol Two opening is in order.

There are two important points to be made in connection with an Acol Two in diamonds. The first is that, since game in a minor suit is such a distant prospect, an opening bid of 2♦ should normally be slightly stronger than a two-bid in a major suit; it should, in fact, contain nine probable playing tricks rather than a bare eight.

Secondly, it is occasionally correct to open 2♦ on a hand which is strictly speaking strong enough for a 2♣ bid. This is because powerful hands based on a long minor suit are often difficult to handle after an artificial 2♣ opening.

    ♠ A K J 4
    ♡ —
    ♦ A K 10 9 5 3
    ♣ A Q 8

Open 2♦. While it is clear that you will almost certainly play this hand in game, the bidding will proceed much more smoothly if you kick off with 2♦ than if you have to go through a 2♣–2♦–3♦ routine, which squanders a valuable round of bidding.

RESPONSES TO AN ACOL TWO

The traditional negative response to an Acol Two is 2NT. However, one of the most significant changes in Acol bidding theory in recent years has been the tendency to substitute Herbert negatives, whereby the responder bids the next-ranking suit on a weak hand, only bidding 2NT if he has the values for a positive response and if his suit is the 'Herbert' suit.

It is generally agreed that Herbert responses lead to greater efficiency. In the first place, the 2NT negative often leads to an eventual no trump contract being played from the wrong side of the table, and always makes it impossible to subside in a no trump part-score; this in turn makes it particularly difficult to handle strong, semi-balanced hands.

    ♠ 7 2
    ♡ A K Q J 5
    ♦ A Q 9
    ♣ K Q 10

This type of hand has always been difficult to deal with in Acol. An opening bid of 2NT will probably work out best, particularly if your partner is armed with the new-style Baron 3♣ convention advocated in the previous chapter. The disadvantage of opening 2♡ is that you will be severely compromised by a negative 2NT response, which will at best lead to 3NT being played from the wrong side. However, 2♡ is much more attractive if you are employing Herbert negatives, for the sequence

2♡–2♠–2NT will describe the hand well and offer the best practical chance of reaching the correct contract.

The other main advantage of Herbert negatives is particularly apparent when the opener has diamonds and spades.

♠   A Q J 9
♡   A 5
♢   A K J 9 7 3
♣   4

Open 2♢, intending to rebid 2♠ over the negative response of 2♡. You can now subside in 3♢ if partner bids 2NT over 2♠, and it is important to notice how much easier the bidding is than if you were compelled to start 2♢–2NT–3♠.

The positive responses to an Acol Two are similar to those to 2♣, except that the high-card requirements are slightly greater: generally speaking, the responder needs 10 or more points for a positive response, unless he has good trump support or can introduce a good suit of his own at the two level.

To respond in a new suit shows a strong four-card suit at the two level or a goodish five-card suit at the three level. It is important to avoid introducing bad suits in this kind of auction, for the opener will generally be interested in where your high-card strength is situated and he will be entitled to expect to find you with at least the king of your suit. For this reason, it may occasionally be correct to respond in a suit in which you hold A–K–x in preference to one as bad as J–x–x–x–x; alternatively, you may be able to jump to 3NT to show scattered values and to avoid bidding a bad suit.

Since an Acol Two opening promises a good suit, the responder can feel free to raise on trump support as poor as Q–x or x–x–x. It is generally agreed that a raise to the three level should guarantee an ace; an immediate raise to four shows useful values, but denies holding a first-round control. This may prevent the opener from going overboard if he has a solid-looking hand lacking primary controls.

OPENER'S REBIDS AFTER AN ACOL TWO
After a positive response, a game-forcing situation is established and the bidding can proceed naturally. A jump rebid by the opener in a sequence of this kind:

2♡   3♣
4♡

shows a completely solid suit and invites the responder to cue bid his controls.

After a negative response, a simple rebid by the opener is not forcing, but the responder will normally push on to game if he has as much as one quick trick. A simple change of suit by the opener, for example:

$$2\heartsuit \qquad 2\spadesuit$$
$$3\diamondsuit$$

is not 100% forcing, but the responder will only pass if the hands are obviously a hopeless misfit. A reverse by the opener after an Acol Two:

$$2\diamondsuit \qquad 2\heartsuit$$
$$3\heartsuit$$

is forcing for one round.

If the opener makes a jump rebid in his original suit after a negative response, he is not showing a solid suit; he is merely indicating that his hand is so strong that he cannot risk being out of game.

A NEW APPROACH TO TWO BIDS

This section must be prefaced by a word of warning. If you are completely satisfied with Acol Two bids in their present form, I can only suggest that you browse quickly through the next few pages. If, on the other hand, you have a sneaking feeling at the back of your mind that perhaps you are not getting as much benefit from your opening two bids as you might, the following paragraphs may provide particularly interesting reading.

The main drawbacks to Acol Two bids in their traditional form may be summarised as follows:

(a) It is clearly extravagant to use three bids ($2\diamondsuit$, $2\heartsuit$ and $2\spadesuit$) to show one kind of hand, that is, a distributionally powerful hand containing eight or more playing tricks.

(b) Acol Twos are a fairly rare species. On grounds of frequency, therefore, there is a strong argument for utilising at least some two bids to describe a more common type of hand; this is, in fact, the case for the Weak Two.

(c) Acol Twos are strangely inadequate in that, while you can show strong hands with spades, hearts or diamonds, hands containing eight or more playing tricks in clubs have to be treated in a different way; you either open a non-forcing 1♣ or force all the way to game by opening 2♣.

(d) The normal Acol structure of two bids does not cater at all for one particularly awkward type of hand: the powerful three-suiter. Hands of the following kind are all too likely to be played at the one level in the wrong suit:

WEST		EAST	
♠	A K 7 2	♠	Q 8 6 4
♡	3	♡	J 10 7 5 2
◇	A K 9 4	◇	5
♣	K Q J 5	♣	10 8 2

As you will see, 4♠ is ice-cold on these hands. Whose fault would it be if an Acol pair were to bid 1◇–No?

THE WEAK TWO

In an effort to eliminate these disadvantages and in pursuance of my normal desire to obtain the best of both worlds, a desire which will be evident throughout this book, I have been experimenting for many years with a completely different structure of two bids. The system has worked so efficiently in practice that I am not ashamed to pass it on for more universal consumption. Briefly, the scheme is as follows.

2♣ is a normal Acol opening, completely forcing to game unless the auction commences 2♣–2◇–2NT.

2♡ and 2♠ are Weak Two bids. They show a goodish six-card suit and a hand which is just below-strength for a light opening one bid; the point count shown can be 5–9, 6–10 or any other range you happen to prefer.

     ♠   A K 10 9 6 4
     ♡   7 3
     ◇   Q 10 5
     ♣   8 2

This is an ideal weak 2♠ opening bid. It is clearly a good tactical weapon, depriving the enemy of valuable bidding space if the hand belongs to them. Furthermore, the Weak Two, being a limit bid, has the advantage of leaving partner in comparative comfort while threatening to make life difficult for the opponents. Partner will almost always be able to judge the combined worth of your two hands, and he can plan his tactics accordingly. If there is no chance of game your way, he can decide whether to increase the pre-emptive effect of the Weak Two by making a further raise, or whether to pass on reasonable values in the hope that the enemy will be lured into the auction. And if the responding hand is strong enough to visualise game, the Weak Two is such a descriptive bid that it does little to hinder the constructive bidding of your side. Even such a devoted Acol-ite as the late 'Skid' Simon, who was himself largely responsible for the development of the Acol Two, admitted that the case for the Weak Two is extremely strong: 'The whole matter of combatting the Weak Two boils down to taking a view. And nobody can take the right view all the time.'* I would not argue with that.

Properly handled, the Weak Two can fulfil a useful role in any organised bidding system, and it is interesting to note that most of the modern artificial club systems incorporate the Weak Two in the major suits into their basic structure. It is perfectly true, of course, that the Weak Two can be a dangerous weapon in certain inexperienced hands,

* *Design For Bidding*, by S. J. Simon.

but that is equally true of other everyday conventions like Blackwood and Stayman and it is not a particularly compelling argument against the bid itself. After all, you would be unlikely to allow a young child to play with a hand grenade.

2◇ covers two other types of hand: the strong two opening in any of the four suits and the strong three-suited hand which is so difficult to deal with in Acol. As is likely with any multi-purpose bid, the bidding after a 2◇ opening contains a number of specialised conventional sequences; as you will see, however, the basic concept is reasonably simple.

THE MULTI-PURPOSE 2◇ OPENING

(a) Requirements for 2◇
Either (a) a strong one-suited hand which would normally qualify for an Acol Two opening; this includes the case which is normally overlooked where the long suit is clubs, or (b) a Roman 2◇: that is, a hand with a 5-4-4-0 distribution and 16-21 points or a hand with a 4-4-4-1 distribution and 17-22 points in the three suits.

(b) Responses to 2◇
2♡ shows 0-7 points; 2♠ shows 8 or more. The 2♠ response is forcing to game.

(c) Opener's Rebid
After a negative response, the opener bids three of his suit if he has an Acol Two opening. This is not forcing and, if the opener is reluctant to stop short of game, he should jump to the four level over 2◇-2♡; alternatively, if he has a solid suit and promising holdings in the other suits, he can jump to 3NT.

If the opener has a three-suited hand, he bids 2♠ with 16-18 and 2NT with 19-21 points in the three suits.

After a positive response, the opener bids 2NT on any Roman 2◇ hand. If he has an Acol Two opening, he bids three of his suit. Since the sequence 2◇-2♠ is forcing to game, an immediate jump to the four level can be used to show a completely solid suit.

(d) The Auction after a Roman 2◇ and a Negative Response
AFTER 2◇-2♡-2♠

2NT by the responder shows 0-4 points and asks the opener to bid the suit above his short suit; 3♣ shows a singleton or void in spades. Thereafter, any bid by the responder is not forcing and suggests the final contract.

3♣ by the responder shows 5-7 points and asks the opener to bid the suit above his short suit; 3NT shows a singleton or void in spades.

Thereafter, any bid of one of the opener's suits by the responder is not forcing.

AFTER 2♢–2♡–2NT

3♣ by the responder shows 0–7 points; the bidding proceeds in the same way as after 2♢-2♡-2♠-3♣.

(e) *The Auction after a Roman 2♢ and a Positive Response*
AFTER 2♢–2♠–2NT

3♣ by the responder asks the opener to bid his short suit; 3NT shows a singleton or void in clubs. The responder will now usually be in a position to determine the final contract. However, if he wants further information about the opener's hand, he can employ a 'relay' bid in the next highest suit. This asks the opener to describe his hand by a series of step responses, as follows:

1 STEP   17–18 points in the three suits and a losing singleton.

2 STEPS   16–18 points in the three suits and a void or singleton ace.

3 STEPS   19–22 points in the three suits and a losing singleton.

4 STEPS   19–22 points and a void. The only exception to this occurs when the opener's short suit is clubs or spades; in this case, he should bid 4♡ on any hand containing a void, for the four-step reply will consume too much valuable bidding space.

(f) *4NT after a Roman 2♢*
4NT by the responder asks for controls on the following basis:

In the three suits

Ace	2 points
King	1 point
Queen of trumps	1 point

In the short suit

Void or singleton ace not already shown	2 points

The responses to 4NT are as follows:

5♣	3–5 points
5♢	6 points
5♡	7 points
5♠	8 points etc.

After 4NT, 5NT by the responder is a grand slam try. If there is no agreed suit, 5NT requires the opener to bid 6♣, over which the responder sets the trump suit; the opener should then bid seven if he has the queen of trumps. If there is an agreed suit, 5NT by the responder asks for queens in the three suits not previously shown. The opener bids 6♣ with no queen, 6♢ with one, and 6♡ with two.

(g) *The System in Action*

That completes an extremely brief summary of the basic framework of the new multi-purpose 2◇ opening. It must be emphasised that it is only a framework, and interested partnerships can certainly spend many happy hours adding some gorgeous twiddly bits of their own; for example, making use of the completely idle sequences like 2◇–2♠–2NT–3◇. Those of you who abhor 'scientific' bidding systems will no doubt be deeply disappointed to find such a convention recommended in a book devoted to the Acol system; you might even be contemplating action under the Trade Descriptions Act. In my defence, however, I must promise that the sequences after a multi-purpose 2◇ are almost the only purely conventional sequences advocated in these pages, and point out that powerful three-suited hands are always extremely difficult to handle by completely natural methods.

The only disadvantage to the proposed new structure of two bids is that it becomes impossible to handle powerful two-suited hands satisfactorily.

♠ A K J 10 7
♡ A Q J 8 3
◇ A 4
♣ 3

Whereas normal Acol Twos allow you to open this hand with 2♠ and rebid 3♡ over a negative response, the auction will become excessively cramped if you are compelled to proceed via 2◇–2♡–3♠. This compulsory jump to show an Acol Two opening matters little if you have a one-suited hand, for you are no worse off than if the bidding had commenced 2♠–3♣–3♠ in normal Acol; however, you have clearly lost valuable bidding space if the opening hand is two-suited. Playing the multi-purpose 2◇, you just have to choose between opening with a lightly frisky game-forcing bid of 2♣ and adopting the conservative approach and starting with the modest bid of 1♠; in actual fact, this latter method is most unlikely to end in disaster, for the shapeliness of your hand suggests that the opponents will also have too much distributional strength to be prepared to let the auction die at the one level.

Even if the necessity to open powerful two-suited hands with a one bid occasionally results in a missed game, this is an extremely small price to pay for all the other advantages which are to be gained from playing the multi-purpose 2◇: the freedom to use 2♡ and 2♠ as Weak Two opening bids, the ability to cope with strong hands containing a powerful club suit, and the comparative ease with which you will be able to handle strong three-suited hands. Just in case there are still some non-believers, let us have a look at one or two examples of the system in action.

WEST	EAST	WEST	EAST
♠ A Q J 10 4	♠ 8		
♡ K 9 7 3	♡ 5	2◇	2♡ (1)
◇ —	◇ 10 8 6 4 2	2♠ (2)	2NT (3)
♣ A Q 8 2	♣ K J 9 7 6 3	3♡ (4)	5♣

(1) 0–7 points.
(2) A Roman 2◇ hand with 16–18 points.
(3) I have 0–4 points. What is your short suit?
(4) Diamonds.

Notice that, under normal Acol methods, this hand might well be played in 1♠.

		WEST	EAST
		2◇	2♠ (1)
WEST	EAST	2NT (2)	3♣ (3)
♠ Q 10 9 5	♠ A K J 6 2	3◇ (4)	3♡ (5)
♡ A K 7 6 4	♡ Q J 3	3NT (6)	4NT (7)
◇ —	◇ K J 4	5◇ (8)	5NT (9)
♣ A K Q 8	♣ 7 2	6♣ (10)	6♠ (11)
		7♠ (12)	

(1) 8+ points and game-forcing.
(2) A Roman 2◇ hand.
(3) What is your short suit?
(4) Diamonds.
(5) Please describe your hand further.
(6) 16–18 points in the three suits and no diamond loser.
(7) How many controls do you have?
(8) Six – two aces and two kings.
(9) Please bid 6♣ so that I can set the trump suit.
(10) Okay.
(11) Spades are trumps. Have you the queen?
(12) Yes.

WEST	EAST	WEST	EAST
♠ J 10 8 7	♠ 9 5 4 2	2◇	2♠ (1)
♡ A K Q 4	♡ J 10 5 3	2NT (2)	3♣ (3)
◇ A K Q 6	◇ J 2	3NT (4)	No (5)
♣ 5	♣ A K Q		

(1) 8+ points.
(2) A Roman 2◇ hand.
(3) What is your short suit?
(4) Clubs.
(5) Ugh.

Notice how difficult it would be to stop in a safe contract if you were not playing the Roman 2◇ convention.

WEST	EAST	WEST		EAST	
♠ A J 9 5	♠ K Q 3	2◇		2♠	(1)
♡ A K 8 6 4	♡ 7	2NT	(2)	3♣	(3)
◇ —	◇ A Q 5 4 2	3◇	(4)	3♡	(5)
♣ A K J 2	♣ Q 10 9 3	4◇	(6)	4NT	(7)
		5♠	(8)	7♣	

(1) 8+ points.
(2) A Roman 2◇ hand.
(3) What is your short suit?
(4) Diamonds.
(5) Please describe your hand further.
(6) 19–21 points and a void in diamonds.
(7) How many controls do you have?
(8) Eight – three aces and two kings.

Notice that it would be difficult to locate the club fit at all under normal methods, for the bidding will probably commence 1♡–2◇–2♠ and the club suit might well vanish in the jungle surrounding the fourth suit.

FOUR NO TRUMPS

An opening bid of 4NT is conventional, asking the responder to identify his ace holding. The replies are as follows:

5♣	to show no ace.
5◇	to show the ace of diamonds.
5♡	to show the ace of hearts.
5♠	to show the ace of spades.
5NT	to show two aces.
6♣	to show the ace of clubs.

Opportunities for this bid are obviously extremely rare. The opener needs an unusually solid hand and, if he is to gain the maximum benefit from the convention, a void in one of the side suits.

♠ A K Q J 10 7 5 2	♠ A K Q
♡ 5	♡ K Q J 10 9 7 5 2
◇ A K Q 9	◇ A K
♣ —	♣ —
HAND A	HAND B

Open 4NT. In each case, a response of 5♡ or 5NT by partner will enable you to bid the grand slam. To show how rare this convention really is, however, it is worth pointing out that Hand A can be handled equally effectively by another method: open 2♣ and jump rebid in spades, showing a completely solid suit and inviting partner to cue bid if he has an ace.

♠ ♠

5. PRE-EMPTIVE OPENING BIDS

THREE OF A SUIT

Little needs to be said in connection with pre-emptive three bids. However, this might be an opportune moment to issue a salutary reminder of the old Culbertson Rule of Two and Three, which applies to all sacrifice bidding. The theory is that, since it can never be a good investment to go down more than 500 to save a game, the pre-emptive hand should be able to win within three tricks of the contract non-vulnerable and within two tricks vulnerable.

That is the theory. In practice, of course, experienced operators recognise that the enemy do not always do the right thing over three bids and that, even if a particularly grisly pre-empt could be punished to the extent of considerably more than 500, the opponents will often throw down the gauntlet and push on to the wrong game or to an unmakeable slam. This being the case, the requirements for pre-emptive opening bids are often reduced to levels which Culbertson would scarcely recognise; in fact, there are occasions on which one might uncharitably assume that the Rule of Two and Three applied not to the number of tricks by which the bidder expects to be defeated, but to the number of tricks he might reasonably expect to make.

There are just four further points to make in connection with opening threes.

(a) The position at the table should be an influencing factor if you are contemplating a shaded three bid. A pre-empt by the dealer is likely to be more effective in that it might make life awkward for either opponent and in that the enemy have no knowledge at all about the strength or nature of each other's holdings. Similarly, third in hand is an ideal position in which to open with a doubtful three bid, for the fact that your partner has already passed means that he is unlikely to be seriously misled by your antics. Incidentally, this point does not apply only to featherweight openings; it is often a good tactical ploy to open three on a surprisingly strong hand.

♠ K 7 2
♡ 6 3
♢ A Q J 9 5 4
♣ J 10

Third in hand, there is a good case for opening 3♢ rather than 1♢ on this hand. You may thereby manage to snatch the part-score or, perhaps more likely, to cause the opponents to misread the situation and bid a little too much.

If you are second in hand, it is advisable to restrict your opening three bids to hands which you would not be ashamed to show to young children. Once one of the opponents has passed, it is a 50–50 chance as to whether it is your partner or your left-hand opponent who has the majority of the outstanding strength, and you are just as likely to make things difficult for your own side if you open with an atypical three bid.

(b) The weakness of the otherwise admirable Rule of Two and Three is the assumption that the only important consideration is the *extent* of the possible loss if the pre-emptive opening is doubled. What matters even more is the likelihood of your loss, balanced against the probability and the size of your gain. In practical terms, this point is reflected in considerations of the vulnerability: if you are vulnerable and the opponents are not, your opening three bid is far more likely to come under the axe than if the vulnerability is in your favour. If they are vulnerable and you are not, the opponents will almost always prefer to make a constructive bid over your pre-empt, even if they could double and take you on a little trip to the cleaners.

(c) Similarly, the level of your bid is an important factor when you are considering its safety. Whereas the opponents will find it temptingly easy to enter the auction over 3♣ or 3◇, they will have more difficulty in contending with an opening bid of 3♠. Since they are always loth to say nothing at all in the face of an opposing pre-empt, it follows from this that they are more likely to double 3♠ than they are to double 3♣. So be warned.

(d) Another factor to be borne in mind if you are contemplating an unsound pre-empt is the nature of the counter-measures which are available to the opponents. If their methods are such that your left-hand opponent is unable to double you for penalties, you will clearly have calmer waters into which to push out the boat.

To summarise. While the Culbertson Rule of Two and Three is eminently sensible, there is considerably more to the theory of pre-emptive bidding than this. As we have seen, the requirements for a third in hand opening bid of 3♣ at favourable vulnerability are by no means the same as for a second in hand 3♠ opening when you are vulnerable and the opponents are not – particularly if the opponents have a penalty double at their disposal.

THREE NO TRUMPS

An opening bid of 3NT in Acol has always shown a long, completely solid minor suit. The significant change in recent years has been that, whereas the opener used to like to hold quite a few bits and pieces in the side suits, it is now recommended that he should have no more than a king or queen in reserve.

♠ 7 5   ♡ 10 4   ◇ Q 3   ♣ A K Q J 7 5 3

Open 3NT. This has the same pre-emptive effect as an opening bid of 4♣, but it makes it possible for your side to play in 3NT if that is the best contract. The advantage of eliminating the need for any guards in the side suits for an opening bid of 3NT is twofold. First, it makes the bid more likely to occur. Second, and more important, it makes it much easier for the responder to judge what to do, especially if the opening bid is doubled.

RESPONSES TO 3NT

(a) The responder should only pass 3NT if he has some kind of guard in three suits, for, playing the bid in the new style, he cannot rely on his partner for anything apart from a solid minor suit.

(b) If the responder elects to sign off in four of the opener's minor suit, he bids 4♣. Partner passes if clubs is his suit; otherwise he converts to 4◇.

(c) Since the responder will always bid 4♣ as a sign-off, even if he is completely certain that his partner's suit is diamonds, a response of 4◇ is idle in a natural sense. Its best use is as a conventional bid enquiring about the opener's distribution for slam purposes. The recommended replies to 4◇ are as follows:

4♡	to show a singleton or void in hearts.
4♠	to show a singleton or void in spades.
4NT	to show a hand containing no singleton or void.
5♣ or 5◇	to show a singleton or void in the other minor suit.

This convention may enable the partnership to reach an excellent slam if the full hands are something like:

WEST	EAST	WEST	EAST
♠ 8	♠ J 7 3		
♡ J 8 3	♡ A 6	3NT	4◇
◇ 7 5	◇ A K Q 10 3	4♠	6♣
♣ A K Q J	♣ 10 6 3		
7 5 4			

Notice the way in which the 4◇ convention makes it comparatively simple for East to bid the excellent slam on minimum values. Even if the opponents cash a top spade and switch to hearts, East knows that his ten of clubs will provide a vital entry card should it be necessary to ruff out the fifth diamond.

(d) A response of 4♡ or 4♠ is natural, showing a good, long suit and a desire to play there.

(e) A raise to 4NT is a slam try, suggesting that the opener should push on if he has a trick to spare: that is, an eighth playing trick not vulnerable or a ninth playing trick vulnerable.

(f) A jump to 5♣ shows a hand on which the responder wishes to be in game in the opener's minor suit. The opener should either pass or convert to 5◇, depending on his suit.

FOUR OF A SUIT

An opening bid of four of a suit is also a pre-emptive gambit. It suggests at least a seven-card suit and seven playing tricks not vulnerable or eight playing tricks vulnerable. However, the general points made earlier in connection with opening three bids all apply with equal force to four bids.

♠   7 2
♡   A Q J 10 8 6 4 2
♢   J 9 5
♣   —

Open 4♡. This is perfectly sound if you are not vulnerable, and it would also be quite reasonable at game all. You might require just a little more at unfavourable vulnerability, particularly if you are in second position.

In traditional Acol, all opening four bids have a similar meaning. 4♣ and 4♢ are rather less useful than four of a major, however, because they have less pre-emptive effect and, more important, because a number of suitable hands can be shown by the opening bid of 3NT which we examined earlier; moreover, to open with four of a minor takes the auction beyond what might well be the correct contract of 3NT. For this reason, a fairly recent innovation is to use opening bids of 4♣ and 4♢ as transfer bids, suggesting that the responder should convert to 4♡ or 4♠ respectively.

The advantage of this idea is that it enables the opener to distinguish between two different types of four bid in a major suit.

♠   A K J 9 7 6 5 3   ♠   A K Q 10 7 4 2
♡   7 5   ♡   J 2
♢   10   ♢   A 8 3
♣   J 6   ♣   4
    HAND A   HAND B

The opener would like to open 4♠ on both these hands, but for different reasons. On Hand A, he is rightly anxious to open with a high-level pre-empt for tactical reasons; and on Hand B, he wants to employ 4♠ as the best constructive opening bid, for the hand is not really strong enough in honour tricks for an Acol Two Bid and yet the opener's rebid will present something of a problem if he starts with a modest 1♠.

If he employs the suggested new methods, the opener has no further problem. He opens 4♠ in the normal way on Hand A. On Hand B he opens 4♢, which shows a 'good' 4♠ opening and is mildly constructive as well as being pre-emptive; 4♢ does, in fact, show a hand on which the opener might have opened with an Acol Two Bid if he had held slightly more honour strength.

Over a Texas opening bid of 4♣ or 4◇, the responder signs off in the opener's known major suit if he has no ambition. If he can visualise a slam opposite his partner's strong hand, the extra space made available by the Texas opening enables the responder to show interest by cue bidding.

WEST	EAST	WEST	EAST
♠ A K Q 10 7 4 2	♠ J 8 5	4◇	4♡
♡ J 2	♡ A K 9 4 3	5◇	5♠
◇ A 8 3	◇ K 7	6♠	
♣ 4	♣ Q 10 2		

Once East has shown mild slam interest by his 4♡ cue bid, West's excellent spade suit and minor suit controls enable him to push on to the unbeatable slam contract.

Part Two

THE FIRST RESPONSE

♠ ♠

This book is not intended to be a primer on bidding. Just as you would
search in vain in these pages for instructions on how to count high-card
points, so will you have to delve elsewhere if you are anxious to find a
detailed exposition on when to respond 1♠ to an opening bid of 1◇.
This section will concentrate solely on some of the more difficult
problems associated with the first response to one of a suit, striving as
always to add a degree of precision to normal Acol methods.

The murky areas of Acol which are directly attributable to the
choice of initial response to the opening suit bid arise when the
responder has strong support for the opener's suit, when he is strong
enough to make an immediate forcing take-out, or, strange as it may
seem, when he has passed originally. These situations are all covered at
length later in this section; we must first run quickly through one or
two general principles.

6. GENERAL POINTS

WHICH SUIT TO RESPOND

With one four-card suit, there is rarely any problem. You always bid it if you can do so at the one level. If your suit is lower-ranking than the opener's, of course, you will only be able to mention it if you have 9 or more points and are strong enough to venture to the two level; with a weaker hand, you will have to conceal your suit and respond 1NT.

There is only one exception to this general rule. This occurs when partner opens 1♠ and your only four-card suit is hearts.

| ♠ J 7 2 | ◇ 9 6 5 | Partner |
| ♡ A Q 8 3 | ♣ A 7 2 | 1♠ ? |

It is generally agreed that, because of the vast amount of bidding space it consumes, a response of 2♡ to 1♠ should guarantee a five-card suit; this enables the opener to raise freely with three-card support and solves an awkward rebid problem if he has quite reasonably opened 1♠ on a 4–3–4–2 distribution. A response of 2♡ is therefore ruled out on the above holding and, since the hand is quite unsuitable for a jump to 2NT, the correct response is 2♣. This may seem at first sight a dangerous manoeuvre, but it is in fact completely safe. The most embarrassing move which the opener can make is to raise to 3♣, but you will then be able to return to 3♠ with no further worries: for partner to raise to 3♣, he must have four-card support; and for partner to open 1♠ when he has a four-card club suit, he must have at least five spades. Q.E.D.

With two or more four-card suits, the general rule is extremely simple: you should bid the cheapest one first. Generally speaking, this rule applies without reference to the quality of the suits involved. Let us take an exaggerated example.

♠ A K 10 9	
♡ J 9 5 4	Partner
◇ J 7 3 2	1♣ ?
♣ 4	

Bid 1◇. This response is both theoretically and practically correct. Since you have such bad support for partner's first suit, it is clearly vital to find any available 4–4 suit fit as soon as possible. 1◇ makes it easy to do just that, for if the opener is not in a position to raise diamonds, he will be able to show a four-card major suit at the one level. Clearly one would like to be able to bid the excellent spade suit first in this situation; however, to respond 1♠ to 1♣ would make it difficult to find a 4–4 fit in either red suit.

There are, in fact, very few exceptions to this general rule that you should respond in the cheapest available four-card suit first. One of the early gospels* suggests an exception when you have a strong hand with two good four-card major suits.

    ♠ K Q 9 7
    ♡ A K 6 2   Partner
    ◇ 10 7   1◇   ?
    ♣ 5 3 2

The suggested solution to this pleasurable problem is that you should bid 1♠, intending to show the heart suit on the next round. I find this argument far from convincing. In the first place, it is not made clear how many hearts you should bid after, say, 1◇–1♠–2◇. 2♡, while generally agreed to be constructive, would certainly not suggest a balanced hand with 12 points; and 3♡ would surely be an exaggeration on a holding of this type. Secondly, there is a serious theoretical objection to bidding 1♠ first on this hand. To respond in spades and then bid hearts on the next round will virtually guarantee a five-card spade suit: since it is normal to bid four-card suits in ascending order, partner will quite reasonably assume from a sequence like 1◇–1♠–2◇–2♡ that the spade suit is longer – and therefore of at least five-card length. Finally, an original response of 1♠ is open to the criticism that, if the opener elects to raise to 2♠ on three-card support, it is possible that a 4–4 heart fit will be lost forever. This could clearly only happen if the opener's distribution is something like 3–4–5–1, but the overall case against 1♠ is quite strong.

My money is therefore on the normal response of 1♡. If partner can introduce spades at this point, your troubles will be over; if he bids 2♣, you can choose between an aggressive 3NT and a pawky 2NT; and if he rebids 2◇, you can show the strength and nature of your hand precisely by making a forcing reverse into 2♠. Partner may assume from this sequence that you have a five-card heart suit, but this is by no means guaranteed: he knows that your policy is to bid four-card suits in ascending order and, since his rebid of 2◇ has virtually denied a four-card spade suit, he should realise that your forcing rebid of 2♠ may be nothing more than a no-trump probe.

There is only one situation where it is theoretically correct not to bid your four-card suits upwards in response to an opening one bid. This is where the responder anticipates a rebid problem and realises that he can keep the auction under closer control by bidding his suits in an unnatural order. For example:

    ♠ K J 7 2
    ♡ 8 5 3   Partner
    ◇ J 8   1◇   ?
    ♣ A K 9 4

* *The Acol System Today*, by Terence Reese and Albert Dormer.

There is a strong case for bidding 2♣ in this sort of situation. If you bid the natural-looking 1♠ and hear 2◇ from partner, you will be in a slightly awkward predicament: 2NT would be misleading with such a weak holding in hearts, while 3♣ both overstates the strength of the hand and invites an unwelcome preference to 3♠ or 4♠. To respond 2♣ initially, however, will leave you better placed on the next round. If partner rebids 2◇, you can now bid 2♠ – thereby keeping the bidding at a more manageable level and leaving the way open for a withdrawal to 3◇ if partner gives preference to 3♣ over 2♠.

With two five-card suits, the general rule is that you should respond in the higher-ranking suit first. This is always true if a major suit is involved.

♠ K 10 7 5 2	◇ A Q J 8 4
♡ 7 2	♣ 3

If partner opens 1♣ or 1♡ opposite this hand, the correct response is 1♠ in either case. The disadvantage of making the apparently cheaper bid of 1◇ over 1♣ is that it will take a long time to convince partner that you have a five-card major suit. On the other hand, the sequence

1♣	1♠
2♣	2◇

guarantees at least five spades; as we saw earlier, you would have bid 1◇ over 1♣ if both your suits were of four-card length.

The only exception occurs when you have two five-card minor suits and an indifferent hand.

♠ 7	
♡ 6 3	Partner
◇ K 10 8 6 3	1♠ ?
♣ A Q 7 5 2	

Bid 2♣. As you only intend to make one bid on this hand (that is to say, you will give way with good grace if partner rebids his wretched suit), it is more constructive to bid 2♣ than the normal 2◇. 2♣ gives partner a chance to raise clubs or rebid 2◇, and it will therefore locate a fit in either minor suit; 2◇, on the other hand, will make it impossible for the partnership to find a club fit unless the opener is strong enough to make a high reverse and bid 1♠–2◇–3♣.

With five-four in two suits, the general rule is that you should respond in the longer suit first. The only genuine exception to this rule occurs when to show your five-card suit would entail going to the two level on inadequate values.

♠ K J 7 2	
♡ 7 5	Partner
◇ 8 2	1♡ ?
♣ K 10 9 5 4	

Bid 1♠. Seven points are not enough to justify an excursion to the two level, and your excellent club suit will have to remain a secret, at least for the time being.

There is a school of thought which makes another exception to the rule in cases where the responder has a five-card minor and a four-card major and a hand which is not strong enough to make two bids.

♠ K 9 6 3	
♡ 7 5	Partner
◇ 8 2	1♡ ?
♣ A Q 10 5 4	

Some players would favour a response of 1♠ in this situation, on the grounds that, since you are not intending to bid again over a minimum rebid from partner, a response of 2♣ will risk missing a 4–4 spade fit if the opener is not strong enough to reverse. There is clearly an element of truth in this argument. However, while it will occasionally result in your playing in the wrong part-score contract, there is also a very good case to be made for a response of 2♣: after all, if you are intending to make only one bid on the hand, it would seem infinitely more helpful to make the one which tells partner (a) that you have at least 9 points, and (b) that your longest suit is clubs. Whereas a response of 2♣ might occasionally lead to the wrong part-score, the pedantic response of 1♠ might even result in a missed game.

♠ A 8 5	
♡ A 9 6 4 2	1♡ 1♠
◇ A Q 10	?
♣ J 3	

If the opener elects to raise to 2♠, an action which could not really be criticised, he will not be too pleased when the post-mortem reveals that the responder's hand is that shown above. The recommended response of 2♣ will lead to an excellent game contract via the auction 1♡–2♣–2NT–3NT.

THE ONE NO TRUMP RESPONSE

Nothing new here. The 1NT response to an opening suit bid shows about 6–9 points and suggests a balanced hand on which you can neither raise the opener's suit nor bid a suit of your own at the one level.

If you are in doubt as to whether to bid 1NT or to raise partner's suit, it is generally advisable to take the latter course of action. With three-card support for partner, it is normally correct to bid 1NT only if your hand is completely balanced or if your strength lies in your short suits.

♠ 9 6 3	
♡ 7 5	Partner
◇ K 9 5 4 2	1♠ ?
♣ A 6 3	

Whereas a 1NT response would be obligatory over an opening bid of
1♡, it is better to raise 1♠ to 2♠. The good top cards and the weak
doubleton holding mean that the hand is better suited to playing in a
trump contract, even if your support is a little inadequate.

While the usual definition of the 1NT response is that it shows a
balanced hand with 6–9 points, the word 'balanced' is perhaps slightly
optimistic. The hand will certainly tend to be balanced in response to
1♣ or 1♢, but it is important to remember that 1NT over a major
suit opening is often little more than a completely conventional response,
showing the values to bid and denying the ability to bid anything else.

♠ 6	
♡ Q 10 4	Partner
♢ 9 7 5 4 3 2	1♠ ?
♣ A J 8	

Bid 1NT. What else? The hand is too strong to pass, but not strong
enough to justify a two level response on such an appalling suit.

It is even possible to devise a situation in which it is correct to
respond 1NT on a hand containing a void.

♠ —	
♡ A J 4 2	Partner
♢ 10 7 6 5 3	1♠ ?
♣ Q 9 8 4	

Bid 1NT. Although a pass could work out best, particularly if partner
is secretly planning to make a violent leap in spades on the next round,
this hand is a little too strong for such pusillanimous action. Furthermore, the 1NT response offers such a good chance of improving the
final contract that it becomes a worthwhile gamble.

One final point about the overworked 1NT response. It has been
suggested that the strength of the response should vary according to
which suit is opened; that is to say, that 1♢–1NT should show a
stronger hand than 1♠–1NT. However, this can be shown to be a
nonsensical suggestion. While it is normal to interpret 1NT in response
to 1♣ as better than minimum, say 8–10 points, this is possible only
because you will always be able to find an alternative bid on a weaker
hand. If 1NT over 1♠ is to mean 6–9 points, the bid must logically
have exactly the same meaning over 1♢ or 1♡; it will otherwise become
impossible to handle certain everyday holdings like:

♠ J 7 6	
♡ K 10 4	Partner
♢ 9 5	1♢ ?
♣ Q 9 8 5 3	

Bid 1NT. Partner should not assume that this response shows a
stronger hand just because it is made over 1♢ rather than over 1♠:
there is no reason at all why you should not have a short diamond

holding and a long club suit which cannot be shown at the two level.

THE TWO NO TRUMPS RESPONSE

One of the least satisfactory parts of the original Acol system is the immediate response of 2NT, showing a balanced hand with 11 or 12 points. As the bid is allotted such a precise meaning, it is difficult to imagine that anything could possibly go wrong with it. In practice the direct 2NT response tends to be avoided like the plague – and used only by players who are trying to hog the bidding opposite a supposedly weak partner. The reasons for this ostracism are as follows:

(a) Even when they have a hand which qualifies for a 2NT response, most players feel an understandable reluctance to eschew the search for a 4–4 major suit fit.

♠ K J 7 4
♥ Q 5 2   Partner
♦ J 4   1♦   ?
♣ A 10 6 3

A balanced hand? Yes. With 11 or 12 points? Yes. So you respond 2NT? Probably not, because of the danger of missing a 4–4 spade fit. This lure of the four-card major suit reduces the frequency of the immediate 2NT response considerably.

(b) The 2NT response has such a cramping effect on the auction that it is rarely welcomed by the opener. For example, it will be the last bid he wants to hear if he has a weakish hand on which he is particularly anxious to find a playable fit.

♠ A 10 6 3
♥ K J 7 4   1♣   2NT
♦ 5   ?
♣ A 7 5 3

There is nothing more galling at the bridge table than to be fixed by one's own partner in an uncompetitive auction . . .

(c) In almost every case, the balanced 11–12 point hand can be shown equally well, if not better, on the second round after a simple suit response on the first. There are very few hands on which it is not possible to make a temporising bid first, intending to rebid 2NT in order to show a balanced, medium-strength hand. Even one of the High Priests of Acol, S. J. Simon, admits* that the principal use of the 2NT response occurs after a minor suit opening when your only four-card suit is partner's suit. He quotes the following example:

♠ A J 6
♥ K J 5   Partner
♦ 9 7 5 3   1♦   ?
♣ K 9 4

* *Design For Bidding*, by S. J. Simon.

If a non-forcing jump to 2NT is not available, this hand certainly presents an awkward problem. You will just have to choose between a misleading raise to 3◇ and a waiting bid of 2♣, neither of which is particularly attractive. Be that as it may, it is possibly slightly extravagant to wait for this kind of hand to come along before you employ an immediate response of 2NT.

For one reason or another, therefore, the traditional Acol 2NT response is used very sparingly. Rather like that dreadful tie you were given last Christmas, it is left gathering dust and cobwebs in the cupboard, although very few people dare to throw it away completely. Maybe this is the time for a little spring-cleaning.

Baron players are among the enlightened minority who have harnessed the 2NT response for a different use: they employ it to show a balanced hand with 15–19 points and a 4–4–3–2 or 4–3–3–3 distribution. They claim, with a great deal of reason, that it is very difficult to find a satisfactory response on this type of hand, for an ordinary jump shift is apt to give partner quite the wrong idea of the shape. Furthermore, this is not the kind of hand on which the responder can take control for, while there are too many points for him to be satisfied with a mere game, there will also be too many gaps for him to be able to visualise a slam.

♠	A J 6	♠	K Q 8
♡	A 10 7 5	♡	A 7 3
◇	K Q 8	◇	A K 9
♣	Q 3 2	♣	J 7 5 2
	HAND A		HAND B

Both these hands are awkward to handle opposite an opening bid of 1♡, for it is always misleading to make a jump shift on a non-existent suit and yet you will have great difficulty in showing the strength of your hand if you improvise with a more modest beginning. A Baron 2NT response is the ideal solution to this kind of problem, and it is strongly recommended that you should consider using the comparatively idle response of 2NT in this way.

My own preference is to reserve the Baron 2NT response specifically for strong 4–3–3–3 holdings; these are the hands with which it is particularly difficult to cope under normal methods. Strong hands with a 4–4–3–2 distribution present less of a problem, for you should always be able to find a suit in which to make a jump shift. Furthermore, you will be much more anxious to locate any available 4–4 fit when you have two four-card suits, and the search will probably not be aided by a conventional jump to 2NT. Finally, it is always much easier for the opener to assess the value of the combined hands if he knows the precise distribution of his partner's hand; to widen the scope of the

2NT response to cover any hand with no five-card suit and no singleton must necessarily reduce the accuracy of the bid.

Against this, to reserve the 2NT response for completely balanced hands reduces the frequency of the bid until it becomes almost as rare as the original Acol 2NT bid. For this reason, I shall not be at all offended if you decide to play the Baron 2NT as the original Baron book suggests; in fact, I shall be delighted if my ramblings persuade you even to consider modernising an obsolete piece of Acol machinery.

7. STRONG RAISES OF THE OPENER'S SUIT

THE LOSING TRICK COUNT

Several different methods have been devised for evaluating the responder's hand when he is contemplating a limit raise in his partner's suit. Most players count high-card points and make some kind of adjustment to take account of good distribution; others compute what they call their 'ace values', taking the honour trick value of the hand and making additions for any distributional values; others favour a method known as the Losing Trick Count.

My own favourite is the Losing Trick Count, which is now generally accepted as a reliable ready reckoner to be consulted when the responder is in any doubt. Since the main theme of this book is how to incorporate precision and accuracy within the Acol framework, it is clearly appropriate to spend a little time on what is probably the most precise and accurate method of hand valuation.

The basic count of losers is as follows:

(a) With a void or singleton ace, count no loser in that suit.

(b) With any other singleton, or A–x or K–x, count one loser.

(c) With any other doubleton, count two losers.

(d) With a three-card or longer suit, count one loser for each missing high honour (ace, king or queen); you should not count more than three losers in any one suit. A suit headed by A–J–10 only counts as one loser. On the other hand, Q–x–x should be counted as three losers unless partner has bid the suit or unless the unsupported queen is 'balanced' by an ace in another suit.

An opening bid should be assumed to show a seven-loser hand. Having ascertained the number of his own losers, therefore, the responder adds it to seven and subtracts the total from the magic number of 18 to see how high he can go.

One example of the system in operation should suffice to show its simplicity.

♠ Q 10 7 3
♥ 6   Partner
♦ A 9 8 6 5   1♠   ?
♣ 7 5 4

This is just the sort of hand on which the inexperienced player would hover between an aggressive raise to 3♠ and a pawky raise to 2♠ – 'but I only had six points, partner!' Let us attempt to solve the problem with the aid of the Losing Trick Count.

		LOSERS
♠	Q 10 7 3	2
♥	6	1
♦	A 9 8 6 5	2
♣	7 5 4	3
		—
		8
		=

And now for the sums. 8+7=15. 18−15=3. So we raise to 3♠ with complete confidence.

With a little practice, you will find it easy to adjust the original count of losers in the light of the previous bidding; for example, you should deduct a loser if you have exceptional trump control, or if your quota of aces and other key features is better than it might be. If you incorporate these vital adjustments, you will find the Losing Trick Count a remarkably accurate guide; it takes into account all the features which really matter once you have found a suit fit.

THE DOUBLE RAISE

A double raise of the opener's suit is not forcing; it shows at least four-card trump support and approximately 8 losers, and it invites the opener to push on to game if he has anything to spare. If the opener's suit is a minor, a double raise tends to show better values than it would in a major. This is because there is further to go to reach game in a minor suit, and because the responder does not normally want to rule out the possibility of settling peacefully in 3NT.

♠ K Q 7 5 4		♠ A 8 3	
♥ A 8 3	Partner	♥ 10 2	Partner
♦ 10 2	1♠ ?	♦ Q 8 6	1♣ ?
♣ Q 8 6		♣ K Q 7 5 4	
HAND A		HAND B	

Hand A is worth a direct raise to 4♠. While Hand B is exactly similar, however, a raise to 3♣ is sufficient: 3NT might easily prove to be the best game contract.

GAME-GOING RAISES

One of the principal areas of bidding in which Acol can be shown to have developed markedly over the years is the raise to game in the opener's suit. Whereas the direct raise from 1♡ to 4♡, or from 1♠ to 4♠, was originally an omnibus bid, covering a wide range of hands, the responder now has the machinery to draw a fine distinction between the various types of game raise.

Let us suppose for the purposes of this analysis that the opener bids 1♡ and that the responder has four-card trump support and a hand which is worth a raise to at least 4♡. He can select any of the following routes to game.

(a) *A Direct Raise* to 4♡ is often partly pre-emptive. It suggests a distributional, rather than a high-card raise, and the hand is unlikely to contain more than 10 or 11 points.

♠	6 3	
♡	Q 10 7 5 2	Partner
◇	K Q 8 6 4	1♡ ?
♣	9	

Bid 4♡. If partner is unable to make the game, you are still likely to do well on the hand by recording a small minus score in 4♡; in that case, the opponents will almost certainly be able to make a contract in one of the black suits.

(b) *The Delayed Game Raise.* Consider the following sequences:

A. 1♡–1♠–2♣–4♡
B. 1♡–1♠–2◇–4♡
C. 1♡–2♣–2◇–4♡
D. 1♡–1♠–2♠–4♡

Since the opener has not guaranteed a five-card heart suit in any of these auctions, the responder's jump to game on the second round must be based on four-card trump support. The inference is that he was too strong for a direct raise to 4♡ on the first round.

A Delayed Game Raise sequence of this kind suggests the high-card strength for an opening bid, 12–14 points, four-card trump support and about 6 losers; furthermore, it is strongly recommended that the suit first bid by the responder should be a good one, so that the opener can count on obtaining a vital discard or two if he has a useful holding like Q–x in the suit and good controls in the two side suits.

♠	7 2	
♡	K Q 7 5	Partner
◇	10 8	1♡ ?
♣	A K J 6 3	

Bid 2♣, intending to follow with a jump to 4♡ on the next round. This sequence shows the values for an opening bid, four-card heart support, and, very important, a good club suit. It may be the only way to reach the excellent slam contract if the full hands are as follows:

	WEST		EAST	WEST	EAST
♠	K 8	♠	7 2	1♡	2♣
♡	A J 9 6 3	♡	K Q 7 5	2◇	4♡
◇	A 9 6 4	◇	10 8	4♣	5♣
♣	Q 5	♣	A K J 6 3	5◇	6♡

This is a good slam to reach on minimum values. It only becomes possible because of West's excellent controls, coupled with the knowledge that he will find a good club suit in dummy.

A Delayed Game Raise sequence can sometimes be frustrated by the opener rebidding his original suit.

♠	A 5 3		
♡	K 10 7 5	1♡	2♣
◇	6	2♡	?
♣	A Q J 9 5		

Whereas the sequence 1♡–2♣–2◇–4♡ would clearly be a Delayed Game Raise, the waters have been muddied by the opener's rebid of 2♡. Now that partner has shown five hearts, a jump to 4♡ at this point might simply be based on three-card trump support and game-going values; it would no longer convey the normal delicate inferences about the four trumps and the good club suit, and it is desirable to have some way of distinguishing between a common-or-garden raise to game and a full-blooded Delayed Game Raise in this murky situation. My suggestion is that you should bid 3♠, an unnecessary jump in a third suit, to show this kind of hand. More of that anon, when we shall be considering the responder's second bid in more detail.

(c) *The Swiss Convention* is designed to cover hands which are too strong for a direct raise to game in the opener's suit, but not suitable for a Delayed Game Raise because of the absence of a good side suit.

The convention involves harnessing two otherwise idle responses. Opposite an opening bid of 1♡ or 1♠, a jump to 4♣ or 4◇ is used to show a good raise to four in the opener's suit: that is, a raise based on high cards rather than on distributional strength. Various precise meanings have been assigned to the two responses. It is, for example, possible to use 4♣ and 4◇ to show a specific number of key cards; to use 4♣ to show two aces and a side-suit singleton; to use 4♣ on a certain point-count range and 4◇ on a slightly stronger hand; to relate 4♣ and 4◇ to the actual holding in the suits themselves; or to the quality of the trump support; and so on. The choice is yours. My only plea is that you should not allot the Swiss response such a rare and precise meaning that you can no longer use it on the sort of hand for which it was originally designed:

♠ K 10
♥ K Q 8 3   Partner
♦ Q 10 6 5   1♥   ?
♣ A 7 2

Bid 4♣ or 4♦, whichever is permitted by your methods. This is an ideal hand for the Swiss convention, for you have a good raise to 4♥ with a full quota of high cards, and yet you have no worthwhile suit to show in a Delayed Game Raise sequence.

It is sometimes possible to employ Swiss to set the trump suit when the responder intends to push on beyond game.

♠ A Q 3
♥ K Q 10 8 5   Partner
♦ A 9 5   1♥   ?
♣ Q 7

This hand is well worth a jump shift, but to force with 3♦ would give partner the wrong picture and to force with 2♠ courts disaster if the auction subsequently drifts irretrievably out of hand. One solution to this awkward problem is to make a Swiss response of 4♣ or 4♦. If partner makes an encouraging move, you will be more than happy to co-operate; and if he attempts to sign off in 4♥, you can proceed by way of 4♠ and see if that will goad him into action.

(d) *Minor Suit Swiss*. The original Swiss convention only applies over an opening bid of 1♥ or 1♠. However, hands with good support for partner's minor suit are even more difficult to handle in traditional Acol. Consider the following holding:

♠ K 10 7 5
♥ K 8 2   Partner
♦ A Q J 3   1♦   ?
♣ 10 5

Under normal methods, you have to respond 1♠ and keep your fingers crossed that the auction will not slip out of your control. It has to be admitted, however, that an immediate response of 1♠ will almost certainly make it extremely difficult for you to show your diamond support later. For example, the bidding might proceed:

(A) 1♦   1♠   (B) 1♦   1♠   (C) 1♦   1♠
    1NT   ?   2♣   ?   2♠   ?

A jump to 3♦ is not completely forcing in either of the first two sequences, and this means that you will have to risk hoisting the bidding beyond 3NT if you are anxious to show your excellent diamond suit. In Sequence C, too, it will be difficult to describe the exact nature of your hand for, even if a return to 3◇ is regarded as forcing at this point, it might be construed as merely being a try for 4♠.

One solution to this, and to other similar problems, is to extend the Swiss convention to cover opening bids of 1♣ and 1◇. Two learned theorists* suggest that 1♣–3◇ and 1◇–3♡ should be equivalent to 1♡–4♣, and that 1♣–3♡ and 1◇–3♠ should equal 1♡–4◇. This is undoubtedly an improvement on normal Acol methods. One example they quote is:

♠	A Q 8	
♡	K 5	Partner
◇	9 7 3	1♣ ?
♣	A J 6 3 2	

This hand is difficult to express in steam-age Acol. The responder would in practice probably resort to an uneducated jump to 3NT, but this could prove to be quite the wrong contract. The recommended Swiss response of 3◇ solves the problem well, and has the merit of putting partner in the picture so that he can assist in the search for the best final contract.

To my mind, however, there is a serious theoretical drawback to the Reese-Dormer version of Minor Suit Swiss. It concerns the fairly common case where the responder has a four-card major suit as well as four-card support for the opener's minor.

♠	10 8	
♡	Q 10 7 2	Partner
◇	A K 9 5	1◇ ?
♣	K Q 3	

This is a difficult hand for the system. If you make the recommended Swiss response of 3♡, you completely rule out the possibility of playing in a 4–4 heart fit; and if you therefore respond 1♡ to 1◇, you run the risk of having to conceal your excellent diamond support if the auction develops in certain ways.

For this reason, I recommend an important change to the system. My theory is that, opposite an opening bid of 1♣ or 1◇, an immediate response of 3♡ or 3♠ should show a four-card major suit as well as four-card support for the opener's minor and the values for an opening bid. This more precise use of the two bids should make it comparatively easy for the opener to judge the correct game contract: he can settle in 3NT, raise to four of the major if he has four-card support, or push on in the agreed minor suit if he has slam ambitions or if he regards it as the best denomination for game. A jump to 3◇ over 1♣, or even a jump to 4♣ over 1◇, can be used in a vaguer Swiss sense, showing that you have the values for game in the opener's minor and that you have neither a four-card major suit nor a minor suit worthy of mention.

* *Bridge for Tournament Players*, by Terence Reese and Albert Dormer.

♠ 10 7
♡ K Q 8 5   Partner
◇ K 10 4   1♣   ?
♣ A Q 7 2

Bid 3♡. This shows the values for an opening bid and a hand
containing at least four clubs and precisely four hearts. The opener
should now be in a good position to judge whether to play in 3NT or
4♡, or whether to push on in clubs; alternatively, he might be able
to investigate no trump possibilities by bidding 3♠ over 3♡

♠ K 7 4
♡ 9 3   Partner
◇ A 10 4   1♣   ?
♣ A Q 10 7 6

Bid 3◇. This hand would be an extremely difficult one to handle
under normal Acol methods, but Minor Suit Swiss provides a good
solution to the problem. 3◇ shows the values for an opening bid and
at least four-card club support, and it denies holding a biddable major
suit; the opener should now be in a good position to judge the correct
final contract.

(e) *The Jump Shift*. Responding hands which contain good support
for the opener's suit and which are too strong for a direct raise to game,
for a Delayed Game Raise, or for a Swiss sequence have to be shown by
first making a jump shift in another suit. But more of this in the next
section.

───────────── ♠ ♠ ─────────────

8. THE JUMP SHIFT

The term 'jump shift' is an American one. It is used to describe a
jump response in a new suit after an opening bid of one of a suit
and, as is often the case with phraseology originating on the other
side of the Atlantic, it is such a concise and descriptive term that it
seems destined to assume a permanent place in international bridge
language. Lest this book on modern Acol might otherwise seem old-
fashioned, therefore, you will find yourself reading about 'jump shifts'
from this point on.

A jump shift is absolutely forcing to game. Furthermore, it should
alert the opener to the possibility of a slam, and this means that, generally
speaking, the responder should make a jump shift whenever he has 16
or more high-card points opposite an opening bid. As with all rules,

however, there are exceptions to this; there are situations in which it is undoubtedly correct to force to game immediately with fewer than 16 points and, perhaps more important, there are situations in which it would be quite wrong for the responder to make a jump shift when he has considerably more than 16.

THE JUMP SHIFT ON MINIMUM HANDS

One case where it may be correct to make a jump shift on fewer than 16 points is where the responder has excellent support for the opener's suit as well as a useful suit of his own.

♠ K Q 7 4		
♡ 8 3	Partner	
◇ 7	1♠	?
♣ A K 10 7 5 2		

Opposite an opening bid of 1◇ or 1♡, 2♣ would be quite enough at this stage. If partner opens 1♠, the hand becomes too powerful for such modest action. Force to game with 3♣ and follow this by supporting spades vigorously; you will otherwise find it quite impossible to express the power of your hand.

You have only to visualise this hand opposite a fairly typical, minimum opening bid to realise its potential strength.

WEST	EAST	WEST	EAST
♠ A J 8 5 3	♠ K Q 7 4	1♠	3♣
♡ A Q 7 2	♡ 8 3	3♡	3♠
◇ J 6	◇ 7	4♠	5◇
♣ 8 4	♣ A K 10 7 5 2	5♡	6♣

Even in the face of an opening diamond attack, the slam depends on nothing more than a 3–1 spade break and a 3–2 club break. However, East will have no hope at all of squeezing any signs of life out of his partner if he fails to make a jump shift on the first round.

It is even more important to force on minimum values when you have good support for partner's minor suit.

♠ 8		
♡ A 7 2	Partner	
◇ K Q J 7 3	1♣	?
♣ K 10 6 5		

Bid 2◇ and follow it up by supporting clubs on the next round. If you fail to force on the first round, the vagaries of the Acol system are such that you may actually have great difficulty in showing your club support at all! Suppose, for example, that you respond 1◇ and hear partner make the likely rebid of 1♠. Since jump preference to 3♣ at this point would not be forcing, you will probably have to resort to a fourth suit manoeuvre and bid 2♡. This will work out satisfactorily if partner is able to show extra values, but you will be back in the mire if he makes a minimum rebid like 2NT: you can clearly bid 3♣ now, but are you completely certain that partner will regard this as forcing? And will he assume that you have such good four-card support for clubs?

You will be faced with similar rebid problems if the auction commences 1♣–1◊–1NT; once again a jump of 3♣ would not be completely forcing, and once again you will have to set off on a mazy, scientific sequence and hope that your partner will be in the right place when the music stops. All these problems will be avoided if you make a jump shift to 2◊ on the first round: the meaning of 1♣–2◊–2NT–3♣ is crystal clear.

You should also force to game on minimal values when you have a good suit of your own.

♠	A K 10 9 5 4	♠	A K Q J 10 7 3
♡	5 3	♡	7 2
◊	A Q 2	◊	K 4 2
♣	10 4	♣	5
	HAND A		HAND B
♠	A K 8 4 2	♠	A K J 9 3
♡	A 8	♡	K 7 5
◊	5 4 3	◊	7 2
♣	A 7 2	♣	A 8 3
	HAND C		HAND D

All these hands are well worth a jump shift to 2♠ opposite an opening bid of one of a suit, even though they all fall short of the generally accepted yardstick of 16 points. The test to employ if you are in doubt about whether or not to force is a simple one: if you make a non-jump response in your long suit, are you going to be faced with an impossible rebid problem on the next round?

For example, consider Hand A. If you make a simple response of 1♠ to an opening bid of 1♡, you will be very poorly placed on the next round if the auction commences 1♡–1♠–2◊. You can keep things ticking over by bidding 3♣, the fourth suit, but you will still have made very little progress towards describing your powerful spade suit and your six-loser hand. The answer is to jump to 2♠ on the first round and then go very quietly thereafter.

Similarly, you will find it virtually impossible to get Hand B across to your partner unless you jump to 2♠ and follow this with a further jump to 4♠. As we shall see later, this type of unnecessary jump bid in a forcing situation guarantees a completely solid, no-loser suit: that is, a suit which will be perfectly playable in a grand slam opposite a void.

Hands C and D are less clear-cut, but the recommended test suggests that the best way of dealing with them is to force with 2♠ and then proceed very quietly thereafter. On Hand C, for example, many players would be content to bid a simple 1♠ over an opening suit bid, but they will subsequently find themselves faced with an extremely difficult rebid problem if the opener makes a minimum rebid. Let us suppose that the full hands are:

WEST	EAST
♠ Q 3	♠ A K 8 4 2
♡ J 4 3	♡ A 8
◇ A 2	◇ 5 4 3
♣ K Q 10 8 6 4	♣ A 7 2

As you will see, 6♣ is an excellent contract. However, it is difficult to see how East will ever be able to goad his partner into showing signs of life unless he makes an immediate jump shift over the opening bid; West will hardly visualise four key cards in the opposite hand if the auction is allowed to commence with a sleepy 1♣–1♠.

Similarly, Hand D will almost certainly become difficult to handle if the responder makes the thoughtless bid of 1♠ over 1♡. He will only have to hear a 2♣ or 2◇ rebid from his partner to start wishing that he had forced on the first round, for there is no longer any way of expressing the power of his hand. In practice, he will probably have to be content with a temporising rebid in the fourth suit, but this is unlikely to help very much. He may still find himself an embarrassed spectator as his partner makes a lot of tricks in no trumps:

WEST	EAST	WEST	EAST
♠ 10 2	♠ A K J 9 3	1♡	1♠
♡ A Q 8 6 4	♡ K 7 5	2◇	3♣
◇ A Q 8 4	◇ 7 2	3NT	
♣ K 10	♣ A 8 3		

East can, of course, solve all his problems by making a jump shift to 2♠ on the first round. Having got the hand off his chest in this way, he can subsequently afford to take thinks very gently; West will now be in a position to make the running, and the partnership should reach the excellent slam contract without too much difficulty.

WHEN NOT TO JUMP SHIFT

As we have seen, there are certain hands on which it is correct to force on minimum values; conversely, there are just as many situations in which the responder would be very ill-advised to make a jump shift on an extremely powerful holding. There are, in fact, hands which are *too* strong for a force.

♠ A Q 10 7 4	
♡ A 3	Partner
◇ A Q 3	1♡
♣ K J 7	

Unfortunately, this is not the sort of problem with which I am often faced. If you ever have the good fortune to hold this kind of hand and hear your partner open the bidding, however, you will find that a simple response of 1♠ will work out better than an immediate jump shift. The reasons for this are twofold.

First, you are clearly on your way to a slam when you hold this gigantic hand opposite an opening bid. The only real questions remaining are whether you are going to play in a suit or in no trumps, and whether you are going to settle in six or seven, and you should realise from the outset that it is you who will have to make the final decision. Even if you jump shift immediately, you will never be able to convey to your partner the extreme power of this hand so that he is in a position to take control of the auction. There is therefore little point in starting to paint a picture of your hand which you can never hope to complete. You will just have to attempt to obtain all the information you can about partner's hand, and this will be easier to achieve if you take things slowly with a gentle bid of 1♠, leaving as much bidding space as possible in which partner can tell you all about his goodies.

The second reason for not forcing on this 20-point hand follows from the first. If you are anxious to build up an exact picture of your partner's hand, you will often obtain more precise information if his rebid is made in a situation which is not forcing to game. For example:

(A) 1♥   1♠   (B) 1♥   2♠
    1NT   2NT

The opener's rebid of 1NT in Sequence A is normally strictly limited; and, even if you favour more flexible methods and play a wide-range 1NT rebid, you will doubtless have some ingenious mechanism at your finger-tips which will enable you to find out all about the opener's point count and distribution. However, can you be as certain about the opener's 2NT in Sequence B? Is he showing a minimum opening bid, or is he merely describing the general nature of his hand and concealing quite reasonable values? Partner's rebid is clearly more informative without the jump shift.

Similarly:

(C) 1♥   1♠   (D) 1♥   2♠
    3♠   3♠

Since the one-over-one response may be based on as little as 6 points and a four-card spade suit, the opener's jump to 3♠ in Sequence C must show a strong hand with four-card trump support. However, no exact inference can be drawn about his raise to 3♠ in Sequence D; he may be trying to be helpful with three-card spade support and a minimum hand, or he may have a full-blooded raise to 3♠ with four trumps and good values. Once again the jump shift muddies the waters around the opener's rebid.

♠ 8 7
♡ A K Q 10 8 4   Partner
◇ A K 7   1♠   ?
♣ K 5

This is another type of hand on which it will simplify your task
if you do not make a jump shift. A slam is almost certain now that
partner has opened the bidding and, since you will never be able to
tell partner the full story of your huge point count and your huge heart
suit, it is you who will eventually have to determine the final contract.
For this reason, it is best to bid a simple 2♡ over 1♠; this gives partner
as much room and as much freedom as possible in which to tell you all
about his modest values.

So much for the gentle approach which you should adopt when you
are in the delightful position of being too strong to make a jump shift.
Another reason for not forcing immediately when you have excellent
values is that you have two suits which you may have difficulty in slotting
conveniently into the auction if you squander too much bidding space.

♠ 10 4
♡ A K Q 4   Partner
◇ A K J 7 3   1♠   ?
♣ 9 3

Opposite an opening bid of 1♣, you would have an automatic
response of 2◇, intending to show both the strength and the distribution of the hand by rebidding 3♡ on the next round. If partner opens
1♠, however, it will not be wise to make a jump shift to 3◇. To do so
will leave you in an awkward position if the auction commences, as
is likely, with 1♠–3◇–3♠. Are you going to see it through with 4♡
now, hoping that partner will find a way of stopping in time if he
has a minimum hand? And, if you decide not to show your heart suit,
are you going to sign off in 4♠ or in 3NT? Either could prove to be
the wrong contract, and the hand will be much easier to handle if you
make a simple response of 2◇ on the first round; no rebid by the
opener will embarrass you, and you will be able to keep things going
with a strength-showing reverse into 3♡ on the next round.

Similarly:

♠ 7 5
♡ A 2   Partner
◇ K Q 10 7 5   1♡   ?
♣ A K J 4

While this hand is well worth a jump shift in terms of high-card
points, it will simplify the subsequent auction if you bid a simple 2◇
over 1♡ or 1♠. The danger of bidding 3◇ will become apparent if
partner rebids his major suit, for you will no longer be able to show your
excellent club suit without hoisting the bidding to the four level – and

beyond what might well be the only safe game contract of 3NT.

Furthermore, there is an important theoretical argument against forcing and then bidding clubs on this hand. As we shall see a little later, a sequence of the following kind:

might well be construed as agreeing the opener's spade suit and showing a club feature for slam purposes. There is a strong case for this interpretation, and this is another reason for not forcing on awkward two-suited hands.

It must not be assumed from the preceding argument that it is never correct to make a jump shift when your hand is two-suited; the important point to remember is that, if he is contemplating an immediate force to game, the responder must think ahead a little and plan his rebid.

♠ A Q J 3
♡ 7 2   Partner
♢ K 4   1♡   ?
♣ A K 9 6 3

On this occasion, there is no reason not to make an immediate jump shift to 3♣. No rebid by the opener can embarrass you. If he rebids 3♡, you can describe your hand precisely by introducing 3♠; and if the auction commences 1♡–3♣–3♢, you have an obvious bid of 3NT at your disposal.

THE CHOICE OF SUIT IN WHICH TO FORCE

Generally speaking, if the responder is planning to make a jump shift on a two- or three-suited hand, he should force in the suit in which he would have made a simple response if his hand were slightly weaker.

♠ K 10 7 2
♡ A Q 8 3   Partner
♢ 8   1♢   ?
♣ A K J 5

Bid 2♡. It is clearly important to locate any available 4–4 fit on this hand, and you should therefore follow normal principles and bid your cheapest suit first. 2♡ will leave the way clear for partner to rebid 2♠ or 3♣, and in either case the search for a fit will be over.

The only controversial theoretical point in this connection concerns the quality of suit guaranteed by a jump shift. Some authorities suggest that a jump shift should only be made on a good suit, but this seems to me to be a dangerous generalisation. It is certainly a sound principle not to force on a bad suit when you have good support for the opener's suit.

♠ Q 7 5 3
♡ A Q J 7   Partner
♢ 7 5   1♡   ?
♣ A K J

This hand is clearly worth a jump shift opposite an opening bid
of 1♡ and, since you are planning to play in a heart contract in any
case, it is best to force with 3♣ rather than 2♠. It is to be hoped
that, when you subsequently show your excellent heart support, partner
will be in a position to move on towards a slam. If he is, he will quite
reasonably expect you to have at least one high honour in the suit in
which you force, and this makes a jump to 2♠ misleading and
dangerous.

The situation is much less clear-cut when the responder does not
intend to play the hand in the opener's suit. If the responder has to
worry about finding a fit as well as telling his partner about the strength
of his hand, he will find himself strangely handicapped if a jump shift
has to guarantee a good suit.

♠ Q 10 7 2
♡ A J 8   Partner
♢ Q 4   1♢   ?
♣ A K 8 5

The answer to this problem depends to a large extent on your
style of bidding opposite a jump shift. If the opener is given complete
freedom to make his natural rebid after a force, the responder can stick
to the good-suit principle and jump to 3♣ on the above hand – secure
in the knowledge that his partner will feel free to rebid an uninhibited
3♠ if he has a four-card spade suit. If your methods are for the opener
to make his normal rebid one level higher after a jump shift (and, as we
shall see shortly, there is a good case for this treatment), the ultra-safe
jump to 3♣ will no longer be sound. Let us suppose, for example, that
the full hands are as follows:

WEST	EAST	WEST	EAST
♠ A J 9 4	♠ Q 10 7 2		
♡ 7 2	♡ A J 8	1♢	3♣
♢ A K 7 5 3	♢ Q 4	3♢	3NT
♣ J 3	♣ A K 8 5		

Apart from the jump shift to 3♣, it is difficult to criticise any of the
bids in this auction, but 3NT is far from the best contract. 6♠ depends
on a finesse and a reasonable break at worst, and yet the suit may not be
mentioned at all if the responder is debarred from forcing without a
high honour in his suit.

To summarise. The principle of not bidding bad suits on good
hands is a good one, and it certainly applies when the responder is
planning a jump shift based on powerful support for the opener's suit.

However, the responder must not adhere to the principle too rigidly when he is still anxious to find a playable trump fit: unless the opener is permitted to make a free-range rebid, there are occasions on which the responder may have to force on an indifferent suit.

OPENER'S REBID OVER A JUMP SHIFT

The general rule here is that opener should make the same rebid over a jump shift as he would have done over a non-jump response – only one level higher. This rule applies particularly to no trump rebids.

    1♡   3♣
    3NT

Since a rebid of 2NT over 2♣ would show 15–16 points, 3NT over 3♣ suggests the same point-count range. This agreement certainly simplifies the opener's rebid problems on balanced hands.

    ♠ K 7 2
    ♡ A Q 10 9   1♡   3♣
    ♢ A 10 4   ?
    ♣ Q 8 3

Bid 3NT, showing a balanced hand and 15 or 16 points. Without the agreement that this rebid shows extra values, you would have a difficult problem in this situation: you would probably have to distort the hand and resort to bidding a three-card diamond suit.

    1♡   2♠
    2NT

If your methods favour a narrow-range 1NT rebid, 2NT over a jump shift will suggest the same values. If your 1NT rebid shows 12–16, you can identify the strength by rebidding 2NT on 12–14 points and jumping to 3NT to show 15–16.

It is, of course, possible to rebid 2NT on considerably more than 14 points, waiting for the responder to describe his hand further.

    ♠ A Q 4
    ♡ J 2   1♢   2♡
    ♢ K 10 8 6 3   ?
    ♣ A K 9

Bid 2NT. A slam is a near-certainty after partner's strong response, and 2NT will give him a chance to show the kind of hand on which his jump shift was based: a strong heart suit, a good fit for diamonds, or general values.

A rebid of the opener's original suit after a jump shift is completely unlimited; it may show a minimum opening bid, or it may be setting the scene on a strong hand. A jump rebid in this situation, for example

    (A) 1♣   2♡   (B) 1♠   3♣
          4♣   4♠

shows a completely solid suit. Furthermore, when the bid is made at the game level, as in Sequence B, the implication is that the hand contains very little apart from the solid suit.

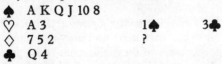

♠ A K Q J 10 8
♡ A 3   1♠   3♣
♢ 7 5 2   ?
♣ Q 4

Bid 3♠. While it would be convenient to show the solid suit by jumping to 4♠, the overall strength of the hand is too great for such action. 4♠ would be the correct rebid if the ace of hearts were transformed into a small card.

A raise of the responder's suit is also unlimited, apart from the one sequence (1♠–3♡–4♡) where the raise is made at the game level. The opener should avoid the common mistake of raising his partner's jump shift suit prematurely.

♠ K Q 7 2
♡ 7 5   1♣   2♢
♢ K J 4   ?
♣ A J 9 3

Bid 2♠, in exactly the same way as you would bid 1♠ after 1♣–1♢. There are two important reasons for this bid. First, an immediate raise of a minor suit always implies four-card trump support. And secondly, there is no reason at all why the responder should not have bid 2♢ on a hand containing four diamonds and four spades; you should therefore not show your secondary support for diamonds until the possibility of a 4–4 spade fit has been ruled out.

A jump raise in this situation

    (A) 1♢   2♠   (B) 1♣   2♢
          4♠   4♢

shows excellent four-card trump support. Once again, the overall strength of the hand is limited if the jump raise takes the bidding to the game level, as in Sequence A above.

♠ K Q 9 5
♡ 7 3   1♢   2♠
♢ A Q J 7 2   ?
♣ 8 4

Bid 4♠. This describes the hand perfectly: a good diamond suit, excellent four-card spade support and a minimum opening bid. The unnecessary jump may be just what partner wants to hear if he has made a jump shift on a nebulous spade suit.

A bid of a new suit after a jump shift is natural. As I hinted earlier, the important theoretical point to be discussed in this connection concerns the meaning of reverse sequences like the following:

(A) 1♢   2♠   (B) 1♢   3♣   (C) 1♠   3♢
     3♡   3♡   4♣

The general principle of bidding after a jump shift is that the opener should respond as he would have done to a non-jump response in the same suit. Applying this tenet to these situations, the opener's rebids should all show the strength and distribution associated with a normal reverse one level lower. This information will clearly be of great assistance to the responder, and this all seems eminently logical and sensible.

However, some authorities suggest that a reverse after a jump shift should show the distribution, but not the strength, suggested by a normal reverse, and this rather surprising view has attracted so much popular support that it is worth a summary consideration. The disadvantage of this treatment is that the uninhibited reverse does not impart as much information to the responder; furthermore, there are many situations in which it actually wastes a round of bidding. Consider the following hands.

WEST	EAST	WEST	EAST
♠ 9	♠ K 10 8 4 2	1♢	2♠
♡ K J 6 3	♡ A Q 7 5	3♢	3♡
♢ K Q J 8 3	♢ A 5	4♣	4♢
♣ A 4 2	♣ K 7	etc.	

Under normal methods, West is not strong enough for a reverse bid of 3♡ over his partner's jump shift to 2♠. He therefore makes an unlimited rebid of 3♢ and, when East shows a four-card heart suit, he can agree hearts and show extra values by making the delicate cue bid of 4♣. The partnership is now able to exchange information in the comfort of the four level.

Now observe what happens if West is permitted by his methods to make an uninhibited reverse over 2♠. The auction will commence:

WEST   EAST
1♢   2♠
3♡   ?

However, East will now be unable to draw any inferences about the opener's high-card strength and, since he has a minimum hand for his jump shift, he will probably have to be content with a simple raise to 4♡. The result is that the partnership has now lost a complete round of bidding and is struggling to exchange information at the five level.

While the uninhibited reverse is patently imprecise regarding strength, its protagonists can clearly claim that it conveys much valuable information concerning the distribution of the opening hand.

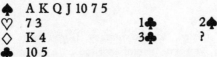

♠ 7 3
♡ A J 8 3   1♣   2♠
◇ Q 4   ?
♣ A Q 10 8 5

My selection here is 3♣. However, if your methods permit a reverse bid of 3♡, you can show five clubs and four hearts by your first rebid. This is undoubtedly extremely satisfying, but have you really gained very much? After all, if there is a 4–4 heart fit between the two hands, the responder will introduce his heart suit after 1♣–2♠–3♣, and the fit will still come to light at the three level. In fact, provided the responder remembers the earlier injunction not to force if he has two awkward suits to show, any available 4–4 fit will always be located at a reasonable level, and there is therefore little advantage to be gained by allowing the opener to show his distribution by his rebid.

The case for the uninhibited reverse is therefore dismissed. It is recommended that a change of suit by the opener after a jump shift should convey exactly the same information as over a simple non-jump response.

RESPONDER'S REBID AFTER A JUMP SHIFT
Generally speaking, the responder's rebid after a jump shift will identify the type of hand on which his force was based.

If the jump shift was based on a good suit of his own, the responder will show this by rebidding it at his second turn. In principle, a rebid of this kind:

      1◇–2♠–3♣–3♠

shows a suit with not more than one loser, but it may occasionally be necessary to rebid a suit no better than A–Q–10–x–x–x. With a completely solid suit, the responder should make a jump rebid on the second round; however, if the jump rebid takes the bidding to the game level, it should show that there is very little else to report apart from the solid suit.

♠ A K Q J 10 7 5
♡ 7 3   1♣   2♠
◇ K 4   3♣   ?
♣ 10 5

Bid 4♠, showing a completely solid spade suit and a minimum hand for the jump shift. If he had a similar hand with another ace, the responder would be too strong for a limited rebid of 4♠ and he would have to take things more slowly by rebidding 3♠.

If the jump shift was based on a fit with the opener's suit, the responder will show this by supporting it on the second round. Jump preference to the opener's first suit shows excellent four-card trump support and a minimum hand for the original force.

♠ K Q J 7
♡ 8 2   1♠   3♣
◇ Q 10 5   3♡   ?
♣ A K 10 8

Bid 4♠. Jump preference in a game-forcing situation shows first-rate four-card spade support and minimum values. Any further move towards a slam must clearly emanate from the opener in this situation, and the knowledge that you have good spades may be just the encouragement he needs if he is conscious of having opened the bidding on a threadbare suit.

The only really murky area of Acol bidding following a jump shift concerns the bid of a third suit by the responder. Consider the following sequences:

(A) 1♡   3♣   (B) 1♡   2♠
    3♡   3♠   3♡   4♣

The meaning of Sequence A is clear-cut; prima facie, the responder is showing a strong hand with at least four spades and at least five clubs, and the opener should proceed accordingly. But what about Sequence B? Does this show, by analogy, a strong hand with a club suit and a spade suit which is as long or longer?

There are many Acol players who would probably answer this question in the affirmative, albeit rather hazily, but there are two serious objections to this interpretation. In the first place, for the responder to show two suits in such an extravagant manner hoists the bidding irretrievably beyond 3NT, and it is difficult to see how the partnership is going to grind to a halt in a safe no trump contract after such an uneconomical sequence. As you will remember, it is for this reason that the responder is enjoined to take things slowly if he has a two-suited hand on which he will be unable to show both suits without climbing to dizzy heights. To recapitulate:

♠ A Q J 5 4
♡ 9 3   Partner
◇ 10 4   1♡   ?
♣ A K Q 10

Bid 1♠. Softlee, softlee, catchee monkey. If you make a jump shift to 2♠ on this hand, you will be embarrassed by a 3♡ rebid from the opener and find yourself unable to show the excellent club suit without venturing beyond 3NT.

The second reason for not taking a new suit at the four level purely at its face value concerns a hand of this kind:

♠ A K 10 6 4
♡ K J 2   1♡   2♠
◇ A K 5   3♡   ?
♣ 7 3

Now that the opener has shown a rebiddable heart suit, this hand is a little too strong for a simple raise to 4♡ – but not strong enough to take over the reins and launch into a 4NT routine. The ideal solution is to make a cue bid of 4◇, and this is such a useful bid in this kind of situation that the following general rule is strongly recommended: following a jump shift on the first round and a simple rebid of his first suit by the opener, any non-jump bid of a new suit at the four level by the responder should be a cue bid, agreeing the opener's suit.

A jump bid in a new suit by the responder is much more simple to analyse.

> (A) 1◇ 2♠   (B) 1◇ 2♡   (C) 1◇ 2♡
>   3◇ 4♡   3♡ 4♠   3♣ 4♠

A jump of this kind shows a void and a hand with strong slam interest. It agrees a trump suit by inference. In Sequence A, diamonds is the agreed suit; in B, hearts; and in C, clubs, the last suit bid by the opener.

> ♠ A 10 4
> ♡ K Q 10 9 3   1♡   3◇
> ◇ K Q J 7 4   3♡   ?
> ♣ —

Bid 5♣, showing a void and agreeing hearts for slam purposes. This hand appeared in a popular bidding competition,* and the director made the valid point that, for the opener to be able to assess his values accurately, he must be certain that the responder's club control is a void. 5♣ tells him just that.

------------------------------ ♠ ♠ ------------------------------

9. BIDDING AFTER PASSING

One of the strangely inaccurate areas of Acol occurs when one of the partnership has made an original pass. It arises as a direct result of an alarming tendency for the opener to back out of the auction prematurely, his only excuse being 'but you had already passed, partner!'

Once the responder has already limited his hand to a certain extent by a first-round pass, there is clearly no reason to play a simple change of suit bid by him as absolutely forcing; on the other hand, there is even less reason for the opener to pass it at the slightest excuse. The nagging fear that the opener might drop out of the auction at an inconveniently early stage means, in effect, that you have to play a completely different structure of responses following an original pass. This is a very curious state of affairs.

* *Bidding Challenge,* by Joe Amsbury; *Bridge Magazine,* May 1973.

♠ J 7 2
♡ A K J 3
◇ 10 3
♣ Q 7 5 4

Opposite an opening bid of 1♠, this hand normally presents little
difficulty: you simply bid 2♣, confident that the opener's rebid will
help you to determine the correct final contract. If he bids 2♡ or 2♠,
for example, you will be able to raise to three; and if he rebids 2◇, a
conversion to 2NT describes both the nature and the strength of your
hand ideally. Now suppose, however, that you have made an original
pass on this hand and that partner has opened 1♠ after two or three
passes. If he has succumbed to the modern epidemic which instils a
compulsive tendency to pass any non-forcing bid in this situation, the
correct response of 2♣ is no longer safe. The haunting fear that you
might be left to play right there in a tenuous 4–3 or 4–2 fit makes the 2♣
response most unattractive, and you can probably think of a number of
partners opposite whom you would feel compelled to resort to the
bucolic response of 2NT. Ugh.

Similarly:

♠ 7 5 2
♡ K 10 3
◇ 9 8 7 2
♣ A K J

If partner opens 1♡, this hand presents an awkward responding
problem at the best of times. 2◇ will probably work out satisfactorily
in practice, and there is also a good case for a response of 2♣, which
at least has the merit of indicating to partner where your high-card
strength lies. If you have passed originally on this hand, however, the
problem becomes even more difficult. Neither 2♣ nor 2◇ will be at all
safe opposite a partner who likes to pass as soon as he is permitted by
the rules to do so, and once again you probably have to take a wild lunge
into either 2NT or 3♡. Once again, ugh.

The solution to these, and similar, problems is refreshingly simple:
the opener should treat a simple change of suit by his partner as a one-
round force, just as it would be if there had not been an original pass.
In my view, the opener should only pass in this situation if he has a
completely minimum, or sub-minimum, hand with at least three-card
support for the responder's suit.

The case for this treatment seems to be unanswerable.

(a) It means that the responder can make his normal, exploratory
response without needing to strain to limit his hand in an unnatural
way. It has always seemed most odd to me that the responder should
be expected to vary his reply according to who happens to be the
dealer: logically, the correct response to a particular bid in one situation

must surely be the correct response to the same bid in another.

(b) It makes the stultifying response of 2NT after passing almost redundant in a natural sense. If partner has chosen to open with a tactical, lead-directing bid in third position, he will not be cheered to hear you make a desperate lurch into 2NT.

(c) It releases the dread 2NT response for another useful purpose. One attractive suggestion is that, after an original pass, 2NT should show the high-card values for a raise to three of partner's suit, four-card trump support, and a completely balanced hand. For example:

♠ K 7 2
♡ A 8 6 3
♢ J 10 7
♣ Q J 4

This type of holding is difficult to handle opposite an opening bid of 1♡. If you have already passed, you can solve the problem neatly by jumping to 2NT.

(d) It means that a response in a minor suit at the two level can be made on a four-card suit in the normal way. If the opener is prone to pass such a response, there is an understandable tendency to assume that a bid of 2♣ or 2♢ shows a five-card suit after passing; this makes certain hands extremely difficult to bid.

(e) It means that the responder does not need to jump to show that he has a maximum hand for his original pass. The jump after passing can, in fact, be given a useful alternative meaning, and we shall be returning to this subject a little later.

Against this, to play a change of suit response as virtually forcing after an original pass means that the opener will have to prepare his rebid if he has the values for a normal opening bid. For example :

♠ A Q J 7
♡ K 4 2
♢ 7 5 2
♣ A 10 8

Assuming that an opening bid of 1NT is precluded by the prevailing vulnerability, the opener might be tempted to open 1♠ on this hand if he is in third or fourth position, intending to pass any response at the two level. If a response of 2♣, 2♢ or 2♡ retains its normal forcing meaning, however, the opener may find himself embarrassed on the second round after an opening bid of 1♠; he must therefore open with the prepared bid of 1♣, just as he would in first or second position.

While it is awkward to have to open on a three-card suit in this situation, this is a small price to pay for the relief the responder will feel if he is permitted to develop his hand in a calm, unhurried way. After all, opening with a prepared bid works well enough in normal circumstances; there is surely no reason to suppose that it will not work equally well once partner has been compelled to pass originally. The change of suit forcing principle is a basic part of any system of approach bidding, and we normally rely on it to reach the correct part-score, game or slam contract. It would therefore be odd if, just because one side has made an original pass, we were expected to reach the correct resting-place without our usual bidding mechanism.

The case rests.

THE JUMP SHIFT AFTER PASSING

Once it is agreed that a simple change of suit after passing is in principal forcing, there is no longer any need for the responder to jump simply in order to show a maximum hand for his original pass. In fact, because of the danger that partner has opened on shaded values third in hand, it is only really safe for the responder to make a jump shift on the second round if he has a good fit for the opener's suit. The modern style is therefore to use a jump shift after passing to show a useful suit *and* good support for the opener's suit, with at least the values for a raise to three.

♠	K 7 4 2		
♡	10 2	No	1♠
◇	A Q 8 6 3	?	
♣	8 3		

Bid 3◇, showing a useful diamond suit and good support for spades. Such a jump is forcing for one round, but no further. This means that, if the opener has the values for game after your strength-showing response, he must either introduce a new suit or jump to 4♠; a simple return to 3♠ at this point can be passed.

The jump shift after passing is clearly more constructive than a jump raise in partner's suit, in that it enables the opener to judge whether or not the hands fit well. For example, let us suppose that the opener holds:

♠	A Q 8 5 3		
♡	A 4	No	1♠
◇	K 10 7	3◇	?
♣	9 7 5		

Opposite a normal raise to 3♠, the opener will only push on to game on this hand if he is desperate for points. Once partner is able to show a good diamond suit as well as spade support, however, prospects of game are considerably brighter, and a jump to 4♠ in this position becomes a very reasonable shot. You have only to imagine this hand opposite the responding hand shown above to see how the excellent diamond fit makes 4♠ a splendid spot.

Furthermore, the jump shift after passing may have the effect of allowing the opener an extra round of bidding in which to make a trial bid.

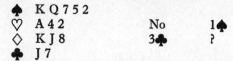

♠ K Q 7 5 2
♡ A 4 2   No   1♠
◇ K J 8   3♣   ?
♣ J 7

With no particular fit for clubs, the opener cannot underwrite 4♠ on this hand. The fate of the contract will probably hinge on partner's holding in diamonds, and this makes a trial bid of 3◇ the best action at this point. Responder will be able to revalue his hand in the knowledge that a little something in diamonds would be most welcome.

It is possible for the responder to make a jump shift even when he has the values for a raise to game in the opener's suit.

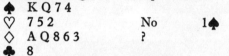

♠ K Q 7 4
♡ 7 5 2   No   1♠
◇ A Q 8 6 3   ?
♣ 8

While you are well worth an immediate raise to 4♠ on this hand, it will probably be helpful to show the nature of your holding by bidding 3◇ first. If partner attempts to sign off in 3♠, you can raise to 4♠; and if he shows extra values by jumping to 4♠ over 3◇, you can make one further effort by cue-bidding your control in clubs. This sequence of bidding may be the most accurate available if the full hands are as follows:

WEST	EAST	WEST	EAST
♠ K Q 7 4	♠ A J 10 6 3	No	1♠
♡ 7 5 2	♡ A Q	3◇	4♠
◇ A Q 8 6 3	◇ K J 5	5♣	6♠
♣ 8	♣ J 5 4		

The hands obviously fit well; what is more, the bidding makes this apparent before dummy is revealed.

Part Three

THE OPENER'S SECOND BID

♠ ♠

The basic philosophy of the various artificial club systems is that the opener should concentrate on showing his approximate strength by his first bid, without worrying too much at that stage about searching for the correct denomination in which to play the hand. Conversely, 'natural' bidding systems like Acol tend to suggest possible trump suits right from the start, and the exact strength of the hand is often only shown by a series of two or more bids. This means, for example, that an opening bid of 1♡, which is limited to 11–15 points in a system like Precision Club, can show anything from 11 to a bad 20 points in Acol.

Let us assume that partner is able to respond to the opening bid of one of a suit. In Acol, the opener generally defines the strength of his hand much more precisely by his second bid. This section looks closer at the various ways in which this can be done.

10. OPENER REBIDS NO TRUMPS

THE ONE NO TRUMP REBID

In the modern Acol style of bidding, a rebid of 1NT by the opener shows the point-count range on which he could not have opened 1NT at the prevailing vulnerability. Thus, if the partnership is using the weak no trump, showing 12–14 points, a rebid of 1NT shows 15–16; and if they are fainter hearts playing the variable no trump, the rebid will show 15–16 not vulnerable and 12–14 vulnerable.

This scheme, which, like so many devices now incorporated into Acol, is an adaptation of an idea introduced in the Baron system, is known as the Reverse No Trump. It has the obvious advantage of mathematical tidiness, neatly slotting every hand into a pigeon-hole according to its point count. For example, let us suppose that your side is playing the weak no trump and that you hold the following hand:

♠ K J 9 8		
♡ Q 6	1◇	1♠
◇ 10 6 3	1NT	?
♣ A 8 7 2		

This is duck soup. Partner's rebid shows 15–16 points and a simple piece of arithmetic will produce the obvious answer: 3NT.

However, it must not be thought that the Reverse No Trump is completely without its problems. Suppose your hand is:

♠ 9 4		
♡ A Q 6	1◇	1♠
◇ A Q 10 7 3	?	
♣ K 6 4		

If you are playing a weak no trump at the prevailing vulnerability, all is well; you can rebid 1NT, describing the hand admirably and showing 15–16 points. But what if your side is vulnerable and your 1NT opening would be strong? The natural-looking rebid of 1NT is now out of the question, for it would show a maximum of 14 points, and you are left with a difficult rebid problem: a problem which can, in fact, only be solved by opening the hand with 1NT – hardly the most accurate description of this holding.

Similarly:

♠ 9 4
♡ J 7 5 4 2
◇ A Q 8
♣ A Q 5

Suppose you are not vulnerable and you hold this hand. What do you open? You would clearly like to open 1♡ and rebid 1NT over the likely response of 1♠, but this is not possible if the 1NT rebid guarantees 15–16. You are therefore left with the choice of opening the hand with 1NT, an extremely risky action with a five-card major suit, and of opening the more natural 1♡ and rebidding 2♡ over a response of 1♠ – clearly a very poor bid in view of the jejune heart suit and the strong tenace holdings in the two unbid suits.

One final example:

    ♠ 8 3
    ♡ A K 9 7
    ◇ 10 6 3
    ♣ A K 7 2

The most descriptive way of handling this holding is clearly to open 1♣, hoping that partner responds 1◇ so that the excellent heart suit can be shown at the one level. If partner makes the inconsiderate response of 1♠ over 1♣, of course, you will have to resign yourself to concealing the hearts and rebidding 1NT. However, this natural style of bidding will not be possible if the Reverse No Trump is being used and the weak no trump is in operation, for to open 1♣ would leave you with an impossible rebid after 1♣–1♠. The opening bid has to be 1NT rather than 1♣, clearly a distortion when all your 14 points are packed into just two suits.

The obvious solution to all these problems is to make the rebid of 1NT a more flexible bid, showing 12–16 points instead of the fashionable restricted point-count range. This will allow the bidding to proceed much more smoothly and naturally on a considerable number of hands, and will often permit you to make the most natural and descriptive opening bid without being restricted by the strait-jacket of the Reverse No Trump.

    ♠ A J 6
    ♡ 8 4
    ◇ K Q 10 7 3
    ♣ K 9 3

Playing the wide-range 1NT rebid, this hand ceases to be a problem. No matter what the vulnerability is, you can open with the natural bid of 1◇, intending to rebid 1NT over a response of 1♡, to raise a response of 1♠ to 2♠, and to rebid 2◇ over a response of 2♣: surely a better way of describing this holding than by treating it as a weak 1NT opening.

Even the flexible 1NT rebid has its disadvantages, of course, and it is here that we must consider a conventional method of overcoming the slight inherent defects. It is time for the commercial break. . . .

THE CROWHURST 2♣ CONVENTION

I have always preferred the comparative freedom offered by a wide-range 1NT rebid. Way back in the mists of time my university partner,

Bryan Boucher, and I devised a simple convention which, perhaps slightly unfairly, has since become associated with my name. In its original, basic form, the convention is as follows.

A rebid of 1NT shows 12–16 points. If the responder is thinking in terms of raising in no trumps, he bids 3NT with 13 or more points and makes an invitational raise to 2NT if he has 11 points or a poor 12. If he has 10 points, or a goodish 9, he is clearly only interested in game if his partner has a near-maximum, and it is here that he employs a conventional enquiry of 2♣.

The responses to 2♣ are fairly natural and straightforward.

  (i) With 15 or 16 points, the opener rebids 2NT.

 (ii) With 12–14 points, the opener has four possible courses of action:

    (a) He can show three-card support for his partner's major suit.

    (b) He can rebid a five-card heart suit.

    (c) He can introduce a four-card heart suit which has previously been concealed.

    (d) If no other bid is available, he bids 2◇.

One or two example hands should help to clarify matters.

♠ A K 7	♠ 10 8 3		
♡ K 8 2	♡ A 7 4	1♣	1◇
◇ J 2	◇ K Q 10 7 6	1NT	2♣ (1)
♣ A 10 6 4 3	♣ 8 2	2NT (2)	3NT

(1) Notice that 2♣ is still conventional after an opening bid of 1♣.
(2) 15–16 points.

A rebid of 2NT over 2♣ by the opener is forcing to game, except in one sequence.

♠ 8 4	♠ K 9 5 3 2	1♣	1♠
♡ A J 7 3	♡ 8 2	1NT	2♣
◇ K 10 4	◇ 6	2NT (1)	3♣ (2)
♣ A K 9 3	♣ Q 8 6 4 2		

(1) 15–16 points.
(2) A return to 3♣ by the responder is not forcing; he just wishes that he had never heard of the Crowhurst 2♣ convention in the first place.

♠ J 8 3	♠ K Q 7 5 2	1♣	1♠
♡ A 10 4	♡ 7 5	1NT	2♣
◇ A 7	◇ Q 9 5 4	2NT (1)	3◇ (2)
♣ A Q 8 7 4	♣ K 3	3♠	4♠

(1) 15–16 points.
(2) Once the 2NT rebid has established a game-forcing situation, the responder is able to investigate the best game contract at his leisure.

♠ Q 8 6	♠ A J 7 4 2		
♡ Q 6 3	♡ 7 4	1♣	1♠
◇ A 10 5	◇ Q 8 3	1NT	2♣
♣ A J 7 4	♣ Q 10 2	2♠ (1)	No

(1) 12–14 points with three-card spade support. Notice that the convention makes it easy for the partnership to alight in the best part-score contract.

♠ Q 4	♠ K J 8 5 3	1♡	1♠
♡ K 7 5 3 2	♡ 8 4	1NT	2♣
◇ A 10 7	◇ K 9 3	2♡ (1)	2NT (2)
♣ K J 8	♣ Q 10 5	No	

(1) 12–14 points with a five-card heart suit.
(2) With such poor support for hearts, the responder elects to play in a no trump part-score.

♠ J 6	♠ A 10 8 5 2	1♣	1♠
♡ K 9 8 7	♡ Q J 6 3	1NT	2♣
◇ A 8 3	◇ K 4	2♡ (1)	3♡ (2)
♣ K Q J 4	♣ 7 6	4♡	No

(1) 12–14 points with a four-card heart suit.
(2) Although he knows that the opener is limited in terms of high cards, the responder is still worth a try for game now that the 4–4 heart fit has come to light.

♠ K 8 5	♠ Q J 7	1♣	1♡
♡ Q 6	♡ A 7 5 3 2	1NT	2♣
◇ A J 4	◇ 8 6	2◇ (1)	2NT
♣ Q J 9 7 3	♣ K 8 4	No	

(1) 12–14 points with a doubleton heart; in fact, the opener's distribution can only be 3–2–3–5 or, just conceivably, 2–2–4–5.

♠ Q 8	♠ K J 9 4 2	1♣	1♠
♡ A J 4	♡ Q 8 3	1NT	2NT (1)
◇ K 10 6	◇ Q 7 2	3NT (2)	No
♣ Q J 10 7 3	♣ K 4		

(1) Here the responder is too strong to employ the 2♣ convention.
(2) Since the raise to 2NT shows at least 11 points, the opener will go on to game unless he is completely minimum.

♠ K 7 3	♠ Q J 10 6 4	1♣	1♠
♡ J 10 5	♡ 8 4	1NT	2NT (1)
◇ A 9 2	◇ K Q 7	3♠ (2)	4♠
♣ A Q 8 4	♣ K 7 2		

(1) Once again the responder is too strong to use the 2♣ convention.
(2) The opener is clearly worth going to game and, as he has such good top cards, he gives his partner a choice of contract.

THE CASE FOR THE CONVENTION

The advantages of this simple convention can be summarised as follows.

(a) It allows a rebid of 1NT to be a completely natural bid, showing a hand on which the opener has no more descriptive rebid available as opposed to a hand which happens to fit into a particular narrow point count range.

```
♠  8 4
♡  K Q 10
♢  A J 9 6 3
♣  K 8 5
```

Whatever the game score and whatever the strength of your opening 1NT, this hand is no longer a problem. Open 1♢, intending to rebid 1NT over the likely response of 1♠, to raise a 1♡ response to 2♡, and to rebid 2♢ over a response of 2♣. Notice that this hand is awkward to handle under normal methods if you are playing a weak no trump: you have to choose between opening a distorted 1NT and opening 1♢ and rebidding 2♢ over 1♠ – neither of which seems a particularly accurate way of bidding what is, after all, a very simple hand.

(b) It means that an opening bid of 1NT can be reserved for suitable hands; it will no longer be necessary to open 1NT with a small doubleton or with a five-card suit, just because you feel it is your last chance to show a particular point count.

```
♠  6 4                    ♠  A Q 8
♡  Q 8 6 3 2             ♡  7 5
♢  K J 4                 ♢  A K 6 4
♣  A Q 5                 ♣  10 7 6 3
   HAND A                    HAND B
```

These two hands both become strangely difficult if you are playing the Reverse No Trump and your opening 1NT would be weak at the prevailing score. On Hand A, you have to choose between opening 1NT, which is hardly ideal in view of the non-existent spade suit and the five-card heart suit, and opening 1♡ and rebidding 2♡ over the likely response of 1♠, which is a complete misrepresentation of the hand. Similarly, on Hand B, you have the alternative of opening 1NT, which is a poor description of a hand containing a small doubleton in one suit and 13 points concentrated into just two suits, and opening 1♢ and introducing the feeble club suit over a response of 1♡, again an awkward way of handling such a balanced hand.

Playing Crowhurst 2♣ these hands become easy and straightforward. You can open 1♡ on Hand A and 1♢ on Hand B in complete confidence, intending to describe your holding accurately by rebidding 1NT if partner responds in the suit in which you hold a small doubleton.

(c) The knowledge that an opening bid of 1NT is reserved for completely suitable hands is invaluable in many ways. For example, if the opponents eventually buy the contract, it will be much easier for the responder to make a fairly tight penalty double if he can be sure that the opener has more than a small doubleton in the trump suit; furthermore, it will subsequently be simpler to defend the hand if it is known that the opening 1NT bid can only have been made on a fairly closely-defined kind of hand. Similarly, if the responder is contemplating a gambling raise to 3NT based on something like A–K–J–x–x–x in a minor suit, he will be able to do so with much greater confidence if he can rely on finding at least Q–x or x–x–x in the opposite hand.

(d) Even if it reveals that the combined hands have insufficient values for game, the 2♣ convention often enables the partnership to play in the best part-score.

♠ Q 7 2	♠ A 10 9 6 4		
♡ Q 8 4	♡ 7 2	1♣	1♠
◇ A 9 3	◇ J 7 4	1NT	2♣
♣ K Q 6 5	♣ A 10 4	2♠	No

The recommended sequence on these two hands, assuming we are vulnerable, leads us to a comfortable part-score in 2♠. Furthermore, it will probably lead us to a good score on the board at Duplicate, for a number of pairs will no doubt linger in the perilous contract of 1NT if West either opens with a weak no trump or opens 1♣ and rebids 1NT, showing 12–14 points.

(e) The 2♣ convention can sometimes be used to locate the best game contract in situations where the total strength of the combined hands is comparatively immaterial.

♠ K J 8 7 3		
♡ 10 7 4	1◇	1♠
◇ A 5	1NT	?
♣ A J 6		

After any variety of 1NT rebid by the opener, this hand obviously has no intention of staying out of game. However, it is still not completely clear as to which is the best game contract; for example, 4♠ could easily be correct if the opener has something like:

| ♠ Q 9 2 | ◇ K J 7 4 |
| ♡ K 8 | ♣ K Q 8 3 |

But how is the responder supposed to investigate the possibility of a 5–3 spade fit? A jump to 3♠ over 1NT is generally regarded as non-forcing, and to invent a forcing continuation like 3♣ might court disaster if he happens to find partner with:

♠ 9 2		
♡ A J 8	1◇	1♠
◇ K Q 7 4	1NT	3♣
♣ K Q 8 3	?	

Could you guarantee that none of your partners would choose to raise to 4♣ at this point? No, neither could I.

Armed with the 2♣ convention, the responder is in no difficulty: he simply makes a strength-asking 2♣ enquiry over the 1NT rebid. If the opener is minimum, he will announce at the same time whether or not he has three-card spade support; and if the opener has 15 or 16 points, he will rebid 2NT and the responder can continue his investigation by making a forcing bid of 3♣.

(f) The wide range of the 1NT rebid will make life extremely difficult for the opponents if 1NT becomes the final contract or if the responder makes a direct raise to 3NT. Hugh Kelsey says in one of his excellent books on defence*: 'Keeping a careful count of declarer's points is a valuable habit that will often show the way to the best line of defence. The bidding sequence usually gives some indication of declarer's values. By relating his bidding to the number of points declarer has shown up with, it will frequently be possible to infer that he must have (or cannot have) a particular honour card.' How much more difficult it will be for the defence to count the hand in this way if the declarer's 1NT rebid can be based on anything from 12 to 16 points – a five-point range.

(g) In addition to its normal application after a rebid of 1NT, the 2♣ convention can also be used to good effect after an overcall of 1NT in the protective position. It is clearly desirable to compete with 1NT on as many hands as possible after the opening suit bid has been followed by two passes; if the responder is armed with the 2♣ convention, it will be practicable to widen the range of the protective 1NT to 10–14, 11–15 or any five-point range you choose. But more of that later.

SUGGESTED MODIFICATIONS TO THE CONVENTION
However biased you may think I am, it must be admitted that there may be one or two bad hands for the Crowhurst 2♣ convention. Not many, just one or two.

One awkward situation arises when the opener has scraped up first an opening bid and then a 1NT rebid on a scrappy 12 count, and his partner summons up an ambitious 2♣ enquiry on a 9-point responding hand, for now the opener may find himself toiling in 2NT when his side only just has the balance of the points. That is unfortunate, but try not to worry too much about it: for one thing, even if your combined point count is only 21, the 2♣ enquiry might still improve the final contract if a 5–3 major suit fit comes to light.

♠	J 6	♠	A 9 7 4 2		
♡	K J 8 6 3	♡	Q 7 2	1♡	1♠
◇	A 7 2	◇	10 6	1NT	2♣
♣	K 10 4	♣	Q J 8	2♡	No

* *Killing Defence at Bridge*, by H. W. Kelsey.

The other difficult situation which arises after a Crowhurst 2♣
enquiry is where the two hands consist of an indifferent 15 points
opposite 9 or a poor 10, for, as the system now stands, the opener is
likely to find himself struggling in 3NT without too much chance of
success. However, this problem can be to a large extent overcome by
a simple modification to the original system: a modification which
we call the Impossible Major. It works as follows. If, in response to a
2♣ enquiry, the opener introduces a major suit not previously bid by
the partnership, he is showing a hand containing a poor to average
15 points; that is to say, a hand on which he only wants to be in game
if his partner has a full-value 10 points opposite. All other replies to 2♣
retain their original meaning, except in the sequence 1♡–1♠–1NT–2♣,
when there is no 'impossible major' reply available. In this one case, the
opener rebids 2NT to show an indifferent 15-point hand and 3♣ to
show a complete maximum.

One or two example sequences should show how simple the new idea
really is:

(a) 2♡ shows 12–14 points with three-card heart support.
(b) 2◇ shows all other 12–14 point holdings.
(c) 2♠ shows an indifferent 15 points.
(d) 2NT shows a good 15 or 16 points.

(a) 2◇ shows 12–14 points with four hearts and two spades.
(b) 2♡ shows 12–14 points with a five-card heart suit.
(c) 2♠ shows 12–14 points with three-card spade support.
(d) 2NT shows an indifferent 15 points.
(e) 3♣ shows a good 15 or 16 points.

What I fear will eventually become known as Extended Crowhurst
may make life easier on awkward hands like the following:

WEST	EAST
♠ K 8 3	♠ J 7 4
♡ J 4	♡ A 8 6 3
◇ A K 7 6	◇ 9 5 4
♣ A 8 7 5	♣ K Q 2

The weakness of the intermediate cards means that nine tricks will
be a very tall order on these hands, and yet 3NT is difficult to avoid
on normal methods. The sequence which we now suggest will at least
put East in a better position to exercise his judgement:

WEST	EAST
1◇	1♡
1NT	2♣
2♠	?

West's response of 2♠, the Impossible Major, shows a sketchy 15 points and suggests that East should only push on to game if he has a completely maximum hand. This information might persuade East to proceed quietly on his emaciated 10 points, and he would certainly put up the shutters if he only had an indifferent 9-count.

In one sequence, 1♣–1◇–1NT–2♣, there are two 'Impossible Major' responses available to the opener. If he is anxious to show an indifferent 15-point hand, therefore, he can describe his holding even more accurately by bidding the major suit in which he has the stronger holding. For example:

♠ A Q 6	♠ K 10 5		
♡ J 8 7	♡ 9 3	1♣	1◇
◇ Q 9 2	◇ K J 7 6 4	1NT	2♣
♣ A Q 7 4	♣ K 6 3	2♠	?

West's rebid is bad news to East for two reasons. It is disappointing to hear that West has, at best, an average-looking 15 count; and it is even more distressing to learn that he has better spades than hearts. However, this information should enable the partnership to avoid the undignified contract of 3NT and East might, in fact, earn himself a very good duplicate score by making a slightly risky retreat into 3◇.

If West rebids 2♡ over the 2♣ enquiry, East has fewer worries on the above hand, and he will probably push on to 3NT even though he knows that his partner does not have a complete maximum. One has only to reverse West's major suit holdings in the above example to see how this simple new idea can give you increased accuracy in the bidding of certain hands.

One final point about the proposed modifications to the system. The conventional use of 'Impossible Major' bids means that it will no longer be possible to place a natural interpretation on two fairly rare sequences.

1♣	1♠		1◇	1♠
1NT	2♣		1NT	2♣
2♡			2♡	

In the original, simple system, 2♡ is a natural bid, showing 12–14 points and a four-card heart suit which had previously been shut out of the auction by the 1♠ response. In the souped-up version of Crowhurst, 2♡ merely shows any indifferent 15-point hand, and the opener must show a completely minimum hand by bidding either 2◇ or 2♠. This is not serious. A concealed heart fit will still come to light, provided that the responder remembers to bid 2♡ en route to a sign off in 2NT.

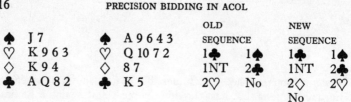

♠ J 7	♠ A 9 6 4 3	OLD SEQUENCE		NEW SEQUENCE	
♡ K 9 6 3	♡ Q 10 7 2	1♣	1♠	1♣	1♠
◇ K 9 4	◇ 8 7	1NT	2♣	1NT	2♣
♣ A Q 8 2	♣ K 5	2♡	No	2◇	2♡
				No	

THE TWO NO TRUMPS REBID

After any response at the one level, and after an immediate raise to two in the opener's suit, a rebid of 2NT shows 17 or 18 points, or occasionally a good 16 points with a five-card suit. It is not forcing. We shall be considering the responder's subsequent action in considerable detail in the next section of the book; suffice it to say at this stage that a simple rebid of the responder's original suit is not forcing but that, unless the initial response was 1NT, no other rebid below the game level may be passed.

After a change of suit at the two level, the meaning of a 2NT rebid is not so obvious. CAB and most artificial club systems say that it shows a minimum opening bid; Baron suggests that it should show the same strength as a jump to 2NT, that is, 17 or 18 points; and traditional Acol recommends that, since partner has guaranteed at least 9 points by bidding at the two level, the requirements for a 2NT rebid can be reduced to 15 or 16 points.

While the Acol method is arithmetically correct, I would be guilty of criminal negligence if I omitted to point out in these pages that the variable 2NT rebid is not theoretically sound. The reason for this is twofold. First, it places too great a strain on the 3NT rebid, which, if the 2NT rebid is devalued to 15–16, has to cover all balanced hands containing from 17 to 20 points; a four-point range for any no trump bid must clearly lead to a loss of efficiency and accuracy.

Secondly, the need to jump to 3NT on 17 or 18 points is in itself inefficient, in that the pre-emptive effect on the auction sometimes makes it more difficult to reach the correct game contract. This is particularly true when a 5–3 major suit fit is available.

	WEST		EAST	WEST	EAST
♠	K J 9 6 3	♠	Q 10 5	1♠	2♣
♡	A K J	♡	Q 8 4	3NT	
◇	A 10 4	◇	7 5		
♣	J 7	♣	A Q 10 6 2		

East is unable to convert to the correct contract over 3NT, for he cannot be sure that his partner has a five-card spade suit. Notice how much easier the auction becomes if the 2NT rebid is permitted to retain its normal strong meaning:

WEST   EAST
1♠   2♣
2NT   3♠
4♠

And another adverse game swing is avoided.

On the other hand, the variable 2NT rebid does have several practical advantages, particularly in that it often solves an awkward rebid problem. For example:

♠ A Q J 7
♡ 10 4
♢ K Q J 8
♣ Q 3 2

Open 1♠ – but only if your methods permit a rebid of 2NT over a response of 2♡. An opening bid of 1♢ would leave you in an embarrassing position over a response of 2♣. Playing a rigid 2NT rebid, therefore, you would have to start with the poor bid of 1♣, allowing the opponents to intervene with hearts at the one level and making very little progress towards painting an accurate picture of your hand.

Similarly:

♠ A Q
♡ A K J 10
♢ J 10 8
♣ 9 7 4 3

The best opening bid on a hand of this type is clearly 1♡, but this will only be possible if you are free to rebid 2NT over a response of 2♢. Playing a rigid 2NT rebid, your opening move will have to be 1♣, which scarcely figures to be a winning gambit.

The 2NT rebid after a response at the two level therefore presents something of a problem. At first sight, it seems as if we have to choose between the rigid 17–18 2NT rebid, which is theoretically correct and more efficient on game-going hands, and the variable 2NT rebid, which has certain practical advantages and can solve a number of awkward rebid problems.

Displaying my customary greed, I have been experimenting with a method which attempts to obtain the best of both worlds. Even playing the variable 2NT rebid, a sequence of this kind:

1♡   2♣
2NT

is very rarely passed. If the responder has poor values and a long club suit, he will retreat to 3♣; and if he has the 9 points normally guaranteed by a two level response, he will almost always push on to 3NT in the hope that his partner has 16.

This being the case, there will be very little loss of efficiency if we play the 2NT rebid as completely forcing, and to do so offers one important advantage. While the responder must assume that the 2NT rebid shows no more than 15 or 16 points, the forcing rebid will enable the opener to conceal a stronger hand if he is anxious to explore other possibilities. For example:

♠ J 10 8		
♡ A K 10 7 3	1♡	2◇
◇ K Q 4	?	
♣ A 2		

Under normal Acol methods, you will probably have to blast straight into 3NT, conscious that 4♡, or even 5◇, could well prove to be a better contract. A forcing rebid of 2NT leaves the way clear for partner to investigate further by bidding, for example, 3♡ on three-card support; if he does this, you can show that the hand is surprisingly strong by cue-bidding 4♣ en route to 4♡.

Provided that one keeps the two level response up to strength and avoids rebidding 2NT on an empty 15-point hand, it seems to me unlikely that the forcing 2NT rebid will lead to much trouble. It certainly simplifies matters for the opener when he has a strong hand on which he cannot be completely certain of the correct final denomination, and it will often make it easier to reach the best game or slam contract. On the other hand, it is possible that the responder's ignorance of the opener's precise point count might prove to be a slight disadvantage in certain situations. I just do not know, but it seems to me that the proposed new method is sufficiently promising to warrant further investigation. Perhaps you will give it a try. But if anything goes wrong, don't blame me: write to your M.P.

THE THREE NO TRUMPS REBID

Nothing new here, for the strength of a jump to 3NT obviously depends to a large extent on what would be shown by a rebid of 2NT.

(A) 1♡ 1NT	(B) 1◇ 1♠	(C) 1♡ 2♡
3NT	3NT	3NT

The rebid of 3NT in these three sequences definitely shows 19 or 20 points. The only controversial point arises in connection with the fourth possible situation:

(D) 1♡   2♣
     3NT

Traditional Acol suggests that 3NT over a response at the two level should show 17+ points; Baron, well supported by pure theory, suggests that it should still show 19–20; and my recommendation is that it shows any hand containing 17 or more points on which the opener knows for certain where he is going – bearing in mind that he can proceed more slowly with a forcing rebid of 2NT if he is still in any doubt.

11. OPENER REBIDS HIS FIRST SUIT

THE MINIMUM REBID

There is little which needs to be said about the minimum rebid of
the opener's suit. It obviously guarantees at least a five-card holding,
but the responder must not expect too much in the way of suit quality –
particularly if his own first response was an uneconomical one. Compare
these two sequences:

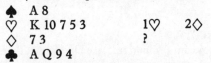

Let us assume in each case that the opener is unable to support
his partner's suit. In Sequence A, he had the opportunity to rebid
1NT, 2♣ or 2◇ over the response of 1♠; the fact that the opener
preferred to rebid 2♡ therefore implies that he has a reasonable suit.
The same inference is not available in Sequence B, where any rebid
other than 2♡ would require extra values.

```
♠  A 8
♡  K 10 7 5 3        1♡      2◇
◇  7 3               ?
♣  A Q 9 4
```

Bid 2♡. Notice how the 2◇ response compels you to rebid an
indifferent suit; if the response had been 1♠, 1NT or 2♣, it would
not have been necessary to rebid 2♡, and the responder should always
bear this point in mind when he is attempting to draw inferences from
his partner's bidding.

A rebid of the opener's suit after a response of 1NT implies a six-card
suit; with a mere five-card holding, the opener will prefer to show a
second suit if he has one or to take his chances in 1NT if his distribution
is 5–3–3–2.

The only debatable point of bidding theory relating to a minimum
rebid of the opener's first suit concerns what is generally known as the
're-raise'.

```
1♡      2♡
3♡
```

Some authorities suggest that the raise to 3♡ in this situation
should be a trial for game based on a long trump suit. However, since
the opener can always introduce a second suit as a Trial Bid if he is
anxious to investigate the possibilities of 4♡, the re-raise to 3♡ is
not really needed in this sense. It is therefore recommended that the
re-raise should be a defensive manoeuvre, designed purely to ensure
that you play the contract your way.

♠	A 7		
♡	K Q 10 8 6 3	1♡	2♡
◇	10 7 5	?	
♣	K 4		

Bid 3♡. You clearly have no hope of game on this hand, but it would nevertheless be extremely thoughtless to make a sleepy pass at this stage. Your left-hand opponent will no doubt be listening to the auction with his ears pricked. If he hears you subside in 2♡, he might well decide to re-open the bidding protectively. Since you have no reason to suppose that the enemy cannot make a spade contract in reasonable comfort, therefore, you should bid 3♡ immediately in an attempt to buy the contract and keep them out.

THE JUMP REBID

A jump rebid in his original suit by the opener is not forcing. It shows a good six-card or longer suit and approximately seven playing tricks.

♠	10 5		
♡	A 6	1♣	1♡
◇	K 8 4	?	
♣	A K Q 10 7 5		

Bid 3♣. A jump rebid in a minor suit usually has 3NT very much in mind. In a major suit, when game in a suit contract is within easier reach, a jump rebid can be made on a hand which is considerably less solid than this one. This is particularly true, of course, when partner has already shown fair values by responding at the two level.

♠	A J 9 8 7 5		
♡	A Q 7	1♠	2♣
◇	6	?	
♣	K 8 4		

Bid 3♠. The hand is too strong for a simple rebid of 2♠, particularly in view of the fact that you appear to have a good fit for partner's club suit.

In practice, sequences of this kind:

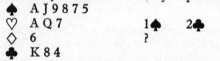

    A. 1◇–2♣–3◇
    B. 1♡–2♣–3♡
    C. 1♡–2◇–3♡
    D. 1♠–2♣–3♠
    E. 1♠–2◇–3♠
    F. 1♠–2♡–3♠

will very rarely be passed; if the responder is strong enough to bid at the two level and the opener has extra values, it is most unlikely that the partnership will choose to linger at the three level. The responder should raise to game on the smell of an oil-rag, only passing the

jump rebid if he has no support for his partner's suit and a completely
minimum hand for his first response.

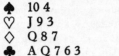

♠ 10 4
♡ J 9 3   1♠   2♣
♢ Q 8 7   3♠   ?
♣ A Q 7 6 3

Bid 4♠. This is a completely minimum hand for a further bid, but
it is unlikely that partner will have no play at all for game. If you imagine
this hand opposite the opener's hand shown above, you will see that,
although neither side has anything to spare, the final contract of 4♠
has excellent chances of success.

Since the opener's jump rebid is such a descriptive bid, the responder's
subsequent action will normally be fairly clear-cut. There are only two
important points to be made in this context. First, any rebid by the
responder below the game level is best played as 100% forcing.

♠ A Q 10 7 5
♡ J 6 4   1♢   1♠
♢ K 3   3♢   ?
♣ 10 8 5

Bid 3♠. 4♠ could well be the best game contract on this hand, and
a forcing rebid of 3♠ gives the opener the chance to raise to four if
he has any kind of concealed support like J–x or x–x–x. Notice that
there would be little advantage in playing a bid of 3♠ as non-forcing
in this situation: since the opener has shown a good six-card suit by
his jump rebid, the responder will not wish to become involved in an
unseemly brawl about which is the correct part-score to play in.

Another advantage of playing all non-game bids by the responder
as forcing is that it will simplify the bidding of minor suit slams.

♠ K Q 9 4 2
♡ A J 5   1♣   1♠
♢ 10 3   3♣   ?
♣ Q 7 2

Bid 4♣, forcing and leaving the way clear for an exchange of cue-
bids. Without the agreement that 4♣ is forcing in this situation, you
would probably have to resort to a bid of 3♡, to be followed by club
support at a later stage; this sequence would have the unfortunate effect
of strongly suggesting a singleton diamond.

The second important point to be made in connection with the
responder's action over a jump rebid concerns the introduction of a
third suit. It is here that we stumble yet again into an uncharted area
of Acol, for the meaning of sequences like the following is far from clear:

(A) 1♣   1♡   (B) 1♡   1♠
    3♣   3♠   3♡   4♣

Does the responder's second bid in these auctions show a suit, a

feature, or a first-round control? It is clearly open to different interpretations, but my own view is that a bid of a third suit by the responder
in these situations should never be assumed to show a suit: to bid a
third suit at the three level, as in Sequence A, shows a guard for no
trump purposes; a third suit at the four level, as in Sequence B, is a
cue bid, agreeing the opener's suit for slam purposes.

♠ 7 5 4		
♡ A 7 3	1♡	2♣
◇ A 2	3♡	?
♣ K Q 10 8 5		

Bid 4◇. This is best played as a cue bid, agreeing hearts and showing
interest in a slam contract. Notice that this hand would be difficult to
bid if 4◇ would show a suit in this situation: it is too strong for a
simple raise to 4♡, and yet there is no other sensible way of making a
slam try.

THE DOUBLE JUMP REBID

A double jump rebid in the opener's suit is a very rare species. If it
occurs in a major suit, the bid will be at the game level. For example:

1♡	2♣
4♡	

While this bid is completely natural, there is an extremely useful
inference to be drawn. Since the opener was content to open with a
mere one bid and has now jumped all the way to game after a minimum
response by his partner, it is almost certain that his hand has been
improved by the bidding. There is therefore a strong inference that
he has a good fit for clubs, and it is safe for the responder to proceed
on this assumption.

♠ Q 10 5		
♡ 2	1♡	2♣
◇ A 6 2	4♡	?
♣ A Q 10 7 5 3		

Bid 6♣. Alternatively, if you are the type who looks under the bed
before going to sleep at night, bid a Blackwood 4NT first and then
bid 6♣. The important point here is that partner's leap all the way to
4♡ implies a good club fit; there must surely be a play for a slam
opposite this hand.

A double jump rebid in a minor suit is normally given a semi-
conventional meaning.

1♣	1♠
4♣	

Since it is most unlikely that he would make such a convulsive
leap without a pretty clear idea of where he is going, a jump rebid
of 4♣ or 4◇ by the opener is generally interpreted as agreeing the

responder's major suit and showing a good six-card suit of his own. This highly descriptive rebid may well enable the responder to move forward if he has a suitable hand.

♠ A Q 10 3
♡ 6   1♣   1♠
◇ J 2   ?
♣ A K J 10 8 5

Bid 4♣, agreeing spades and showing a powerful six-card club suit. This may be the key bid in a successful slam sequence if the full hands are something like:

WEST	EAST	WEST	EAST
♠ A Q 10 3	♠ K J 8 5 2	1♣	1♠
♡ 6	♡ J 9 4	4♣	4◇
◇ J 2	◇ A 7 5	4♡	4NT
♣ A K J 10 8 5	♣ Q 3	5♡	6♠

♠ ♠

---

12. OPENER RAISES RESPONDER'S SUIT

THE SINGLE RAISE

This should be a comparatively straightforward section, for there is very little abstruse theory to be found under this heading. The only point which warrants a brief consideration concerns the minimum trump support needed for a single raise.

There has in the past been a great deal of muddled thinking about direct raises, and there are a number of players who still cling to the impractical principle that an immediate raise should always guarantee four-card trump support. In so doing, they create far more serious problems for themselves; even the most straightforward hand becomes strangely difficult.

♠ A Q 8
♡ 6 2   1♣   1♠
◇ A 9 5   ?
♣ Q 8 5 4 3

Bid 2♠. Even if a rebid of 1NT is permitted by your methods, it would be a poor choice on this hand: your bleak holdings in the red suits make it desirable that any no trump venture should be played from partner's side of the table. It is clear that an immediate raise to 2♠ will work out well if partner has a five-card spade suit, which is, incidentally, quite likely when he bids 1♠ over 1♣. Moreover, even if he only has a four-card suit, the hand should play quite well in spades, for partner should be able to negotiate a heart ruff in the hand with the shorter trump holding. And if partner does only have four spades, it is virtually certain that he will not have more than three hearts – in which case the opponents will have an obvious attack against a no trump contract.

One more everyday example should serve to prove the folly of restricting your immediate raises to hands with four-card trump support.

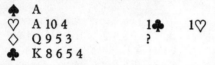

A raise to 2♡ is surely the best practical rebid on this hand. The only possible alternative is to rebid the barren club suit, but this is open to several unanswerable objections: it overstates what is, after all, a very poor suit; it is much less constructive than an immediate raise of partner's suit; and, most important, 2♣ is unlikely to be the correct contract – ruffing spades in the long trump hand will be far less productive than using your small hearts for ruffing purposes.

The case for permitting a raise of a major suit on three-card support is therefore overwhelming. Conversely, there is a strong argument for reserving immediate raises of minor suits for hands with four-card support.

    A. 1◇–2♣–3♣
    B. 1♡–2♣–3♣
    C. 1♠–2♣–3♣
    D. 1♡–2◇–3◇
    E. 1♠–2◇–3◇

In sequences like these, where the single raise takes the bidding to the dizzy heights of the three level, so much bidding space has been squandered that it is essential to be sure that an eight-card trump fit has been found; it will make the subsequent bidding much simpler if the responder can rely on the opener having a minimum hand with four-card trump support. This applies particularly if the responder is comparatively weak:

    ♠ A J 6
    ♡ 8 4   1♡   2♣
    ◇ Q 6 4 2   3♣   ?
    ♣ K 10 7 5

No bid. The lack of room for manoeuvre in this kind of auction illustrates the advantage of allocating a very precise meaning to the opener's rebid of 3♣. If it could conceal extra values, the responder might feel tempted to have a shot at 3NT at this stage: and the temptation to try to improve the final contract will be even stronger if he is not absolutely certain that there are four clubs in the opposite hand. This is certainly not the type of hand on which he would look forward to toiling in a 4–3 trump fit at the three level.

The responder will welcome the same reassurance if he is slightly stronger.

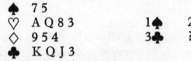

Bid 3♡, inviting the opener to convert to 3NT if he has a good holding in the unbid suit, diamonds. However, this delicate exploratory bid will only be sound if the responder can be sure that there is an eight-card club fit between the two hands – so that the opener can return to 4♣ or 5♣ if he has a poor holding in diamonds.

To summarise. It is perfectly sound for the opener to raise his partner's major suit response if he has reasonable three-card trump support and an unbalanced hand. However, there are a number of reasons for insisting that a simple raise of a minor suit response should guarantee at least four-card support. First, while it is quite possible to play in a major suit game with a 4–3 trump fit, it is very rarely correct to play in 5♣ or 5♢ when you have only seven trumps in the combined hands. Secondly, it is not safe to hoist the bidding to the three level unless you are certain that you have an eight-card trump fit between the two hands. And finally, to raise a minor suit response to the three level consumes so much valuable bidding space that the responder will be in difficulties unless he has a fairly exact knowledge of the opener's hand; he must be able to proceed on the assumption that the opener has four-card trump support and a minimum hand.

THE JUMP RAISE

A jump raise of the responder's major suit shows four-card trump support and approximately six losers; a double jump shows five losers. The high-card strength of a jump raise and of a jump to game is approximately equal to that for a jump to 2NT or 3NT respectively, but you must obviously take the distribution of the hand into account.

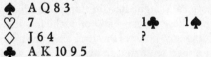

Bid 3♠. While you would never dream of jumping to 2NT on as few as 14 high-card points, the excellent distribution of the hand makes it too strong for a simple raise to 2♠. If you are ever in doubt in this kind of situation, the Losing Trick Count which we considered in an earlier section of the book will provide a useful guide on how high to raise partner: once you are assured of an eight-card trump fit, you can do your sums on the assumption that he has nine losers for a response of 1♡ or 1♠.

Once again, a jump raise in a minor suit is less straightforward. A jump raise to the three level, as in the sequence

    1♣   1◇
    3◇

is exactly similar to the sequence 1♣–1♡–3♡. A jump raise to the four level, on the other hand, is best played as completely forcing.

    A. 1◇–2♣–4♣
    B. 1♡–2♣–4♣
    C. 1♠–2♣–4♣
    D. 1♡–2◇–4◇
    E. 1♠–2◇–4◇

Once the responder has the values for a two level response and the opener has strong enough support for a jump raise, it is almost inconceivable that the jump to 4♣ or 4◇ in these sequences will ever be passed. In view of this, there is little point in playing the jump to four of a minor as non-forcing, and the forcing treatment of these bids makes it easier to investigate slam possibilities if the opener is strong.

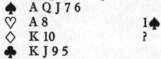

  ♠ A Q J 7 6
  ♡ A 8   1♠   2♣
  ◇ K 10   ?
  ♣ K J 9 5

Bid 4♣, forcing. There must be a good chance of a slam on this hand, and 4♣ sets the scene and leaves the way clear for an exchange of cue bids. 4♣ may, in fact, be the key bid in a neat sequence to reach the excellent slam contract if the full hands are something like:

	WEST		EAST	WEST	EAST
♠	A Q J 7 6	♠	K 3	1♠	2♣
♡	A 8	♡	J 9 5	4♣	4◇
◇	K 10	◇	A Q 4	4♡	4♠
♣	K J 9 5	♣	Q 10 8 7 2	4NT	5◇
				6♣	

All right so far. However, any eagle-eyed readers who have stayed the course will have noticed a slight flaw in this persuasive argument. It must be admitted that there is one – and one which is conveniently overlooked in most bidding text-books. However, since the main purpose of this exercise is to remove as many ambiguous, hazy sequences as possible from Acol and to produce a streamlined, supercharged version which will compare favourably with the most precise of the new modern systems, I must be brave and face reality.

If, in the interests of accuracy, a single raise of a minor suit response is reserved for a minimum opening hand with four-card trump support and if, as we have just decided, a jump raise to 4♣ or 4◇ is reserved as a forcing slam try, what happens if the unfortunate opener has a hand which is too good for a single raise but not strong enough to force to game?

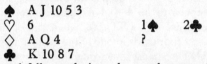

This hand falls neatly into the gap between 3♣ and 4♣, and it is clearly extremely difficult to cope with under Acol methods. I regret to admit that there is no straightforward solution to the problem. Playing with a confirmed overbidder, you can bid 3♣ and hope that he does not choose this moment for one of his rare passes. Otherwise, my choice is 2◇. If this bid ends the auction, you may have to pretend that you had your hand mis-sorted in a rather curious manner. However, if partner manages to find another bid over 2◇, you should be in a much better position to judge the correct final contract or to reveal your excellent support for clubs.

It may sometimes be possible to get an awkward hand off your chest by concealing your four-card trump support and rebidding 2NT.

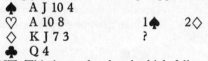

Bid 2NT. This is another hand which falls awkwardly between two stools. You are too strong for 3◇ but by no means strong enough to invite a slam by jumping to 4◇. The best solution is to rebid 2NT; this keeps the excellent diamond suit a secret, but it at least advertises a balanced hand with 15 or 16 points.

13. OPENER BIDS A SECOND SUIT

AFTER A 1NT RESPONSE

As we have already seen, a 1NT response to any opening bid apart from 1♣ is often little more than a conventional reply, showing the values to bid and denying the ability to bid anything else. It must not be assumed that it shows an overwhelming desire to play in no trumps, and this means that the opener should continue the search for the best contract unless he himself has a balanced hand which is ideally suited for playing in 1NT.

Assuming that the opener has no real interest in game, the general rules for bidding after a response of 1NT are as follows:

(a) Rebid a six-card suit.

(b) Pass any hand containing no five-card suit. This may, of course, mean that you have to settle for 1NT on a hand containing a singleton, if your distribution happens to be 4–4–4–1. This cannot be helped. Apart from the one sequence 1◇-1NT-2♣, when the opener *knows* that his partner has at least four cards in one of the minors, to introduce a second suit after a 1NT response must guarantee five cards in the opener's first suit, for the responder may be compelled to give preference on doubleton support if he is not keen on the opener's second suggestion.

(c) Pass any 5–3–3–2 hand, unless you choose to rebid a five-card major suit in order to achieve a pre-emptive effect.

(d) Bid a second, lower-ranking suit if you are at least 5–4 in your two suits.

This last point is a particularly important one, and one which is in general insufficiently understood. This is partly the result of what I consider to be the misleading advice which appeared in an earlier book on Acol.* The authors suggest that the opener should tend to stick it out in 1NT even if he has a weak, unbalanced hand: that is, unless he can calculate that the responder is unlikely to have length in his own short suits. This theory leads them to some surprising conclusions.

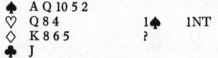

```
♠  A Q 10 5 2
♡  Q 8 4                1♠        1NT
◇  K 8 6 5              ?
♣  J
```

They suggest that you should pass in this situation, no doubt sadistically settling back in your chair to watch partner toiling in 1NT. Their principal argument is that you cannot be certain that you will improve your chances of a plus score by removing 1NT on this kind of hand, but this seems to me to be an unnecessarily pessimistic and cowardly view.

While you clearly cannot be 100% sure that the hand will play better in 2◇, 2♡ or 2♠, you can be fairly certain that things will be sticky in 1NT, when your unsuitable hand will be on the table for all to see. In my view, therefore, a rebid of 2◇ stands to gain far more than it loses. Consider three typical hands for the responder.

```
♠  J 6            ♠  6 4            ♠  6
♡  10 7 5 3       ♡  K 10 5         ♡  A J 10 5 2
◇  Q 10 4         ◇  Q J 7 2        ◇  Q 3
♣  A 7 5 4        ♣  Q 8 5 4        ♣  10 8 6 4 2
   HAND A            HAND B            HAND C
```

* *The Acol System Today,* by Terence Reese and Albert Dormer.

These hands all constitute fairly typical 1NT responses to 1♠, and two of them contain length in the opener's short suits, as we are led to expect. In each case, however, 1NT is far from the best resting-place, and the theoretically correct rebid of 2◇ will lead to the superior final contract of 2♠, 2◇ and 2♡ respectively. The fact that the responder might well be short in spades is not in itself a compelling reason to play 1NT; since the main feature of the opener's hand is his strong spade suit, partner is unlikely to find seven tricks very easy to accumulate if he cannot harvest the spades.

Generally speaking, therefore, it is recommended that the opener should remove 1NT if he has a 5–4–3–1 or 5–4–2–2 distribution and if his four-card suit can be shown without reversing. This stands to improve the final contract in one of three possible ways: if partner has four-card support for the opener's second suit, if he is in a position to give preference to the opener's five-card suit, or if he is able to introduce a long suit of his own. In my view, the only occasion on which it is correct to pass a 1NT response on an unbalanced hand is when a large proportion of your high-card strength lies in your short suits.

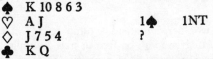

```
♠  K 10 8 6 3
♡  A J              1♠      1NT
◇  J 7 5 4           ?
♣  K Q
```

No bid. Since so much of your strength is concentrated in your doubleton suits, this hand will probably play reasonably well in no trumps. Even now, however, a rebid of 2◇ could lead to a better contract, and the opener should always be extremely reluctant to pass 1NT when he has a 5–4 distribution and can introduce a lower-ranking suit.

A reverse after a 1NT response shows the same strength as after a one-over-one suit response. It is not completely forcing but, since the responder has already denied four cards in the opener's second suit by his original 1NT reply, he is most unlikely to pass at his second turn.

```
♠  A 10 9 5
♡  A K J 7 3         1♡      1NT
◇  K Q 4             ?
♣  2
```

Bid 2♠. Partner is not likely to hold a four-card spade suit, but there is still no reason not to make the most descriptive rebid on this hand. Furthermore, 2♠ suggests that you are crying out for preference to 3♡ or 4♡.

E

A jump in a second suit after a 1NT response is forcing in a minor suit.

♠	A 6		
♡	A Q 8 7 5	1♡	1NT
♢	K Q J 4 2	?	
♣	2		

Bid 3♢. In traditional Acol, a jump shift of this kind was forcing to game. The modern practice, however, is to make it forcing for one round only; this means, for example, that you can pass if the responder gives simple preference to 3♡ in this situation. It is unarguably reassuring to be equipped with brakes of this kind. However, it is extremely doubtful whether anyone has ever had sufficient willpower to apply them.

Theoretically, this new interpretation of the jump to 3♣ or 3♢ over a 1NT response means that you can employ it on hands with 5–4 distribution in your two suits.

♠	A Q 8 7 5		
♡	A J 6	1♠	1NT
♢	K Q J 4	?	
♣	2		

Some authorities would recommend a jump to 3♢ at this point, adding complacently that you will be free to pass a simple preference bid of 3♠. This is fine if partner is in a position to raise diamonds or to give preference to spades, or if he is strong enough to push on to 3NT. The further outlook will not be so bright, however, if he has, let us say, a 1–4–3–5 distribution and no more than 6 or 7 points; your jump to 3♢ will probably be less favourably received in that case. There is therefore much to be said for concealing the diamonds in the above situation and making the simple, quantitative raise to 2NT. My view is, in fact, that a jump to 3♢ should be reserved for two different types of hand: a hand strong enough to go to game in any event, or a strong hand containing two five-card suits.

A jump shift to three of a major after a 1NT response is even less straightforward. It can, in fact, only occur in one sequence:

1♠	1NT
3♡	

It is here that we stumble once again into unexplored Acol territory. The soothsayers suggest that 3♡ in this sequence should be a one-round force, with the opener free to pass a simple return to 3♠ by the responder. One illustrative example is the following:

♠	K J 8 7 6		
♡	A Q 10 2	1♠	1NT
♢	4	?	
♣	A Q 5		

Reese and Dormer recommend* a bid of 3♡ at this point, urging you to pass if partner can say no more than 3♠. But can partner rely on your having this kind of hand? What would you rebid over 1NT on the following holding?

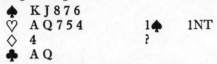

♠ K J 8 7 6		
♡ A Q 7 5 4	1♠	1NT
♢ 4	?	
♣ A Q		

If you would also bid 3♡ on this hand, your unfortunate partner is going to have great difficulty in judging what to do for the best. If he has a three-card heart holding, for example, he will have to guess whether you have four or five hearts, so that he can decide whether to raise to 4♡ or give false preference to 3♠.

Furthermore, even if partner assumes that the jump to 3♡ is based on a four-card suit, as the authorities seem to imply, it still does not follow that he will be in complete command of the situation. Let us suppose that the unfortunate fellow has:

♠ 10		
♡ 7 5 4	1♠	1NT
♢ K Q 9 7 2	3♡	?
♣ J 10 9 3		

What now? If the opener's 3♡ rebid could be based on 5–4 in the major suits, the responder is faced with an unenviable problem on this kind of hand. He has to choose between a sporting raise to 4♡ and a desperate return to 3NT, neither of which will prove a conspicuous success if the opener has the first hand mentioned above.

This problem does illustrate a serious flaw in the concept of playing 3♡ as a one-round force. The responder is equipped with brakes which enable him to stop if he prefers the opener's first suit, but he has no similar machinery to allow him to grind to a halt short of game if he either prefers the second suit or has no marked preference for either. Unless he is able to return to 3♠, the responder has no alternative but to raise to 4♡ or return to 3NT, which may be the last thing on earth he wants to do.

The whole thing is, in fact, a theoretical muddle, and this is just the sort of imprecise situation which earns Acol a bad name. And there is worse to come. Suppose the opener has a hand of this kind:

♠ A K 10 7 3		
♡ K Q 4	1♠	1NT
♢ K 10 6	?	
♣ A 2		

This is an awkward hand for Acol methods. Unless you dare to risk the confusion which might ensue from an exploratory leap to 3♣, you

* *The Acol System Today*, by Terence Reese and Albert Dormer.

just have to blast into 3NT. You must realise, however, that this might well not be the correct spot, for either 4♡ or 4♠ could easily prove to be a superior contract. Suppose, for example, that the responder has made an eminently reasonable 1NT response on one of the following hands:

♠	9 8 2	♠	8 4
♡	J 10 7	♡	J 10 9 7 3
◇	A Q 7 5	◇	A 9 5 4
♣	10 6 4	♣	J 7
	HAND A		HAND B

If the opponents are mean enough to lead a club, partner is most unlikely to make 3NT on either of these hands – and yet 4♠ is an odds-on contract on Hand A and 4♡ is almost ice-cold in Hand B. Clearly not a good hand for the system.

It is at this point that the U.S. Cavalry appear on the horizon. There is a solution to most of these difficulties. It lies in incorporating a new piece of machinery into the Acol framework: a conventional 3♣ bid to enquire about the responder's holdings in the major suits after the sequence 1♠–1NT. This convention is based on a little-known idea devised, I think, by Alan Truscott and Tony Priday some years ago.

After 1♠–1NT–3♣, the responder replies as follows:

(a) 3◇ to show 3 or 5 hearts. 3♡ by the opener now asks for further clarification:

    3♠ shows 3–3 in the majors.

    3NT shows 3 hearts and 0–2 spades.

    4♡ shows 5 hearts.

(b) 3♡ to show 4 hearts.

(c) 3♠ to show 3 spades and 2 hearts.

(d) 3NT to show no more than a doubleton in both majors.

After a reply of 3◇ or 3♡, a rebid of 3♠ by the opener shows a five-card suit and asks the responder to show three-card support.

The only disadvantage of this simple convention is, of course, that you will no longer be able to rebid 3♣ on a strong hand containing both black suits. However, 3♣ is an extremely rare bid in this natural sense, and there are considerable theoretical and practical advantages to be gained by allotting a conventional meaning to the 3♣ rebid.

(a) It releases a rebid of 3♡ as a non-forcing game try, showing two five-card major suits and a hand not strong enough to insist on game.

♠	A K 10 7 5		
♡	K Q 6 4 2	1♠	1NT
◇	K 8	?	
♣	7		

Bid 3♡, which describes the hand precisely. The responder can now raise to 4♡ or 4♠ if he has a suitable holding. Furthermore, he is now equipped with a really efficient set of brakes: 3♡ is not completely forcing, and partner can either pass 3♡ or convert to 3♠ if he is unable to rustle up any enthusiasm for the whole affair.

(b) It enables the opener to search for the best game contract if he has a game-going hand with both majors.

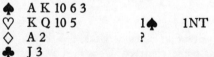

♠ A K 7 6 3
♡ A Q 8 2   1♠   1NT
◇ A 2   ?
♣ Q 4

Bid 3♣, asking partner about his major suit holdings. If he bids 3♡, showing a four-card suit, you raise to 4♡; if he bids 3♠, showing three spades and two hearts, you push on to 4♠; if he bids 3NT, showing shortage in both majors, you pass; and if he replies 3◇, showing three or five hearts, you can investigate further by rebidding 3♡. In each case, you can be sure of reaching the correct contract.

(c) It enables the opener to locate a 5–3 major fit which would normally be lost forever.

♠ A K 7 3 2
♡ A Q 5   1♠   1NT
◇ K Q 10   ?
♣ J 2

Bid 3♣, in an effort to find a 5–3 fit in either hearts or spades. Under normal methods, you would probably have to raise 1NT to 3NT without further ado; the 3♣ convention enables you to investigate the various possibilities much more accurately.

Unfortunately, this is not a perfect world. The above convention, admirable as it is, leaves one problem unsolved: the opener still has no precise way of making a try for game when he has five spades and four hearts.

♠ A K 10 6 3
♡ K Q 10 5   1♠   1NT
◇ A 2   ?
♣ J 3

This is very difficult. The hand is not suitable for a game-forcing bid of 3♣, and to make a non-forcing jump to 3♡ would show at least 5–5 in the major suits. The best rebid is probably 2NT, which conceals the heart suit but which at least shows 17 or 18 points. If the hand were slightly weaker, my choice would be 2♡, which will not often end the auction; if partner does manage to find another bid, you will be able to make a further effort over a return to 2♠ and push on to game if he raises 2♡ to 3♡.

This situation is admittedly not completely satisfactory; however, one slightly unsatisfactory situation is negligible compared with all the muddles which are liable to occur in Steam-Age Acol when the opener has a strong hand and the bidding commences 1♠–1NT.

AFTER A 2NT RESPONSE

For the more conservative of you who still claim to use an immediate 2NT response in the original Acol sense, showing a balanced hand with 11 or 12 points, it is important to remember that a bid of a second suit by the opener is forcing.

3♡ is forcing in this sequence, suggesting that you are not overjoyed at the prospect of playing the hand in no trumps. However, it is not completely forcing to game, and the opener is free to pass a simple return to 3♠; this means that the responder must bid the full value of what is left of his hand after the 2NT response.

AFTER A 3NT RESPONSE

An immediate response of 3NT has such a stultifying effect on the auction that it is best reserved for perfectly balanced 3–3–3–4 or 3–3–4–3 hands containing 13 or 14 points. If it is allocated this precise meaning, the opener should be able to determine the best final contract without too much difficulty.

> 1♠   3NT
> 4◇

Any rebid below the game level is forcing and is obviously a slam try: the opener already knows for certain that there is three-card spade support in the opposite hand, and he will therefore never need to bid 4◇ in an attempt to find the best game contract.

There is only one really murky patch in this particular area of the Acol jungle. This concerns the specific sequence:

> 1♠   3NT
> 4♡

Does 4♡ in this situation show a weak 5–5 hand, offering the responder a choice of game contract? Does it show a strongish two-suiter? Or is it merely a forcing bid, showing interest in a slam?

This is just the sort of sequence which causes trouble at the table but which is rarely covered in the text-books. We must put that right without further delay, and we can arrive at the correct conclusion best by a process of elimination.

First, 4♡ is not needed to show a weak two-suited hand.

♠ A J 7 4 2		
♡ K J 10 6 5	1♠	3NT
◇ J 2	?	
♣ 4		

Bid 4♠. 4♡ seems the obvious rebid here, but a little thought shows that it is not absolutely necessary. You know that partner has three-card support for both majors, and the hand should therefore play just as well in 4♠; in fact, you may gain some advantage in the play if you keep the five-card heart suit a closely guarded secret.

And 4♡ is not absolutely essential as a slam try on a hand with 5–4 in the majors.

♠	A Q 10 7 2		
♡	K J 7 5	1♠	3NT
◇	8	?	
♣	A Q 3		

Bid 4♣. Partner's bid of 3NT is most unlikely to conceal a biddable four-card heart suit. While it would be satisfying to make a slam try by bidding 4♡, therefore, 4♣ will probably work out just as well. In fact, since you are contemplating playing in 6♠ in any case, 4♣ will leave partner more space in which to cue bid if he has a suitable hand for slam purposes.

This leaves us with one other type of hand.

♠	A Q 8 6 3		
♡	K J 7 4 2	1♠	3NT
◇	A 5	?	
♣	7		

There are excellent chances of a slam on this hand. Its success will depend on how well the responder's high cards are working, and it is therefore important to be able to bid 4♡ in this situation to show the exact nature of your hand. It is, in fact, recommended that the sequence 1♠–3NT–4♡ should show precisely this kind of hand: 5–5 in the majors and sufficient general strength for there to be good hopes of a slam opposite a good fit.

Even if this sequence is primarily to be interpreted in this way, it is advisable to play the 4♡ bid as absolutely forcing, bearing in mind that the opener can always stand a return to 4♠ if the responder is not interested in better things. If this is agreed, the opener can afford to rebid 4♡ on even stronger hands on which a slam is much more than a faint hope.

♠	A Q 9 5 3		
♡	A Q 8 6 3	1♠	3NT
◇	2	?	
♣	A 4		

Bid 4♡, forcing. If partner can show some immediate enthusiasm, there may even be a grand slam on this hand. If he attempts to sign off in 4♠ over 4♡, you can try again with a 5♣ cue bid; partner will now warn you off a slam only if he has a completely unsuitable holding.

AFTER A SINGLE RAISE: TRIAL BIDS

1♡   2♡

3♣

After his first suit has been raised to two, a simple bid of a second suit by the opener is forcing. Its first meaning is to invite the responder to push on to game if he has a suitable hand; the 3♣ bid in this sequence is therefore called a Trial Bid.

Since the initial raise to two may have been made on three-card trump support, a Trial Bid by the opener will normally be based on a five-card holding in his first suit. This means that, if the opener only has a four-card suit, he should generally make a try for game by rebidding 2NT.

♠	A J 7		
♡	A Q 8 3	1♡	2♡
◊	K Q J 4	?	
♣	J 5		

Bid 2NT. While the club holding is far from ideal for this action, it is the most descriptive bid available, suggesting a balanced hand with 17 or 18 points. The alternative bids of 2♠ or 3◊ would both imply a more shapely hand with at least five hearts.

There are, of course, hands on which the opener may have to make a Trial Bid when he has no more than four cards in the agreed suit, notably when he has a 4-4-4-1 distribution. This cannot be helped. The important point is that a Trial Bid implies a five-card trump suit, and the responder will be entitled to proceed accordingly.

In traditional Acol, a Trial Bid is made in the suit in which the opener would particularly welcome a little assistance. The suit will almost always be a three-card or longer holding, and it will usually contain two losers.

1♡   2♡

3◊

The 3◊ bid in this sequence invites the responder to jump to 4♡ if he has a maximum for his 2♡ bid, and to sign off in 3♡ if he has nothing to be proud of; if the responder's hand is neither minimum nor maximum, he should judge what to do by reference to his holding in diamonds, the suit in which the opener particularly needs help.

Trial Bids in this form owe much to the late Iain Macleod, who was one of the pioneers in their development. It would be churlish, therefore, not to dip into his excellent book* to find an example of the Trial Bid in action.

* *Bridge Is An Easy Game,* by Iain Macleod.

WEST	EAST	WEST	EAST
♠ 7	♠ J 6 5		
♡ K Q 10 8 6 2	♡ A 7 5 3	1♡	2♡
◇ K 8 4	◇ Q J 6 2	3◇	4♡
♣ A 10 2	♣ 9 5		

Notice that it is the excellent fit in diamonds which makes this such a good game contract. If East's spade and diamond holdings were reversed, for example, there would be almost no play for ten tricks; but in that case East would not be tempted to bid more than 3♡.

There are two important points to be made in connection with Trial Bids after a major suit has been raised to two. The first concerns two specific sequences:

    (A) 1♡   2♡   (B) 1♠   2♠
        2♠   3♡

The opener's second bid in both sequences is obviously a Trial Bid. It is also just possible that it is based on a four-card suit and, if the responder decides to go to game in any case, he should remember to proceed via a raise to 3♠ or 4♡ if he has a four-card suit. After Sequence A, for example, 4♠ might well prove to be the correct game contract if there is a 4–4 spade fit and a 5–4 heart fit.

WEST	EAST	WEST	EAST
♠ A K 7 3	♠ J 8 6 4	1♡	2♡
♡ A J 7 5 2	♡ Q 9 6 4	2♠	3♠
◇ K 9 4	◇ A 7 3	4♠	
♣ 7	♣ Q 2		

Since East is worth a jump to 4♡ over 2♠, he can mention his four-card spade suit en route. Notice that, while West would probably lose one trick in each suit in 4♡, he will almost certainly make 4♠ if the trumps are 3–2, for he can throw dummy's diamond loser on the fifth heart.

The other point arises in a sequence of this kind:

    1♠   2♠
    3♣   3◇

The responder's 3◇ bid is a Return Trial Bid. It suggests that, while he would be loth to sign off in 3♠, he has not sufficient strength or a sufficiently good fit in clubs to justify a jump to 4♠. It does, in fact, pass the buck back to the opener, who will now have to make the final decision himself.

♠ A 10 2			
♡ 7 5		1♠	2♠
◇ K 10 8 5 3		3♣	?
♣ J 9 4			

Bid 3◇. While you are not completely minimum for your raise to 2♠, your holding in clubs is not sufficiently inspiring to justify a jump to 4♠. It is best to consult partner by making a further Trial Bid of 3◇. The fate of 4♠ will probably depend on the opener's holding in diamonds, and he should be in a better position to judge what to do. Furthermore, it will now appear to be his fault if you end up in 3♠+1 or 4♠−1. . . .

If the opening bid is a minor, a Trial Bid acquires a slightly different meaning.

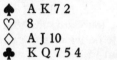

The opener's 2♠ bid here is still a Trial Bid, in the sense that it cannot be passed, but his eyes may not be fixed solely on the distant objective of 5♣. He may be seeking a cheaper game contract in 3NT or 4♠, and the responder should therefore bear in mind the possibility that the opener has introduced a four-card major suit on the second round.

<table>
<tr><td>♠ A K 7 2</td><td></td></tr>
<tr><td>♡ 8</td><td>1♣   2♣</td></tr>
<tr><td>◇ A J 10</td><td>?</td></tr>
<tr><td>♣ K Q 7 5 4</td><td></td></tr>
</table>

Bid 2♠, the best forward-going move available. While you are quite prepared to play in 5♣ if partner has a little to spare, you should investigate the other possible game contracts first. If partner attempts to sign off in 3♣ over 2♠, you can make a further move towards 3NT by trying again with 3◇.

Short suit trial bids. One recent innovation in this field is the so-called Short Suit Trial Bid. Under this method, the opener moves on towards game after a single raise by bidding his shortest side suit rather than the suit in which he particularly needs help.

<table>
<tr><td>♠ A K 10 7 3</td><td></td></tr>
<tr><td>♡ A 4 2</td><td>1♠   2♠</td></tr>
<tr><td>◇ 6</td><td>?</td></tr>
<tr><td>♣ K J 8 5</td><td></td></tr>
</table>

Playing Short Suit Trial Bids, the opener bids 3◇, warning the responder to discount any values he holds in that suit when he is assessing the prospects of 4♠. This method works well on hands of this kind, where the opener has a small singleton in a side suit; its accuracy is not as impressive when his shortest suit is something like K–x. But maybe I am biased. Traditional Acol Trial Bids have always worked pretty well for me.

A jump bid in a second suit after a single raise is a slam try.

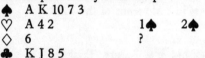

The jump to 4♣ in this sequence is best played as a cue bid, showing a void in clubs. This should enable the responder to judge whether his modest values are suitably placed for slam purposes; if they include wasted strength in clubs, he will sign off in 4♡ without further ado.

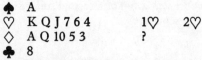

WEST	EAST	WEST	EAST
♠ A J 10	♠ 7 5	1♡	2♡
♡ A Q J 9 6 4	♡ K 8 7 3	4♣	4◇
◇ K Q 7 2	◇ A 8 4	6♡	
♣ —	♣ 10 7 6 4		

Although East's hand only contains one ace and one king, it becomes quite suitable for slam purposes when West is known to have a void in clubs. He is therefore able to co-operate by showing the ace of diamonds, and this enables West to take a shot at the excellent slam contract.

It is, of course, unlikely that the opener will be interested in a slam after nothing more than a single raise, particularly if he has no void among his controls. On those rare occasions where he is anxious to make a mild slam try, he can proceed by way of a normal Game Trial Bid.

♠ A		
♡ K Q J 7 6 4	1♡	2♡
◇ A Q 10 5 3	?	
♣ 8		

Bid 3◇. Partner will, of course, assume that this is a normal Trial Bid. However, his reaction to it will be helpful to you in your search for a slam. There are three key cards which are of crucial importance: the two missing aces and the king of diamonds. If partner has two of these cards, he will certainly jump to 4♡ over 3◇ and you can go on from there. If he attempts to sign off in 3♡ over 3◇, you should abandon the hunt for a slam and settle for 4♡. Partner will then realise that your 3◇ bid was a trial bid for a slam rather than for a game.

AFTER A DOUBLE RAISE

After a jump raise of a major suit, a bid of a second suit by the opener is a slam try.

     1♡   3♡
     4♣

Since it commits the side to game in any case, the opener's 4♣ bid in this sequence is clearly a try for 6♡. As so often seems to be the case in Acol, the bid is open to two interpretations. Both of them are perfectly sensible, but it is absolutely vital to know what we are doing in situations of this kind.

One possible meaning of the 4♣ bid is that it is a cue bid, showing the ace of clubs and inviting the responder to cue bid in turn if he has a suitable hand. This is clearly a perfectly playable method, and it has one obvious advantage: 4♣ *sounds* like a cue bid.

In my view, however, it is preferable to use the 4♣ bid in this sequence as a kind of Trial Bid. Just as the sequence 1♡–2♡–3♣ suggests that the opener would particularly welcome a little assistance in clubs for game purposes, so the sequence 1♡–3♡–4♣ can be used to direct partner's attention to clubs for slam purposes. This interpretation of the bid will be particularly useful on hands of this type:

♠	A		
♡	A K 10 7 5	1♡	3♡
◇	K Q 7	?	
♣	Q 10 9 5		

Bid 4♣. This might be described as a Polo bid, showing the suit with the hole. Cue bidding alone is unlikely to be a great deal of help in this situation; a slam will probably depend on the responder's holding in clubs, and 4♣ announces that you would welcome a good honour holding or a pronounced shortage in that suit.

After a jump raise of a minor suit, a bid of a second suit by the opener is a Trial Bid for game. The sequence

1◇	3◇
3♡	

is exactly analogous to the sequence 1♡–2♡–3◇, and the responder should use the same principles in deciding between 4◇ and 5◇. It is possible, of course, that the opener has a slam in mind when he bids 3♡; however, the responder must not proceed on that assumption until he receives further confirmation.

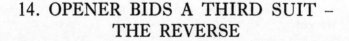

14. OPENER BIDS A THIRD SUIT – THE REVERSE

The reverse has always been surrounded by such an aura of mystique and confusion that it is advisable for any new analysis of the subject to start from the rudimentary principles. The plan of campaign in this chapter is to spend some time on the important basic points, before adding one or two new ideas to the general theory of bidding after a reverse.

DEFINITION

Let us start at the very beginning with a definition. The opener is said to 'reverse' if he bids two suits in such an order that his partner is forced to go to the three level in order to express simple preference for the first. That sounds simple enough. However, if you were to ask the average player in the average bridge club for a definition, it is extremely unlikely that you would hear anything remotely resembling this version. There is, for example, a common belief that a reverse bid has something to do with bidding a low-ranking suit before a higher-ranking one, but this is patently not so: the sequence 1♣–1♢–1♠ is clearly not a reverse, and yet the sequence 1♠–2♢–3♣ most certainly is.

There are two kinds of reverse available to the opener.

A Low Reverse is where the opener's second suit is bid at the two level. There are eight possible situations:

A. 1♣–1♡–2♢
B. 1♣–1♠–2♢
C. 1♣–1♠–2♡
D. 1♢–1♠–2♡
E. 1♢–2♣–2♡
F. 1♢–2♣–2♠
G. 1♡–2♣–2♠
H. 1♡–2♢–2♠

A High Reverse is where the opener's second suit is bid at the three level. This happens in only four sequences:

I. 1♡–2♢–3♣
J. 1♠–2♢–3♣
K. 1♠–2♡–3♣
L. 1♠–2♡–3♢

REQUIREMENTS FOR A REVERSE

A Low Reverse forces the responder to go to the three level in order to sign off.

   1♢   1♠
   2♡   3♢

Since the responder may have no more than 5 or 6 points and three small diamonds in this sequence, it is clear that the opener needs a strong hand to hoist the bidding up in this way. The generally accepted minimum for a Low Reverse is 17 points, the same as for a jump to 2NT, but this may be shaded a little if the opener has compensating values: for example, a partial fit for his partner's suit or a six-card suit of his own.

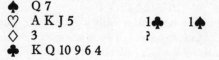

♠ Q 7
♥ A K J 5   1♣   1♠
♦ 3   ?
♣ K Q 10 9 6 4

Bid 2♥, but only just. It is strongly recommended that you should not shade your requirements for a reverse any further than this. For example, if your holdings in spades and diamonds were transposed, there would be a strong case for a modest rebid of 2♣.

So much for the high-card strength required for a Low Reverse. The other essential ingredient is the correct distribution, and it is in this connection that a great deal of muddled thinking occurs. The rule is simple: a Low Reverse guarantees that the first suit is the longer and that it is of at least five-card length; a reverse does, in fact, tell the responder more about the opener's distribution than it does about his strength.

To understand why this is so, consider the following sequence:

1♦   1♠
2♥

If the opener had equal length in the red suits, he would clearly open 1♥. The fact that he has chosen to open 1♦ must indicate that his diamonds are longer than his hearts, and the responder can therefore infer three important items of knowledge from this reverse sequence: that the opener has approximately 17 points, that he has at least five diamonds, and that he has longer diamonds than hearts.

To digress briefly for a moment, there may actually be one case in which the opener should open 1♦ when he has four diamonds and four hearts.

♠ A J 9
♥ 10 7 4 2
♦ A Q 8 5
♣ A Q

There is a strong case for ignoring the anaemic heart suit and opening 1♦ on this hand. If you do, however, you must rebid in no trumps if partner replies anything but 1♥; it would be a serious error to bid hearts on the second round, for a reverse must always show the shape as well as the strength of your hand.

It is not difficult to understand why a Low Reverse guarantees greater length in the first suit when the opener holds 'touching' suits. The same point also applies, however, in the two sequences in which the opener's suits are not adjacent.

(A) 1♣   1♠   (B) 1♦   2♣
     2♥   2♠

In each case, the opener is implying a five-card minor suit by inviting preference at the three level. This means, of course, that there are certain situations in which the opener should select his opening bid with great care.

♠ A Q 10 7
♡ 7 3
◇ K Q J 8
♣ K J 4

If you open 1◇ on this hand, you will be slightly embarrassed by a response of 2♣. The correct opening bid is 1♠, intending to rebid 2NT over 2♡ and to introduce the diamonds if partner responds 2♣

A High Reverse shows approximately the same strength as a Low Reverse. It does not, however, convey the same precise message about the shape of the hand for, while the first suit is always of at least five-card length, the second suit can occasionally be as long.

♠ A K J 8 4
♡ Q 4   1♠   2♡
◇ K Q J 7 3   ?
♣ 8

Bid 3◇. A High Reverse of this kind is forcing. It guarantees at least five spades, but in this type of sequence the responder cannot be certain that the diamond suit is shorter.

It must not be assumed from this that the opener's second suit is never shorter when he executes a High Reverse. There are situations in which the second suit can even be a three-card holding.

♠ A K Q 7 3
♡ 7 2   1♠   2◇
◇ K 9 5   ?
♣ A Q 8

Bid 3♣. The opener has a difficult rebid in this situation, for, while he clearly wants to be in game, he cannot be sure whether the hand belongs in 3NT, 4♠ or 5◇. The best rebid is a High Reverse of 3♣. This will force the responder to find another bid, and the picture should be clarified as a result.

BIDDING AFTER A LOW REVERSE
If the responder has bid at the one level, a reverse is not absolutely forcing – even if the occasions on which the responder will elect to pass are admittedly very few and far between. Moreover, the opener certainly does not guarantee to find another bid, and the responder must avoid making a minimum rebid if he can visualise game after the reverse.

1◇   1♠
2♡   ?

The responder has three non-forcing bids available in this situation:

(a) 2♠ which shows a goodish six-card spade suit and very little else.

(b) 2NT which shows a guard in the unbid suit but denies the values to bid 3NT.

(c) 3◇ simple preference to the opener's first suit.

The responder must avoid these courses of action if he can visualise game opposite his partner's strength-showing rebid. If he is unable to bid game direct, the following sequences are best played as forcing, leaving space to investigate game and slam possibilities.

(a) *A raise of the opener's major suit*

This sequence is described as limited and non-forcing in traditional Acol. In practice, however, the opener will only pass 3♡ once in a blue moon, and we can therefore increase the efficiency of our bidding by defining a raise of the opener's major as 100% forcing. This will ease the responder's task if he is anxious to make a waiting bid in order to keep various options open.

Furthermore, the fact that a simple raise of the opener's major suit is forcing releases a jump raise as a specific type of slam suggestion.

Bid 4♡. Since 3♡ would have been forcing in this situation, the unnecessary jump to 4♡ shows a hand with interest in a slam and, more important, with first-rate trump support. This may come as good news to the opener if he has rebid 2♡ on a powerful hand containing a feeble heart suit.

(b) *A jump rebid of the responder's original suit*

Once again it is almost inconceivable that the opener will pass this sequence, and it is therefore best to define the jump rebid as absolutely forcing. This will simplify matters if the responder has a six-card suit but is still not certain about the best game contract.

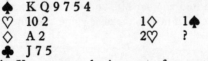

Bid 3♠. You want to be in game after partner's reverse, but the

correct denomination is not yet clear. 3♠ shows a goodish six-card
suit and makes it possible to play in 4♠ or 3NT – or even in 5◇.

(c) *Jump preference to the opener's first suit*

> 1◇   1♠
> 2♡   4◇

Since simple preference to 3◇ would not be forcing in this sequence,
it must not be assumed that the responder is enormously strong for
this jump to 4◇. It is, however, possible that he is setting the scene
before investigating slam possibilities.

	WEST		EAST	WEST	EAST
♠	K 5	♠	A Q J 7 2	1◇	1♠
♡	K Q 10 7	♡	A 3	2♡	4◇
◇	A Q 10 7 5	◇	K 9 4 2	5♣	5♡
♣	A 7	♣	8 5	5♠	5NT
				7◇	

Once West has shown the ace of clubs and the vital king of spades
by cue bidding, East is able to suggest a grand slam by bidding 5NT,
inviting his partner to bid seven if he has two of the top three trump
honours. Notice how the forcing jump to 4◇ makes all this possible
at a reasonable level.

(d) *A bid of the fourth suit*

> 1◇   1♠
> 2♡   3♣

You will find a detailed analysis of the theory of Fourth Suit bidding
in the section on the Responder's Second Bid. For the time being, it
will be sufficient to say that, following a reverse, a bid of the fourth
suit by the responder is absolutely forcing. It may be a temporising
move on a powerful hand; or it may be an exploratory manoeuvre on a
game-going hand on which the responder's destination is not yet clear.

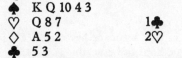

> ♠ K Q 10 4 3
> ♡ Q 8 7   1♣   1♠
> ◇ A 5 2   2♡   ?
> ♣ 5 3

Bid 3◇. You clearly want to be in game on this hand, but it is by
no means certain that 3NT is the best spot, particularly played from
your side of the table. 3◇ gives partner a chance to bid no trumps if
he can help in the diamond department; it also leaves the way clear for
a final contract of 4♡ or 4♠ if he is short in diamonds.

(e) *A jump bid in the fourth suit* has little value in a natural sense. It is
probably best played as a cue bid agreeing the opener's second suit,
just as it is after a non-reverse rebid by the opener. For the sake of

simplicity, I suggest that a jump in the fourth suit should show the ace if it is at the three level and a void if it is at the four level; that is in line with the suggested interpretation of jumps in the fourth suit in non-reverse situations which is explained in a later chapter.

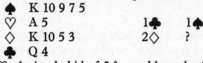

♠ K 10 9 7 5		
♡ A 5	1♣	1♠
◇ K 10 5 3	2◇	?
♣ Q 4		

Bid 3♡. A simple bid of 3◇ would not be forcing in this situation and, while a raise to 4◇ is a reasonable alternative, the hand can be shown more economically and more accurately by a jump to 3♡. This agrees diamonds, pin-points the ace of hearts, and shows a hand with slam interest – all in one bid.

♠ A J 9 6 4 2		
♡ K J 6 5	1◇	1♠
◇ J 8 3	2♡	?
♣ —		

Bid 4♣, agreeing hearts and showing a void in clubs. There must be a good chance of at least a small slam on this hand, and the knowledge that you are void of clubs should enable the opener to judge accurately how well his high cards are working and how far to proceed.

If the responder has bid at the two level, a reverse is best played as forcing; it is inconceivable that, if the responder has the values for a bid at the two level, he will be anxious to pass a strength-showing rebid by his partner.

The only difference in the responder's rebids in this situation is that certain bids which can be passed after an initial one level response now become forcing. This applies to two principal situations.

(a) *A rebid of 2NT by the responder is forcing*

1◇	2♣
2♠	2NT

To play 2NT as forcing in this sequence has certain advantages if the responder still has a vague hope of better things.

♠ 10 4 2		
♡ A Q 6	1◇	2♣
◇ J 2	2♠	?
♣ K Q 10 8 5		

Bid 2NT. Since the two hands seem to fit rather poorly, you may eventually have to settle for a mere game contract. However, if partner is able to reveal some support for clubs, prospects of a slam will be considerably brighter; the forcing rebid of 2NT gives him a chance to bid 3♣.

(b) *Simple preference to the opener's suit is forcing*

1♥	2♣
2♠	3♥

The fact that 3♥ is forcing in this situation releases the jump to 4♥ for use as a slam suggestion. The most valuable meaning to assign to unnecessary jump preference is that it shows a hand with excellent trump support and with interest in a slam.

♠ 10 3
♥ K Q 2   1♥   2♦
♦ A K 9 5 2   2♠   ?
♣ 7 5 3

Bid 4♥. This shows strong interest in a slam and surprisingly good trump support. It might be just what the opener wants to hear if he is conscious of having opened the bidding on a fragile five-card heart suit.

To summarise. After an initial response at the two level and a reverse by the opener, a virtual game-forcing situation has been created; the responder can therefore afford to take his time if he is anxious to explore all the various possibilities. In fact, the only rebid by the responder which can be passed in this situation is a simple rebid of his original suit.

♠ 7 5
♥ 6   1♥   2♣
♦ 10 9 6 3   2♠   ?
♣ A Q J 9 7 4

Bid 3♣. The original response of 2♣ was a dubious move in itself. You must now warn partner that your only reason for responding at the two level was a good six-card suit and a distaste for any other contract. If partner chooses to pass 3♣, you can be certain that you are in the correct contract.

BIDDING AFTER A HIGH REVERSE

A High Reverse is forcing. Furthermore, it promises another bid from the opener, and this means that the responder can afford to take things slowly if he is not yet certain where the best game contract lies.

♠ J 3
♥ A J 9 6 4   1♠   2♥
♦ K 7 3   3♦   ?
♣ J 10 5

Bid 3♠. If the opener is able to bid 3NT over 3♠, that will almost certainly be the correct game contract. Notice that, if 3♠ was not regarded as forcing, you would have an extremely awkward decision at this point; since to introduce the fourth suit would hoist the auction to the four level, you have no other sensible way of investigating the various possible game contracts.

The fact that any rebid below the game level by the responder is forcing enables him to employ an unnecessary jump to show a good suit. For example:

♠	Q 5		
♡	K Q J 10 7 3	1♠	2♡
◇	7 5	3◇	?
♣	K 8 4		

Bid 4♡. Since 3♡ would be forcing in this situation, the unnecessary jump to 4♡ suggests that, although your hand is not particularly powerful, your heart suit is an excellent one, almost self-supporting. Similarly:

♠	7 5 4		
♡	K Q 3	1♡	2◇
◇	K 10 7 6 3	3♣	?
♣	A 7		

Bid 4♡. Unnecessary jump preference of this kind shows slam interest and first-rate trump support. It may be the key bid if partner has a powerful hand in all but the heart suit.

	WEST		EAST	WEST	EAST
♠	A Q	♠	7 5 4	1♡	2◇
♡	J 10 8 7 5	♡	K Q 3	3♣	4♡
◇	A J	◇	K 10 7 6 3	4♠	5♣
♣	K Q J 4	♣	A 7	5◇	5♡
				6♡	

Notice that, while the West hand is in many ways very suitable for slam purposes, he would be extremely loth to move forward without the assurance that East has excellent heart support.

15. OPENER BIDS A THIRD SUIT – WITHOUT REVERSING

THE SIMPLE CHANGE OF SUIT

Most rebids by the opener after a simple response in a new suit by his partner represent a serious attempt to limit his hand within a fairly narrow range. For example, all no trump rebids by him are non-forcing and show a precise point-count; rebids of his original suit and raises of the responder's suit either show great strength (for example, 1♡–2♣–4♣ or 1♣–1♡–4♣), or they limit the hand in a non-forcing situation.

In fact, the only completely unlimited rebid available to the opener is a simple non-reverse bid in a new suit. Consider the following completely dissimilar hands:

♠ K Q 7 2				♠ A Q J 7			
♡ 7 3	1♣	1◇		♡ 7 4	1♣	1◇	
◇ J 8 4	?			◇ A 3	?		
♣ A Q 9 5				♣ A Q J 8 5			
HAND A				HAND B			

In each case, the correct rebid is 1♠. It may seem odd that you should be enjoined to bid the same way on a gigantic 18-point hand as on an emaciated 12-point collection, but Hand B is not quite strong enough to force to game by jumping to 2♠ and there is no other way in which to express the value of the hand while at the same time continuing the search for the best final denomination.

A simple change of suit by the opener is not, of course, forcing in Acol. However, the wide range of hands covered by the rebid means that the responder should be reluctant to pass at his second turn. As we shall see in the forthcoming section on the Responder's Second Bid, he should do all he can to give the opener another chance to define the nature of his hand more precisely.

There are even occasions on which the opener may choose to make an unlimited rebid in a three-card suit on the second round. We have already discovered one such situation in our discussion of the immediate raise of a minor suit response at the two level. To recapitulate.

♠ A J 10 5 3		
♡ 6	1♠	2♣
◇ A Q 4	?	
♣ K 10 8 7		

Bid 2◇. The hand falls neatly into the gap between a pawky raise to 3♣, which should suggest a minimum opening hand, and a full-blooded raise to 4♣, which is best played as forcing and slam-orientated. Unless you are of a nervous disposition, therefore, the best rebid on the above hand is an exploratory 2◇; providing that partner emerges with another bid, this should enable you to judge the situation much more accurately on the next round.

A similar situation arises when your hand is fairly balanced but not suitable for a limited rebid in no trumps.

♠ 4 2		
♡ A J 10 5 4	1♡	2♣
◇ K Q 3	?	
♣ A J 2		

Bid 2◇. Here again there is no accurate way in which you can limit your hand. You are worth 2NT in terms of values, but that would be a distortion in view of the non-existent spade suit. To raise clubs would mislead partner both about your overall strength and about the length of your club suit; and to rebid 2♡ would be pessimistic in the extreme in view of your 15 high-card points and your good fit in clubs. In the absence of a better solution, therefore, cross your fingers and rebid 2◇; as we have seen, it is impossible to limit this hand at this point, and 2◇ is the only unlimited rebid at your disposal.

It is also possible to find hands on which you would like to raise partner's major suit to two-and-a-half. Since this is contrary to the laws of the game, the answer may be to temporise with a three-card suit.

♠	K 10 7		
♡	7 2	1◇	1♠
◇	A K 9 5 3	?	
♣	A Q 8		

Bid 2♣. The hand is clearly too good for a simple raise to 2♠. However, 3♠ would be an exaggeration on such inadequate trump support, and, since there is no other way of limiting your hand at this point, a temporising bid of 2♣ is the best solution to the problem. If partner finds another bid, you will be able to show your hand exactly by showing your spade support on the next round. For example, the sequence:

1◇	1♠
2♣	2◇
2♠	

shows a hand with three-card spade support which was too strong for an immediate raise to 2♠; in fact, just the sort of hand we devised above.

Finally, to bid a three-card suit may be the best solution if you cannot accurately limit an essentially one-suited hand.

♠	Q		
♡	7 5 3	1◇	1♠
◇	A Q J 9 7 5	?	
♣	A Q 8		

Bid 2♣. A simple rebid of 2◇ would scarcely do justice to this hand. However, you are not worth a jump to 3◇, which might encourage partner to essay an undignified 3NT contract, and the best rebid is the unlimited one of 2♣.

It must be emphasised that these three-card suit bids are not completely sound. They rely on the fact that partner will only pass a simple change of suit if he is quite unable to find another bid and, very important, they assume that partner has read the chapter on false preference which appears later in this book. With these reservations, a rebid in a three-card suit is theoretically correct in a number of situations. However, please do not write to me if you have an unpleasant mishap as a result; I have enough troubles of my own.

THE JUMP SHIFT BY THE OPENER

A jump bid in a third suit by the opener is forcing to game.

> 1♣   1♡
> *2♠*

The opener's jump to 2♠ in this sequence can be based on three different types of hand:

(a) A hand containing general values and approximately 19 high-card points; however, this requirement can be reduced if partner has guaranteed good values by responding at the two level.

> ♠ A J 7 3
> ♡ K Q 6   1♣   1♡
> ◇ K 4   ?
> ♣ A Q 9 3

Bid 2♠. You are worth a jump to 3NT in this situation, but such action would be premature; 4♡ or 4♠ could prove to be a better game contract.

(b) A powerful hand containing two strong suits.

> ♠ A Q J 7 3
> ♡ Q   1♣   1♡
> ◇ 4   ?
> ♣ A K J 9 6 5

Bid 2♠, intending to show the distribution of the hand by rebidding 3♠ on the next round.

(c) A game-going hand with strong support for the responder's suit.

> ♠ A K 6
> ♡ A Q 7 3   1♣   1♡
> ◇ 2   ?
> ♣ A J 10 8 4

Bid 2♠. You are clearly worth a raise to 4♡ in this situation, but it costs nothing to show the extreme power of your hand by making a jump shift to 2♠ first. Furthermore, when you proceed by subsequently supporting hearts vigorously, this sequence has the advantage of showing a pronounced shortage in diamonds.

The jump reverse deserves special consideration. There are three different types of jump reverse available to the opener:

> (A) 1♣   1♡   (B) 1◇   2♣   (C) 1♡   2◇
>   3◇   3♡   4♣

In Sequence A, a rebid of 2◇ by the opener would not be absolutely forcing. The jump reverse of 3◇ is therefore completely natural, showing game-going values and implying a five-card or longer club suit and a shorter holding in diamonds.

♠ 7 2
♥ A J   1♣ 1♥
♦ A K 7 2   ?
♣ A Q J 8 3

Bid 3♦. You want to play in game now that partner has scraped up a 1♥ response, and a simple rebid of 2♦ would not be 100% forcing in this situation.

In Sequence B, on the other hand, a rebid of 2♥ would be forcing, bearing in mind that the responder's bid at the two level has guaranteed good values. The jump reverse in this sequence can therefore be used as a mild slam suggestion, agreeing partner's suit and showing a feature in the suit bid.

♠ 7
♥ A J 4   1♦ 2♣
♦ A K 7 5 3   ?
♣ K J 8 5

Bid 3♥. This shows strong support for clubs and a top honour in hearts. It is important to draw a distinction between this sequence and the sequence 1♦–2♣–4♣ which was discussed at length earlier in this section. The suggestion is that the latter sequence should be construed as the stronger; since the jump reverse in a forcing situation enables the opener to describe his hand extremely accurately, the responder might possibly judge it best to apply the brakes at a low level – even in 3NT if the responder's main strength lies in the suit in which the opener has implied shortage.

Finally, the jump to 4♣ in Sequence C above cannot be a natural bid, because a forcing bid of 3♣ is available in a situation of this kind. Following the general pattern recommended in all analogous sequences, it is recommended that an unnecessary jump reverse at the four level should agree the responder's suit and show a void for slam purposes.

♠ A J 7
♥ A Q 10 8 3   1♥ 2♦
♦ K 10 8 5 2   ?
♣ —

Bid 4♣, agreeing diamonds and showing a void in clubs and a hand with strong slam interest.

THE DOUBLE JUMP SHIFT

1♥ 1♠
4♣

A double jump in a new suit by the opener once again agrees the responder's suit and shows a void. This sequence can be compared with others in which there is an unnecessary jump to the four level. For example:

(A) 1♡ 2◇   (B) 1◇ 1♠   (C) 1♠ 2◇
    4♣   2♡ 4♣   2♡ 4♣

These sequences are all analysed elsewhere in this book, and you will find that they all agree partner's last-named suit and show a void for slam purposes. Simple, isn't it?

♣ ♣

Part Four

THE RESPONDER'S SECOND BID

♠ ♠
———————————————

Generally speaking, the opening bid and the first response are quite straightforward in any bidding system. The same is true to a lesser extent of the opener's second bid, but it is on the second and later rounds of the auction that doubt and uncertainty begin to creep in for all but the most keenly-tuned partnerships. This is unfortunately true of all too many rank-and-file Acol players up and down the country. For example, the meaning of the responder's second bid is often far from clearcut, and the object of this section of the book is to analyse the various bidding situations which occur under this heading, renovating some little-used sequences, giving new clarity to others, and generally removing the ambiguity from everyday auctions.

It is assumed for the purposes of this analysis that the opener has started with one of a suit and has either (a) rebid in no trumps, (b) made a simple raise of the responder's suit, or (c) made a simple rebid in his original suit or in a new suit. The situations which arise when the responder either raises the opener's second suit or makes a quantitative raise of the opener's no trump rebid are quite straightforward and do not require further discussion. However, other rebids by the responder are by no means as clearcut, and it is proposed to analyse these in the following seven chapters.

CHAPTER 16. No trump bidding.
CHAPTER 17. Rebidding his suit.
CHAPTER 18. Preference.
CHAPTER 19. Belated support.
CHAPTER 20. Bidding the second suit.
CHAPTER 21. Bidding the third suit.
CHAPTER 22. Bidding the fourth suit.

16. NO TRUMP BIDDING

I am afraid there are few sparkling pearls of wisdom here. Unless the opener has shown extra values by his rebid, no trump bids by the responder on the second round are natural and limited, suggesting the same values as if he had made the same bid one round earlier.

1NT ON THE SECOND ROUND

There are just two small points to make in this context. Whereas an immediate response of 1NT may be little more than a conventional bid, made on any hand which is too strong to pass but which does not contain the values for any other action, 1NT on the second round is always natural. It shows some kind of guard in the unbid suit; without one, the responder will always have an alternative rebid available.

♠	J 7		
♡	K J 9 5 3	1♣	1♡
◇	7 5 3	1♠	?
♣	Q 9 4		

If partner had opened the bidding with 1♠, the correct response would clearly have been 1NT. Now that three suits have been suggested, however, a return to 1NT should be reserved as a completely natural bid, guaranteeing a guard in the fourth suit. The correct bid in the above situation is therefore 2♣, simple preference to partner's first suit.

The second point concerns the strength of the responder's rebid of 1NT. Although there are occasional 6-point hands on which 1NT seems the obvious rebid, especially at match-point duplicate, 1NT is best played as fractionally stronger on the second round than on the first round; the recommended range is 7–10.

♠	J 5 2		
♡	K 7 5 4 2	1♣	1♡
◇	A Q 3	1♠	?
♣	6 4		

Unless you find yourself in a situation where to miss a game at this juncture would be a disaster, 1NT is probably enough. While you should normally try to avoid bidding 1NT on as many as 10 points, this hand is very weak in intermediate cards, and the auction so far suggests that you will have to struggle with something of a misfit.

2NT ON THE SECOND ROUND

Whereas 1NT becomes, if anything, slightly stronger when it is bid at the second attempt, a rebid of 2NT by the responder on the second round often tends to be devalued.

1♣	1♡
1♠	2NT

A delayed jump to 2NT shows the same values, if not the same hand, as an immediate 1♣–2NT; that is to say, anything from a good 10 to a bad 12 points.

If the opener has rebid at the two level, however, the responder may sometimes have to stretch slightly to bid no trumps on the second round. Let us take the last example hand and do a little juggling with the suits.

♠	K 7 5 4 2		
♡	6 4	1♡	1♠
◇	J 5 2	2◇	?
♣	A Q 3		

Bid 2NT. While you would really prefer not to bid 2NT on such an emaciated 10-point hand, the fact that the bidding has been pushed to the two level leaves you with very little choice: not to bid no trumps when you have such a good holding in the unbid suit would be disloyal to your partner.

━━━━━━━━━━ ♠ ♠ ━━━━━━━━━━

17. REBIDDING HIS SUIT

A SIMPLE REBID AT THE TWO LEVEL

A simple rebid of the responder's original suit at the two level is always limited and weakish, showing a six-card or longer suit and a strong desire to play in it. However, certain simple rebids carry with them a vague hint of encouragement, and it is important to distinguish those sequences in which the responder will not be too upset if his partner toils on with a further effort.

After a rebid of 1NT by the opener, a simple rebid of his suit by the responder can be very weak.

♠	Q 9 7 6 4 3		
♡	K 7 3	1♣	1♠
◇	10 7 5	1NT	?
♣	8		

Bid 2♠. This should end the auction without your needing to place your hand face downwards on the table and reach for your score-card.

If the opener has rebid his suit or made a simple rebid in a new suit, however, the responder should try to avoid repeating his own suit on a completely minimum hand. Let us metamorphose the last hand.

♠	10 7 5		
♡	Q 9 7 6 4 3	1♣	1♡
◇	K 7 3	1♠	?
♣	8		

Pass. While the hand could well play better in 2♡, it would be dangerous to bid again on such an appalling collection of cards; the prudent action is to pass before the storm-clouds start to gather.

The advantage of keeping the simple rebid well up to strength in these situations is that you will then be able to show slightly better hands without needing to make a reckless leap.

♠	K J 10 8 6 3		
♡	J 5	1◇	1♠
◇	7 2	2◇	?
♣	A 8 3		

Bid 2♠, which is vaguely constructive in this situation. With a weaker hand and six spades, you should pass and let partner make the best of things in 2◇; in any case, it is by no means certain that you would do any better in spades than he will in diamonds.

A SIMPLE REBID AT THE THREE LEVEL

Here again the precise meaning of the rebid depends to a certain extent on the nature of the opener's actions.

      1◇   1♡
      2NT   3♡

3♡ in this sequence is weak, showing a long suit and a hand which is severely lacking in high cards. The opener will only pursue the matter with good support for hearts and good top cards.

After an initial response at the two level, however, a simple rebid of the responder's suit is always constructive; the opener will be looking out for an opportunity to convert to 3NT.

♠	7		
♡	K 10 4	1♠	2◇
◇	A K J 9 5 3	2♠	?
♣	8 7 5		

Bid 3◇, a constructive bid in this sequence. It is, after all, difficult to imagine what else you can possibly bid if you are anxious to encourage partner to have a shot at 3NT with a suitable hand.

A JUMP REBID AT THE THREE LEVEL

Unless the opener has shown extra values by reversing, a jump rebid at the three level by the responder is not forcing; it is, however, highly encouraging, showing a robust six-card suit and values approaching those for an opening bid.

♠	6 3		
♡	A K J 10 7 5	1◇	1♡
◇	8 5	2◇	?
♣	K 9 2		

Bid 3♡, inviting partner to push on to game if he has the slightest excuse for doing so. It is important to have a healthy suit for a jump rebid of this kind, for the opener should feel free to raise to game with meagre trump support.

A jump rebid has a similar meaning if the opener either rebids 1NT or makes a simple change of suit rebid. In these cases, however, the minimum values for the bid are slightly lower, for the opener is now less likely to have made a light opening bid for tactical reasons.

A JUMP REBID AT THE FOUR LEVEL

A jump to game in a major suit on the second round means exactly what you would expect: having listened to the auction to date, the responder believes that the best game contract is in four of his suit. It is clearly based on an extremely good six-card or longer suit, and a hand which was slightly too strong for an immediate jump to game on the first round and yet not strong enough to force to game over the opening bid.

♠	6		
♡	A Q J 10 7 5 2	1◇	1♡
◇	8 5	2◇	?
♣	A 7 3		

Bid 4♡, a contract which you will almost certainly make if partner has anything remotely resembling an opening bid.

A jump to four in the responder's minor suit, on the other hand, is a forcing, forward-going bid. After a rebid of 2NT or 3NT by the opener, 4♣ or 4◇ is a slam try, showing a good six-card suit and inviting partner to make an encouraging noise if he has a suitable hand.

♠	A 4		
♡	7 5	1♠	2♣
◇	A Q 6	2NT	?
♣	K J 9 8 6 3		

Bid 4♣. There must be excellent chances of a successful slam contract now that partner has shown extra values by his 2NT rebid. 4♣ is the best way of putting him in the picture and testing his reaction.

After a minimum rebid by the opener, a jump to four of a minor is a little-used bid. How often have you come across sequences like the following?

1◇	2♣	1♠	2◇
2◇	4♣	2♡	4◇

I suspect that the answer is probably 'never', for this is an area of the bidding jungle which Acol explorers have never really penetrated. It seems to me, however, that these second-round jumps to 4♣ or 4◇ can serve an extremely useful purpose, describing hands which are otherwise almost impossible to show accurately. Consider the following hand.

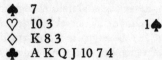

This is a very powerful hand now that partner has opened the bidding, but how do you plan to convey the good news about your solid club suit? If the suits were reversed, of course, there would be little difficulty, for the sequence

shows that the original force was based on a solid spade suit and very little else. The same approach is simply not possible when the suit is a minor, for to force with 3♣ and then jump to 5♣ in order to show a solid suit would expend so much bidding space that there would be no room left in which to investigate matters further: one more slight move by the opener, and the partnership will virtually be committed to a slam.

One possible solution to this problem is to use the second-round jump to four of a minor, which is almost idle under normal bidding methods, to show a completely solid suit and the kind of hand on which the responder would have forced to game on the first round had he been able to do so at the two level. The corollary to this is, of course, that a sequence like:

1♠   3♣
3♠   4♣

would imply a non-solid club suit, and yet again an important element of accuracy has been added to Acol bidding methods.

In case there are still one or two non-believers, let us look at just one example hand.

WEST	EAST	WEST	EAST
♠ A K J 10 6 5	♠ 9	1♠	2♣
♡ 10 5	♡ A 8 3	2◇	4♣
◇ A K 8 5	◇ 7 2	4◇	4♡
♣ 9	♣ A K Q J 10 7 4	4NT	5♡
		7♣	

Once East's 5♡ response to Blackwood confirms the ace of hearts, West has sufficient information to enable him to have a shot at the grand slam in clubs; there must be an excellent chance of setting up the spades, no matter what partner's holding in the suit is.

♠ ♠

18. PREFERENCE

Let us assume that the opener has made a simple change of suit bid on the second round. If the responder is not able either to bid no trumps or to rebid his own suit at this stage, he will normally content himself with expressing his preference between the opener's two suits. This may in itself sound like a reasonably straightforward matter, but so much woolly thinking becomes evident in the field of preference bids in Acol that it will probably prove worthwhile to run quickly through the important principles involved.

SIMPLE PREFERENCE

Simple preference by the responder means exactly what it says: he is expressing his choice between the two suits offered to him by the opener, while at the same time not showing any greater strength than he promised by his original response. A simple change of suit bid by the opener is not forcing in Acol, and this means that preference for the opener's second suit can occasionally be shown by passing.

♠	Q 8 7 4 2		
♡	6	1♡	1♠
◇	J 10 3	2◇	?
♣	K 6 4 2		

Pass. It is just possible that 2♠ might prove to be a better contract, but it would be dangerous to rebid such a bad suit. By far the safest action is to pass and let partner play in 2◇; this hand looks like being an awkward misfit, and this may be your last chance to stop in a playable contract.

The only other important point to make about simple preference is that you should always put partner back to his first suit if you have equal length in his two suits, regardless of the relative strength of your holdings.

♠	8 4		
♡	10 7 5 3	1♠	2♣
◇	K J	2◇	?
♣	K Q 10 7 5		

Bid 2♠. Even though you actually prefer diamonds to spades, you prefer to play the hand in spades, for the simple reason that partner probably has greater length in his first suit. You only have to visualise a fairly typical holding for the opener

♠	Q J 10 7 5
♡	Q 2
◇	A 9 8 3
♣	A 6

to realise what a struggle your unfortunate partner will have if he is left to toil in 2◇. 2♠, on the other hand, should prove to be a fairly comfortable contract.

JUMP PREFERENCE

We saw earlier that simple preference by the responder denies extra values. If he has more than his initial response promised, he must try to convey the good news to his partner on the second round; one of the ways of doing just this is by giving jump preference to the opener's first suit.

Whereas simple preference may not show more than tolerance for the opener's first suit, jump preference always shows genuine support. If it is a major suit, of course, you will only have three-card trump support, for you would have made an immediate limit raise on any hand of that strength containing four or more trumps.

♠ K 7 2		
♡ 8 5 4	1♠	2♣
◇ Q 5	2◇	?
♣ A Q 9 5 3		

Bid 3♠. This hand is too strong to give simple preference to 2♠, and 3♠ describes it well: it contains the values for an immediate raise to three, but only has three-card trump support.

If the jump preference is made to the opener's minor suit, it could well be based on four-card trump support; it is clearly not obligatory to make an immediate limit raise in clubs or diamonds.

♠ A J		
♡ K 10 7 5 2	1◇	1♡
◇ Q 9 6 4	1♠	?
♣ 7 5		

Bid 3◇. This hand was worth a limit raise to 3◇ on the first round, but it was correct to show the major suit first. Now that partner has not been able to support hearts, you can put the final touches to an accurate picture of your hand by giving jump preference to 3◇. Partner will half expect this to be based on four-card trump support, for, with a slightly more balanced hand with only three diamonds, you would probably prefer to investigate the hand further by bidding 2♣ – that is, if fourth suit forcing is part of your scene. However, this is not the time for red herrings of that kind: the theory of bidding the fourth suit will be the subject of a separate chapter later in this section.

Just one final thought on jump preference. There are one or two rare situations in which it is correct to give jump preference after you have already limited your hand.

♠ J 7 2
♡ A 6 4   1♠   1NT
◇ K J 4   2◇   ?
♣ 8 6 3 2

This hand is maximum for the original response of 1NT; it is only the appalling quality of the club suit which makes 1NT a better bid than the more encouraging response of 2♣. Now that partner has rebid 2◇, the hand has become even stronger, and you can express this by jumping to 3♠. Partner can hardly misunderstand this jump, in view of your original limited response of 1NT. He will realise that you have a maximum hand for your first response, together with a good fit for spades and diamonds, and this knowledge should enable him to push on to the excellent game contract if he holds something like:

♠ K Q 9 6 3
♡ 10 5   1♠   1NT
◇ A Q 8 2   2◇   3♠
♣ A 5   4♠

FALSE PREFERENCE

So much for simple preference and jump preference. Nothing very new or very difficult has arisen so far, but we must now sail on into the comparatively uncharted waters of false preference. Newcomers to this idea will doubtless find it extremely odd that they should be enjoined to express a preference for a suit which, at first sight, they do not really prefer, but I hope to be able to convince them that false preference is an invaluable aid to good bidding.

Let us first consider an elementary example.

♠ 10 5
♡ J 7 2   1♠   1NT
◇ A K 6 5   2♡   ?
♣ 8 6 4 3

An inexperienced player will tend to pass at this point, without giving the matter too much thought. After all, partner has invited you to choose between the two major suits and, since you have more hearts than spades, why should you not express this preference by passing 2♡? We hinted at the answer to this question when we were considering simple preference earlier: the preference we are asked to express is not merely between our holdings in the two relevant suits, but between the two alternative contracts of 2♡ and 2♠. The indications are that 2♠ will prove a more manageable contract than 2♡. You know that partner has a five-card spade suit to bid in this way, but his heart suit might well be a four-carder; if this is so, the 5–2 spade fit will play much better than the 4–3 heart fit, particularly if the opener is vulnerable to a forcing attack in clubs.

♠ K J 9 6 2   ♦ 7 3
♥ A Q 8 5   ♣ A 2

If partner's hand is something like this, 2♥ will be a difficult contract to manage, particularly on an opening club lead and continuation. On the other hand, the opener should be able to scramble home in 2♠, for the simple reason that the five-card trump suit will be able to withstand a forcing defence so much better.

This, then, is the primary reason for giving false preference: that the hand will play better in partner's five-card suit. However, there is more to it than that. There are certain hands where you may have to give false preference to what might only be a four-card suit.

♠ A 9 7 5 4
♥ 10 3   1♥   1♠
♦ Q J 4   2♣   ?
♣ Q 8 6

Bid 2♥. There are two reasons for giving false preference on this hand. The first is the obvious one that partner may well have five hearts and four clubs and a weak hand, in which case 2♥ will probably be the best contract. The second argument for bidding 2♥ is a more difficult one. It is that, although partner's hand is limited to a certain extent by his simple rebid, he could still be concealing quite a reasonable holding. For example, he may be looking at something like:

♠ K 8 2   ♦ 9
♥ A Q 9 6 5   ♣ A K 10 4

After 1♥–1♠, the opener has a difficult rebid on this hand. 2♠ would be pusillanimous to a degree, and yet a jump to 3♠ would be misleading and dangerous on such meagre three-card support. By far the best rebid is 2♣, intending to show the spade support, and therefore a good hand, at a later stage. However, such a delicate bidding sequence will not be available to the opener if there is a danger of your passing 2♣ on the responding hand shown above.

It does not follow from this that a simple change of suit by the opener is 100% forcing; it is a fundamental Acol principle that it is not. Nevertheless, it should also be a general principle of good bidding that the responder should be very loth to pass a change of suit at his second turn, and to give false preference is often the only possible answer when he appears to be in systemic difficulties over the opener's rebid.

♠ 10 6
♥ Q 8 3   1♠   2♦
♦ A K 7 4 2   2♥   ?
♣ 6 4 2

This hand is discussed in an earlier text-book on Acol.* The learned authors suggest that the correct bid in this difficult situation is 3♥, and they add the comment that 'it is better to risk over-balancing than to

* *The Acol System Today*, by Terence Reese and Albert Dormer.

leave partner suspended in mid-air'. Admirable sentiments, but false preference to 2♠ gives partner another chance to speak while at the same time keeping both feet firmly anchored to the floor; 3♡ is unlikely to prove a sparkling success if partner has an average hand with only four hearts, particularly if he can be got at in clubs.

One more example should suffice.

WEST	EAST	WEST	EAST
♠ K J 2	♠ A 10 7 6 4	1◇	1♠
♡ 5	♡ Q 8 3	2♣	2◇
◇ A K 8 6 4	◇ Q 3	2♠	4♠
♣ K Q 9 3	♣ J 6 5		

A good bidding sequence, the key to which is East's false preference to 2◇ over 2♣. This enables West to revert to 2♠, showing three-card support and a goodish hand – with a weaker hand, West would prefer a direct raise to 2♠ rather than the more delicate bid of 2♣.

Finally, it is possible to devise a situation in which it is correct to give false preference even though you have *four-card* support for the opener's second suit.

♠ K Q 9 5		
♡ 8 3	1◇	1♠
◇ K 7 2	2♣	?
♣ 8 6 4 2		

This is a difficult problem. A raise to 3♣ would be an exaggeration on so few high-card points and such bad clubs, and yet to pass 2♣ would be equally risky, particularly at rubber bridge or team of four scoring. After all, partner will not be amused to find himself playing in 2♣ if he has any of the following hands:

♠ A J 4	♠ A 4	♠ 8
♡ 10 4	♡ 4	♡ A Q
◇ A Q 8 3	◇ A Q 8 5 4	◇ A Q 8 5 4 3
♣ K Q J 5	♣ A J 10 7 3	♣ A 9 5 3

Opposite the responding hand shown above, these hands will probably make 4♠, 5♣ and 3NT respectively, and yet it would be difficult to criticise the opener's rebid of 2♣ after 1◇–1♠.

The solution is to give false preference to 2◇ over 2♣. This will occasionally lead to a slightly inferior part-score contract if the opener is weak, but this is unlikely to be serious. 2◇ at least gives partner an opportunity of emerging from the bushes if he has been experimenting with a delicate bidding sequence on a strongish hand.

♣ ♠

19. BELATED SUPPORT

There is an important distinction to be drawn between giving belated support to the opener's first suit and merely expressing preference for it: whereas simple preference may be a forced, involuntary effort, belated support is always to some extent constructive.

Strictly speaking, a delayed game raise sequence like 1♡–1♠–2♣–4♡ could be described as belated support, but the term is usually only applied to two situations in connection with the responder's second bid: where the opener has rebid in no trumps and where the opener has made a simple raise of the responder's suit.

THE OPENER REBIDS 1NT

1♡   1♠
1NT   2♡

While it is in no way forcing, there is a vague hint of encouragement about the responder's bid of 2♡; with a completely minimum hand, he would almost certainly have preferred an immediate raise to 2♡. The belated support sequence could, in fact, be based on a hand as good as:

♠	A J 10 7 2		
♡	K 9 3	1♡	1♠
◇	5 2	1NT	2♡
♣	7 6 4		

Belated support for a major suit shows three trumps; with four-card trump support, the responder would have made an immediate raise to 2♡ or 2♠ on the first round. In a minor suit, however, there is no such inference, and it is quite likely that belated support to 2♣ or 2◇ will be based on four trumps.

♠	K 10 7 5 3		
♡	7 2	1◇	1♠
◇	Q 9 8 3	1NT	2◇
♣	J 6		

The responder was correct to show his five-card spade suit on the first round, and his return to 2◇ over 1NT is a mere rectification to the correct final contract. Belated support to 2♣ would, of course, have a similar meaning; that is, unless you are able to find a better use for a bid of 2♣ over a 1NT rebid. . . .

A delayed jump to three in the opener's minor suit is encouraging, but not completely forcing; it shows four-card support and the sort of hand on which you would have made an immediate limit raise to three if the suit were a major.

♠	K J 10 7 3		
♡	7 3	1♢	1♠
♢	A Q 8 3	1NT	?
♣	9 6		

Bid 3♢, which, although not forcing, is highly invitational. This sequence shows four-card support for partner's minor suit, and there is also an inference that the hand contains a five-card spade suit: with a more balanced hand and 4–4 in the two suits, the responder would probably prefer to make a quantitative raise in no trumps on the second round.

A delayed jump in the opener's major suit, on the other hand, is best played forcing.

♠	K J 10 7 3		
♡	A Q 4	1♡	1♠
♢	7 2	1NT	?
♣	Q 9 5		

Bid 3♡. This is a forcing sequence when both major suits have been bid. You have the values for game on this hand, but 4♡ or 4♠ could be a better contract than 3NT; the only way to investigate all the possibilities is to bid a forcing 3♡.

A belated jump to four of a major suit constitutes a delayed game raise sequence, which we have considered in some detail elsewhere. A delayed jump to four of a minor shows a similar hand and indicates strong slam interest.

♠	A Q 9 8 3		
♡	K 7 2	1♢	1♠
♢	K 10 9 4	1NT	?
♣	7		

Bid 4♢, forcing and expressing an interest in a diamond slam. A delayed jump to 4♣ or 4♢ in this kind of sequence implies a distributionally powerful hand with a five-card major suit, particularly if the partnership is employing the Minor Suit Swiss convention which we introduced in an earlier chapter.

THE OPENER REBIDS 2NT

Any belated support by the responder is forcing after a 2NT rebid by the opener. The advantages of this method are obvious when the support is for a major suit.

♠	Q J 8		
♡	7 4	1♠	2♣
♢	K 6 2	2NT	?
♣	A 10 9 7 5		

Bid 3♠. This must clearly be forcing, showing three-card spade support and offering the opener a choice between 4♠ and 3NT.

Belated support for the opener's major suit is also forcing when the opener has raised the original response of 1NT to 2NT.

♠	A 7 2		
♡	Q 8 3	1♡	1NT
◇	Q 10 9 5	2NT	?
♣	6 5 3		

Bid 3♡, just in case partner has a five-card heart suit and judges it best to play in 4♡, even though he knows that your hand is balanced. The opener may not be completely balanced, despite his 2NT rebid, and the full hands might easily be something like:

	WEST		EAST		WEST	EAST
♠	K Q 4	♠	A 7 2		1♡	1NT
♡	K J 9 7 5	♡	Q 8 3		2NT	3♡
◇	A J 3	◇	Q 10 9 5		4♡	
♣	A 2	♣	6 5 3			

3NT is a very poor contract on these cards, but it is difficult to see how the partnership is to reach the ice-cold 4♡ without the benefit of belated support.

♠	A Q 7 5 3		
♡	7 2	1♣	1♠
◇	6 4 3	2NT	?
♣	K 8 5		

Here again it will make the bidding much easier if you are able to investigate the hand fully with a forcing bid of 3♣. 3♣ invites the opener to give belated support to spades, in which case it is quite likely that 4♠ will be the best game contract. Suppose, for example, the full hands are something like:

	WEST		EAST		WEST	EAST
♠	J 8 4	♠	A Q 7 5 3		1♣	1♠
♡	A 10 5	♡	7 2		2NT	3♣
◇	K Q J	◇	6 4 3		3♠	4♠
♣	A Q 10 4	♣	K 8 5			

As you will see, 4♠ will probably make in comfort, while 3NT is almost certainly doomed to defeat. It is difficult to see how the partnership is going to reach the correct contract if belated support to 3♣ is not regarded as forcing.

Similarly:

♠	7		
♡	10 6 5	1♣	1◇
◇	A Q 9 5 2	2NT	?
♣	K 7 4 3		

Once again the benefits of a forcing 3♣ rebid are apparent. It will enable the partnership to reach the correct game contract if it is 5♣. . . .

WEST	EAST	WEST	EAST
♠ Q 9 3	♠ 7	1♣	1◇
♡ A Q 4	♡ 10 6 5	2NT	3♣
◇ K 8	◇ A Q 9 5 2	3♡	4♣
♣ A Q 9 6 2	♣ K 7 4 3	5♣	

... or 3NT.

WEST	EAST	WEST	EAST
♠ A Q J	♠ 7	1♣	1◇
♡ A Q	♡ 10 6 5	2NT	3♣
◇ 7 4 3	◇ A Q 9 5 2	*3NT*	
♣ A J 8 6 2	♣ K 7 4 3		

THE OPENER REBIDS 3NT

Belated support by the responder after the opener has rebid 3NT is always forcing, for it is impossible to imagine a hand on which you would be anxious to rescue partner after he has made such a strong rebid.

A return to four of partner's minor suit is an obvious slam try. It may be based on four-card trump support, but the opener must not assume this without receiving further confirmation. The responder may have no better bid available when he has only three-card support.

♠	J 7 4		
♡	A Q 10 7 5	1♣	1♡
◇	6 5	3NT	?
♣	K 10 4		

Bid 4♣. This hand warrants a slam try of some kind, and 4♣ is by far the most helpful move at this stage. 6♣ could easily be the best slam if the opener has a five-card club suit.

WEST	EAST	WEST	EAST
♠ A Q 3	♠ J 7 4	1♣	1♡
♡ K 4	♡ A Q 10 7 5	3NT	4♣
◇ A 10 3	◇ 6 5	4◇	4♡
♣ A Q 8 7 5	♣ K 10 4	4♠	5♣
		6♣	

After an opening diamond lead, 6NT depends entirely on a favourable heart break. In a contract of 6♣, on the other hand, the play is much more flexible and, given a 3–2 club break and a 4–2 heart break, you should be able to discard two diamond losers on dummy's hearts and eventually concede a spade trick. Alternatively, you can play to ruff a diamond in dummy and rely on either a favourable heart break or a successful spade finesse for your twelfth trick.

A return to four of partner's major suit after 3NT is also forcing. It may be based on a similar hand to that on which we bid 4♣ in the

previous example, but it may also conceal a hand on which the responder was planning to effect a delayed game raise sequence.

♠	7		
♡	K J 9 3	1♡	2♢
♢	K Q 10 7 3	3NT	?
♣	A 5 4		

Bid 4♡. This hand is almost certainly worth a slam now that partner
has made a strength-showing rebid, and 4♡ leaves the way clear to
fully investigate all the possibilities. 7♡ could be an excellent contract
if the opener has the right cards.

	WEST		EAST	WEST	EAST
♠	A J 3	♠	7	1♡	2♢
♡	A Q 7 5 2	♡	K J 9 3	3NT	4♡
♢	A 4	♢	K Q 10 7 3	4♠	5♣
♣	Q 10 6	♣	A 5 4	5♢	5NT
				7♡	

THE OPENER RAISES THE FIRST RESPONSE

There are four categories of belated support after the opener has raised
the responder's suit, the determining factor being the rank of the suits
involved.

CATEGORY A	1.	1♣–1♢–2♢–3♣
	2.	1♢–2♣–3♣–3♢
CATEGORY B	3.	1♡–1♠–2♠–3♡
	4.	1♠–2♡–3♡–3♠
CATEGORY C	5.	1♡–2♣–3♣–3♡
	6.	1♡–2♢–3♢–3♡
	7.	1♠–2♣–3♣–3♠
	8.	1♠–2♢–3♢–3♠
CATEGORY D	9.	1♣–1♡–2♡–3♣
	10.	1♣–1♠–2♠–3♣
	11.	1♢–1♡–2♡–3♢
	12.	1♢–1♠–2♠–3♢

Opinions differ about which of these sequences should be regarded
as forcing and which should merely be encouraging. It is generally
agreed that the first two categories listed above, where the suits involved
are both minors or both majors, should be forcing.

♠	K 10 8 3		
♡	A Q 3	1♡	1♠
♢	A 4	2♠	?
♣	9 7 6 2		

Bid 3♡, giving the opener a choice of game contract. Unless it is the
first move on a strong hand, belated support of this kind implies four
spades and three hearts, for the responder would otherwise not be in

any doubt regarding the correct final denomination. The opener might therefore choose to bid 3NT over 3♡ if he is also four-three in the major suits.

♠ 10 7 2
♡ A 8   1◇   2♣
◇ K Q 9 4   3♣   ?
♣ A J 7 3

This is a good example of the sort of hand on which a belated support sequence can be employed to investigate slam possibilities. A forcing bid of 3◇ in this situation will make it possible to reach an excellent slam contract if the full hands are:

WEST	EAST	WEST	EAST
♠ A 5	♠ 10 7 2	1◇	2♣
♡ 7 3	♡ A 8	3♣	3◇
◇ A J 8 5 2	◇ K Q 9 4	3♠	4♡
♣ K Q 9 2	♣ A J 7 3	4NT	5♠
		6♣	

East's 5♠ response to West's Byzantine 4NT enquiry shows two aces and the king-queen of an agreed suit, and it enables West to bid the slam with complete confidence. Notice the importance of playing the hand in the 4–4 fit rather than the 5–4 fit; the discard of a heart on dummy's fifth diamond is essential for the slam.

Playing 3◇ as forcing in this kind of sequence also makes it possible for the partnership to berth in the safe harbour of 3NT if the hands fit less well.

WEST	EAST	WEST	EAST
♠ A J	♠ 10 7 2	1◇	2♣
♡ Q 10 4	♡ A 8	3♣	3◇
◇ A J 7 2	◇ K Q 9 4	3NT	
♣ Q 6 5 4	♣ A J 7 3		

The third category of belated support sequences shown above covers the case where the responder returns to the opener's major suit after his original minor suit response has been raised. It is generally agreed that these sequences should be non-forcing, and one example hand should be sufficient to show that this treatment is undoubtedly best.

♠ K Q 6
♡ 7 5   1♠   2◇
◇ A J 9 5 3   3◇   ?
♣ 8 7 2

It is difficult to see how you are to bid this hand if a non-forcing bid of 3♠ is not available at this point. 3♠ in this sequence shows the values for an immediate raise to 3♠, but with only three-card trump support. It should enable partner to push on to game if he has a little something in reserve.

WEST	EAST	WEST	EAST
♠ A J 9 5 4	♠ K Q 6	1♠	2◇
♡ A 10	♡ 7 5	3◇	3♠
◇ K Q 7 4	◇ A J 9 5 3	4♠	
♣ 10 4	♣ 8 7 2		

But it leaves him free to pass if he has exhausted all his resources with his first two bids:

WEST	EAST	WEST	EAST
♠ A J 7 3 2	♠ K Q 6	1♠	2◇
♡ Q 8	♡ 7 5	3◇	3♠
◇ Q 7 6 4	◇ A J 9 5 3	No	
♣ K 3	♣ 8 7 2		

Furthermore, a non-forcing bid of 3♠ may enable the opener to make a cowardly return to the responder's minor suit if he does not relish the prospect of toiling in a 4–3 spade fit.

WEST	EAST	WEST	EAST
♠ A 9 7 5	♠ K Q 6	1♠	2◇
♡ A 8 3	♡ 7 5	3◇	3♠
◇ K 10 7 2	◇ A J 9 5 3	4◇	
♣ Q 4	♣ 8 7 2		

The meaning of the fourth category of belated support sequences, where the responder returns to the opener's minor suit after his own major suit response has been raised, is less obvious.

1◇	1♠
2♠	3◇

The advantage of playing this sequence as non-forcing is that it allows you to describe accurately a hand with four spades and four diamonds and the values for an immediate raise to 3◇. However, there are other hands on which a forcing treatment is preferable.

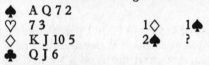

♠ A Q 7 2		
♡ 7 3	1◇	1♠
◇ K J 10 5	2♠	?
♣ Q J 6		

This problem would not exist if you were playing the Minor Suit Swiss convention which was recommended in an earlier chapter. As it is, however, it is vital to have a forcing bid of 3◇ available in this situation; the correct game contract could still be 4♠, 5◇ or even 3NT, and it is difficult to see how you are to investigate all the possibilities if you have to make a limited bid at this point.

While belated support to 3♣ or 3◇ will normally imply a four-card major suit holding, there are also situations in which a return to the opener's minor suit is the best way of trying for game in the agreed major.

♠ A 10 9 5 3
♡ 7 4   1◇   1♠
◇ K 10 6   2♠   ?
♣ K 9 3

While it would be possible to make a game try by bidding 3♠ in this position, a forcing bid of 3◇ is likely to be more helpful to partner. Furthermore, even if he is unable to jump to 4♠ himself over 3◇, his reaction to your belated support should enable you to judge the situation better on the next round.

Since our bidding methods are, generally speaking, geared to reaching good game contracts rather than to alighting on a pin's head in the correct part score, my own view is that belated support to a minor suit should be 100% forcing. However, the alternative interpretation is clearly perfectly playable, and the important point really is that regular partnerships should consider the two possibilities and decide which treatment they prefer. This is the only way to introduce a vital element of precision into Acol.

            ♠ ♠

20. BIDDING THE SECOND SUIT

AFTER AN ORIGINAL RESPONSE OF 1NT

There are three situations in which the responder might wish to introduce a new suit on the second round after responding 1NT at his first turn. The first is a most unlikely one, and it occurs after the opener has rebid his original suit.

      1♡   1NT
      2♡   3♣

It is difficult to imagine the sort of hand which would justify this action. The only possible explanation is that the responder's original 1NT bid was an involuntary effort based on a weakish hand with a long minor suit, and that he has now decided that perhaps he had better play the hand after all.

♠ 8 6 4
♡ —   1♡   1NT
◇ J 9 4 2   2♡   ?
♣ K Q 10 9 5 3

There was a good case for either passing or bidding 2♣ on the first round, but you cannot be criticised for bidding 1NT in an attempt to improve the contract. Now that partner has chosen to rebid his wretched heart suit, what was always an unpleasant situation has turned into a really ugly one. While the prudent action at this stage is to pass before it is too late, the more daring among you might try to gamble your way out of trouble by converting to 3♣; if you are fortunate enough to find partner with two or three clubs, you are likely to derive more pleasure from playing in 3♣ than from watching partner's death throes in 2♡.

The other two cases in which the responder bids a new suit on the second round after first bidding 1NT occur when the opener makes a limit raise to 2NT.

1♡	1NT
2NT	3♣

This situation is clearcut: the responder is showing a poor hand and a weakish six-card suit which he was unable to bid on the first round.

♠	K 4		
♡	7 5	1♡	1NT
◇	8 6 3	2NT	?
♣	Q J 9 8 6 2		

Bid 3♣, which should prove to be a much safer contract than 2NT. 3♣ is in no way forcing, and the opener will almost certainly pass. However, the knowledge that you have a six-card suit may improve his hand so much that he will be spurred into further action. For example:

♠	A 10 7		
♡	A 8 6 3	1♡	1NT
◇	Q J 9	2NT	3♣
♣	A K 4	?	

Bid 3NT. Now that partner has advertised a six-card club suit, there must be an excellent chance of running nine tricks in no trumps. You have only to imagine this hand opposite the responder's hand which we discussed earlier to see that the play in 3NT is merely a question of how many overtricks.

The situation is not quite the same if the suit introduced by the responder is hearts.

1♠	1NT
2NT	3♡

It is possible to play the 3♡ bid in exactly the same way as you would an escape into 3♣ or 3◇, but my own view is that this is not the most efficient interpretation of the sequence; after all, now that partner has shown 17 or 18 points, you might choose to have a stab at 4♡ if you have a concealed six-card heart suit. It is important to consider another type of hand.

♠	7 4		
♡	K 8 7 5 4	1♠	1NT
◇	8 2	2NT	?
♣	A 10 9 3		

This hand is just about worth a push to game after partner's raise, but there is a distinct possibility that 3NT might not be the best spot. Suppose, for example, that the full hands are something like:

WEST	EAST
♠ A K 8 5 3	♠ 7 4
♡ J 10 9	♡ K 8 7 5 4
◇ A 4	◇ 8 2
♣ K Q 7	♣ A 10 9 3

A diamond lead will torpedo 3NT, but there are excellent chances of making 4♡ against any defence. The solution must be to play 3♡ as forcing in this one sequence (1♠–1NT–2NT–3♡), showing a five-card heart suit and the values for game.

AFTER RAISING THE OPENER'S SUIT

Nothing new here.

1♡	2♡
2NT	3♣

This sequence is exactly analogous to the sequence 1♡–1NT–2NT–3♣ which we discussed earlier.

♠ 10 4		
♡ Q 7 5	1♡	2♡
◇ 8 6	2NT	?
♣ K J 9 8 6 2		

Bid 3♣, which shows a six-card club suit and a weakish hand with three-card heart support. The opener will normally pass, but he might choose to play in 3♡ if he has a good five-card suit of his own; furthermore, he might be in a position to make another effort if he has a good fit in clubs.

Similarly, the sequence:

1♠	2♠
2NT	3♡

is probably best played forcing, in the same way as 1♠–1NT–2NT–3♡.

♠ Q 7 2		
♡ K 10 8 5 3	1♠	2♠
◇ 9 4	2NT	?
♣ K 6 5		

Bid 3♡. This shows five hearts and three spades, and offers partner the choice of three possible game contracts: 3NT, 4♡ and 4♠.

21. BIDDING THE THIRD SUIT

Murky situations often seem to arise in Acol when the responder introduces a third suit at his second turn. In this chapter, I shall attempt to shine a light along some of the darker passages, considering all the possible situations in turn.

RESPONDER HAS FIRST BID 1NT

This first situation is a slightly unusual, but nevertheless important one. It occurs after the responder has been compelled to bid a distorted 1NT on the first round, concealing a long suit because he was not strong enough to bid at the two level.

♠	7 2		
♡	K 8 3	1♠	1NT
◇	K J 10 8 6 4	2♣	?
♣	10 4		

1NT is a gruesome response on this hand, but what else do you suggest? It would be dangerous to pass on as many as 7 points, yet you are not strong enough to respond at the two level. You therefore have to bid 1NT and hope that the auction does not get completely out of hand. As it turns out, you can uncross your fingers and breathe a silent sigh of relief. Partner's rebid of 2♣ has made it possible for you to describe your hand precisely; you can now bid 2◇, showing a long diamond suit and inadequate values to make the same bid on the first round.

Some authorities suggest that to bid a third suit in this sort of sequence implies mild preference for the opener's first suit: in other words, that to bid 2◇ in the above situation merely shows a five-card or longer suit 'on the way' to 2♠. This has always seemed to me to be an inefficient interpretation of the bid, however, and I like to allot a bid of a new suit in this kind of auction one meaning, and one meaning only: that the original 1NT bid was an involuntary action and that the only possible resting place in which to play the hand is in two of the responder's long suit.

It might even be possible for the responder to bid a third suit at the three level after first bidding 1NT.

♠	7		
♡	Q 9 4 2	1♠	1NT
◇	6 3	2◇	?
♣	K Q 10 9 5 3		

Ugh. Bid 3♣. This hand does not seem likely to be a sparkling success in 2◇, and to give false preference to 2♠ would be to punish partner for something he has not really done. You are in serious trouble now that your 1NT response has elicited such a disappointing rebid from the opener. All you can do is to make one last desperate attempt to improve the final contract; the one point on which you can be absolutely certain is that your hand will make many more tricks in clubs than it will in either of partner's wretched suits.

OPENER REBIDS HIS SUIT

Generally speaking, a bid of a third suit by the responder after his partner has rebid his original suit is 100% forcing. The only exception to this occurs when the suit is bid at the two level and the responder has not reversed.

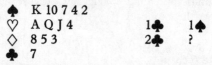

♠	K 10 7 4 2		
♡	A Q J 4	1♣	1♠
◇	8 5 3	2♣	?
♣	7		

Bid 2♡. This is not forcing, but the opener will regard it as a constructive effort. You should avoid bidding in this way on a weak hand just because you have two five-card suits; if you do not reserve this sequence as vaguely constructive, you will experience great difficulty in handling all those hands which are not worth a full-blooded jump to 3♡ on the second round.

For the responder to bid a third suit either at the three level or as a reverse is completely forcing.

♠	A Q 10		
♡	7 5 2	1♣	1◇
◇	K Q 8 6 4	2♣	?
♣	J 3		

Bid 2♠, a responder's reverse and therefore forcing. It is perfectly safe to bid a three-card suit in this position, for partner is most unlikely to raise: his rebid of 2♣ has already denied the possession of a four-card spade suit. 2♠ is by far the best exploratory bid at this point. It shows the values for 2NT, at least, and directs partner's attention to the weakness in hearts.

♠	J 6		
♡	A J 10 8 3	1◇	1♡
◇	Q 4	2◇	?
♣	K Q 7 5		

Bid 3♣. This is forcing, as is any new suit at the three level by the responder. Since this kind of sequence forces the opener to bid game if he chooses to bid no trumps at this point, the responder must guarantee a stronger hand than he does by a simple reverse at the two level. He is also implying a five-card heart suit, for his partner may have to give preference at the three level on a doubleton.

♠ 7
♡ 10 4   1♠   2♣
♦ K Q J 3   2♠   ?
♣ A Q J 8 5 2

Bid 3◇. A responder's reverse at the three level is the strongest of all these third-suit sequences, for the opener may have to give preference to clubs at the four level. The hand shown above is a good example; it is clearly worth going to game, and it may even produce a slam if a fit can be found.

A jump in a third suit after the opener has rebid his original suit is forcing to game. Its meaning varies according to the suits involved. This may sound splendidly confusing, and it is, in fact, a situation in which a great deal of muddled Acol thinking exists. Fortunately, the rule is extremely simple: if to bid the same suit without a jump would not be forcing, to jump in a third suit is completely natural.

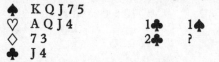

♠ K Q J 7 5
♡ A Q J 4   1♣   1♠
♦ 7 3   2♣   ?
♣ J 4

Bid 3♡, natural and forcing to game. As we saw earlier, a bid of 2♡ in this situation would be constructive, but not completely forcing. As this hand is powerful enough to insist on game, therefore, you must put partner in the picture by jumping to 3♡ at your second turn.

If the responder could have made a forcing bid in the same suit without needing to give a convulsive leap, the jump in a third suit can be given a special meaning: to promise the values for a delayed game raise in the opener's suit, to show a feature in the bid suit, and to suggest a shortage in the unbid suit.

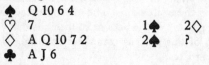

♠ Q 10 6 4
♡ 7   1♠   2◇
♦ A Q 10 7 2   2♠   ?
♣ A J 6

Bid 4♣. When partner first opens 1♠, this hand seems a fairly easy one to handle: you plan to respond 2◇ and subsequently jump to 4♠, showing a good diamond suit and a hand with four-card trump support which was too strong for an immediate raise to 4♠. This is the so-called delayed game raise sequence which we came across earlier. When the opener rebids 2♠ over 2◇, however, your original plan lies in ruins. If you attempt to see it through by raising to 4♠ now, partner will no longer recognise this as a delayed game raise. From his point of view, there is no reason why you should not have a less powerful hand with only three-card trump support; now that the opener has

shown a rebiddable spade suit, you would be quite happy to raise to
4♠ on:

♠ Q J 4
♡ 10 4   1♠   2◇
◇ A Q J 6 3   2♠   4♠
♣ Q 8 7

In order to distinguish between this kind of hand and the frustrated
delayed game raise, and thereby to remove yet another imprecise,
ambiguous sequence from the Acol repertoire, the suggestion is that an
unnecessary jump in a third suit should be reserved to show the strong
hand with four-card support for the opener's suit. This will occasionally
enable you to reach the sort of slam which Acol players all too often
write off as being unbiddable, while at the same time registering −13
IMPs on their score-card. Suppose, for example, that the full hands
are:

WEST	EAST	WEST	EAST
♠ A K 9 8 2	♠ Q 10 6 4	1♠	2◇
♡ J 8 3	♡ 7	2♠	4♣
◇ K 4	◇ A Q 10 7 2	?	
♣ K 9 5	♣ A J 6		

Since 3♣ would have been 100% forcing over 2♠, the unnecessary
jump to 4♣ shows a delayed game raise in spades, including a good
diamond suit, and some kind of club holding. With no wasted values in
hearts, West's modest hand begins to grow in stature, and he is worth
a mild slam try with 4◇. East will confirm his heart control by bidding
4♡, and West can now show the other vital king by cue-bidding 5♣.
The excellent contract of 6♠ will be reached in this way. The hands are
a good fit; furthermore, the bidding tells us so.

One important point about the suggested semi-conventional use of
a jump in a third suit in these situations. The more conservative among
you may have a niggling worry in the back of your minds that you would
prefer to keep a jump of this kind as completely natural. Maybe you
have in mind something like:

♠ J 4
♡ A Q 7 6 3   1♠   2♡
◇ 8   2♠   ?
♣ A J 9 5 4

If 4♣ would show a strong raise to 4♠, as is suggested, you clearly
have to content yourself with a modest 3♣ on this hand. But do you
really want to make a 'natural' jump to 4♣ at this point? 3♣ will almost
certainly make it easier to investigate the correct game contract. Let us
suppose that the two hands are as follows:

WEST	EAST	WEST	EAST
♠ A Q 7 6 5 2	♠ J 4	1♠	2♡
♡ J 5	♡ A Q 7 6 3	2♠	3♣
◇ K 6	◇ 8	3♡	3♠
♣ K 7 2	♣ A J 9 5 4	4♣	

Notice that the additional round of bidding made available by the gentle bid of 3♣ enables the partnership to investigate all the possible game contracts before alighting in the correct one. A natural jump to 4♣ by the responder on the second round would be far from helpful.

There is no reason why a jump in a third suit should not convey the same message if the opener's suit is a minor, for the Acol system has always found it difficult to bid hands on which the responder has good support for his partner's clubs or diamonds.

♠ A 10 7			
♡ 5		1◇	2♣
◇ Q J 8 4		2◇	?
♣ A Q 7 6 5			

Once again 3♠, the unnecessary jump in a third suit, describes the hand well: values for game in the opener's suit, a feature in the bid suit, and shortage in the unbid suit. 3♠ should enable the opener to assess what the best final contract is likely to be, and if he has wasted values in hearts and a fairly balanced hand, he will be able to end the auction while there is still time with a bid of 3NT. For example:

WEST	EAST	WEST	EAST
♠ J 4	♠ A 10 7	1◇	2♣
♡ K Q J	♡ 5	2◇	3♠
◇ A 10 7 5 3	◇ Q J 8 4	3NT	
♣ J 10 4	♣ A Q 7 6 5		

If the opener's suit is a minor, there are situations in which the responder can make a *double* jump in a third suit without taking the bidding beyond the game level. Following the usual principles, this is best used to agree the opener's suit and to show a void in the suit bid.

♠ K 9 6 3			
♡ —		1◇	2♣
◇ Q J 6 4		2◇	?
♣ A Q J 7 3			

Bid 4♡. 3♡ and 4♡ both agree diamonds in this situation; 3♡ shows a heart feature and suggests a shortage in spades, and 4♡ shows a void in hearts. This information should make it easy for the opener to evaluate his hand for slam purposes, and he will be fully entitled to don his rose-coloured spectacles if he has no wasted values in hearts.

OPENER RAISES RESPONDER'S SUIT

Consider the following sequence.

    1◇   1♠
    2♣   3♣

It scarcely seems possible that any confusion could exist over this simple situation, but are *you* completely certain that you know what 3♣ means? It is clearly a try for game, but is the responder showing a club guard and looking for 3NT, or is he making a trial bid for a game in spades? There *are* hands on which it will not matter what partner has in mind.

    ♠ K Q 8 4
    ♡ 7   1◇   1♠
    ◇ A J 9 7 3   2♣   3♣
    ♣ Q 10 5   ?

Bid 4♠. A more forward bidder might well have jumped to 3♠ on the previous round, and you must clearly push on to game now that partner has shown distinct signs of life.

However, let us suppose that the opener has a different kind of hand.

    ♠ K 10 3
    ♡ A J 9   1◇   1♠
    ◇ K J 8 7 3   2♣   3♣
    ♣ 7 5   ?

It is now absolutely vital to know what partner is trying to say by his 3♣ bid. If he is looking for 3NT, it would be disloyal not to bid it with A–J–9 in the unbid suit. If, on the other hand, his 3♣ bid is simply a trial bid for game in spades, your minimum hand with only three trumps and no fit in the trial bid suit could hardly be worse, and a prompt return to 3♠ is in order. The question is which of the following hands partner is likely to have?

♠ Q 9 8 6 4	♠ A 8 7 4
♡ 7 5	♡ 10 6 2
◇ A 2	◇ Q 5
♣ K 10 6 4	♣ A Q J 4
HAND A	HAND B

You have only to imagine each of these hands opposite the opening hand shown above to see how important it is to guess right in these situations. It you bid 3NT over 3♣ and find partner with Hand A, we can only hope that you have been going to church regularly; and if you sign off in 3♠ and your unfortunate partner has Hand B, the post-mortem should make interesting listening.

The opener's problems do not end there. Let us give him a slightly different kind of hand and put him in the same murky situation.

♠ K 8 7
♡ 9 3   1◇   1♠
◇ A Q 8 6 4   2♣   3♣
♣ K Q 5   ?

What do you suggest now? If partner's 3♣ bid is a trial bid with a
spade game in mind, this hand has improved considerably and there is
a good case for jumping to 4♠. This should play quite well if the
responding hand is something like:

♠ A 9 6 4 2   ♠ Q J 9 6 3
♡ 10 4 2   OR   ♡ K 4
◇ 7   ◇ 7 5
♣ A J 7 3   ♣ A 10 8 2

A well-bid hand. However, I wonder whether partner will say the
same if he finds himself in 4♠ opposite the opening hand shown above
when he has:

♠ A 6 4 2
♡ 10 7
◇ K 3 2
♣ A J 10 9

He will make 4♠ on a lucky day, but I am sure he would rather be a
spectator as you take the obvious eleven tricks in diamonds after the
auction:

     1◇   1♠
     2♠   3♣
     3◇   4◇
     5◇

As always, the solution to this problem is simple. Difficulties of
interpretation and hand-evaluation will be removed if the bid of a
third suit by the responder in these situations is *always* a try for game in
no trumps. Thus the sequence

     1♣   1♡
     2♡   2♠

shows a balanced hand with at least 10 or 11 points and a good holding
in spades; it invites the opener to convert to no trumps if he has a
guard in diamonds, bidding a non-forcing 2NT on a minimum hand
and jumping to 3NT if he has a suitable hand with extra values.

Similarly, the sequence:

     1◇   1♠
     2♠   3♣

is a definite try for game in no trumps, showing the values for an
opening bid including a good holding in clubs.

If the responder is anxious to make a try for game in his suit after a
simple raise by the opener, he merely makes a further raise to three.

♠ Q J 9 6 4
♡ A 7 2   1◇   1♠
◇ K 4   2♣   ?
♣ 10 8 3

Bid 3♠, showing a five-card suit and inviting the opener to go on to game if he has anything to spare. The absence of a trial bid in this situation may lead to an occasional loss of efficiency if a thin game contract depends on the two hands being a precise fit; however, the improved definition of the various game tries available to the responder after the opener has made a simple raise of his initial response more than compensates for this, and yet another of Acol's notoriously murky areas should no longer contain hidden terrors.

A jump bid in a third suit in the situation under review is much simpler to analyse.

     1♣   1♡
     2♡   3♠

After the partnership has located a fit, a jump of this kind can have no useful meaning in a natural sense. It is best used as some kind of control-showing bid, and my own view is that a jump in a third suit after the partnership has already agreed a suit should show a void. You may prefer to expand this slightly to mean any suit with no losers, that is, to treat a holding like singleton ace as though it were a void; however, this occasionally leads to slight confusion, particularly if the opener is tempted to assume that his partner has certain honour holdings in the other suits or if he downgrades his hand because he holds the king of the suit bid.

A void-showing jump can sometimes simplify the bidding of the kind of slam which so often passes us by. For example:

	WEST		EAST	WEST	EAST
♠	J 7 2	♠	—	1♣	1♡
♡	K 10 6 3	♡	Q J 9 7 4 2	2♡	3♠
◇	K 4	◇	A 10 7 3	4♣	4◇
♣	A Q 8 5	♣	K 4 3	4NT	5◇
				6♡	

East's jump to 3♠ comes as music to West's ears, for it begins to look as if all the partnership's high cards are pulling their full weight. He tests the market with a gentle cue bid of 4♣ and, once he is re-assured regarding the ace of diamonds, there is no holding him back: when it becomes clear that East is missing the ace of hearts, it is almost certain that he has the king of clubs to justify his strong bidding. This hand brings out the point I made earlier about distinguishing a void from a singleton ace. If East's jump to 3♠ could be based on a hand of this sort:

♠ A
♡ Q J 9 7 4 2
◇ A 10 7
♣ J 4 3

the bidding will become much more difficult to handle, and there is a grave danger of the partnership's reaching 6♡ and losing one heart and one club trick.

If we interpret a jump in a third suit in this kind of situation as showing a void, we must consider how the responder is to investigate slam possibilities if his side-suit controls take the form of aces and kings rather than voids.

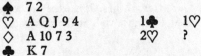

♠ 7 2		
♡ A Q J 9 4	1♣	1♡
◇ A 10 7 3	2♡	?
♣ K 7		

It begins to look as if this hand might be the kind of fit which produces a slam on comparatively few high-card points, and you would clearly like to make a mild slam try here. The answer is to bid 3◇. As we discussed at length earlier, partner will interpret this initially as a try for no trumps, but your actual motives will soon become apparent. If he bids 3NT, for example, you can revert to 4♡ and all will be revealed; if he attempts to sign off in 3♡, you can push on to 4♡ and it will be clear that 3◇ was not, after all, a try for game; and if partner jumps to 4♡ over 3◇, you can see it through with a further cue bid of 5♣ and leave the rest to partner. This last sequence might be taken from its wraps if these are the two hands:

WEST	EAST	WEST	EAST
♠ A 8 3	♠ 7 2	1♣	1♡
♡ K 10 7 3	♡ A Q J 9 4	2♡	3◇
◇ 9 4	◇ A 10 7 3	4♡	5♣
♣ A Q J 5	♣ K 7	5♠	6♡

OPENER REBIDS 1NT

Any consideration of the responder's second bid after a rebid of 1NT by the opener must take into account the strength and, more important, the range of the rebid. If, as I hope, common-sense has prevailed and you are playing a wide-range 1NT rebid, the responder's second bid on hands on which he hopes to progress further will often be a conventional strength-asking enquiry, the name of which escapes me for the moment. Leaving that aside, however, the general meaning of bids of a third suit after a 1NT rebid are standard; for the sake of argument, let us assume that the rebid shows 15–16 points.

1♡	1♠
1NT	2◇

A non-reverse bid in a new suit is not forcing; it merely shows a weak, distributional hand and invites the opener to express a preference between the responder's two suits. On the other hand, a responder's reverse after a 1NT rebid is forcing for one round.

♠	K Q 9 4		
♡	A J 7 6 3	1♣	1♡
◇	7 2	1NT	?
♣	8 5		

Bid 2♠. Partner has almost certainly denied holding a four-card spade suit by his failure to rebid 1♠ over 1♡, but you cannot be too careful; furthermore, there can be no harm in showing both your distribution and where your strength lies. If partner chooses to give preference to hearts over 2♠, 4♡ could well be the best game contract. The full hands may be:

	WEST		EAST	WEST	EAST
♠	A 10 7	♠	K Q 9 4	1♣	1♡
♡	Q 10 8	♡	A J 7 6 3	1NT	2♠
◇	Q 5 4	◇	7 2	4♡	
♣	A K 9 3	♣	8 5		

And so we come to the only really badly-defined area of Acol following a 1NT rebid. This is a jump bid in a new suit, especially where the responder has bid both majors in a sequence like:

1♣	1♠
1NT	3♡

It is generally suggested that this sequence should be a one-round force. Terence Reese, in his younger, Acol days,* gives the following hand as an example of a jump to 3♡ opposite a 13–15 1NT rebid:

♠	A K 10 4 2		
♡	Q 10 7 5 2	1♣	1♠
◇	6	1NT	3♡
♣	8 3		

Furthermore, the point is made that, if partner can only bid 3♠ over 3♡, the responder should pass; this means that the opener should bid game whenever he has a fair holding in either of your suits.

However, it is far from clear that this is the best treatment of the sequence. For one thing, I have never fully understood the logic behind one-round forces of the kind advocated here: it is comforting to feel that you will be able to stop in 3♠ if the opener merely gives simple preference, but is it not a little incongruous that you cannot also remain in 3♡ if partner happens to have an unenthusiastic preference for hearts? After all, your holdings in the major suits could be absolutely identical, and it is doubtful whether you improve the accuracy of the bidding very much by equipping the opener with a set of brakes which can only be applied if he happens to prefer your first-bid suit. In fact,

* *The Acol System Today*, by Terence Reese and Albert Dormer.

if you choose to use a jump to 3♡ to show a hand like the one shown above, there must be a good case for making 3♡ a non-forcing game try, enabling the opener to pass, convert to 3♠ or bid game in either major, depending on the nature of his hand and on how good a fit he has for your suits.

Unfortunately, while this suggestion would probably be an improvement on existing methods, it does not overcome the second objection to playing 3♡ as a one-round force. If a jump to 3♡ is to be used to show two five-card suits, as the text-books imply, what is the responder supposed to bid if he has a four-card heart suit?

♠ A K 10 4 2		
♡ K J 7 3	1♣	1♠
◇ 6 2	1NT	?
♣ 8 4		

Even if the 1NT rebid guarantees 15 or 16 points, it is still by no means clear what the best game contract is. The opener could easily hold any of the following hands:

♠ Q 7 3	♠ J 7	♠ Q 7
♡ A Q 4	♡ A Q 8 4	♡ Q 8 4
◇ Q 9 7	◇ A 7 3	◇ A Q J
♣ K Q 6 5	♣ K Q 9 3	♣ K J 10 6 5
HAND A	HAND B	HAND C

The correct contract opposite these hands will be 4♠, 4♡ and 3NT respectively, and yet it is difficult to see how the responder is supposed to investigate all the possibilities if he is not allowed to make a game-forcing jump to 3♡ on a hand containing five spades and only four hearts.

For this reason, I recommend that, while a jump bid in a minor suit might well be based on a five-card suit, the sequences

1♣	1♠	1◇	1♠
1NT	3♡	1NT	3♡

should be reserved for game-going hands containing five spades and *four* hearts. If the responder has two five-card major suits he will just have to decide for himself whether or not the hand is worth a shot at game; after all, he knows the strength of the opposite hand within one point and he can rely on the opener having three cards in at least one of the major suits. He should therefore be in a good position to determine the level of the final contract, whereas it is extremely doubtful whether the opener can really judge the situation accurately enough to be able to alight on a pin's-head in a sequence like 1♣–1♠–1NT–3♡–3♠. Let us return to the hand we considered earlier.

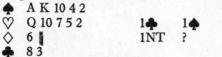

♠ A K 10 4 2		
♡ Q 10 7 5 2	1♣	1♠
◇ 6	1NT	?
♣ 8 3		

Bid 4♡, showing two five-card suits and inviting the opener to choose between 4♡ and 4♠. The opener is most unlikely to have rebid 1NT on a 2–2–4–5 distribution, and it would be difficult to construct a hand on which partner's bidding is sensible and on which there is no play for a major suit game.

OPENER REBIDS 2NT OR 3NT

All bids of a new suit after a 2NT or 3NT rebid by the opener are forcing. They are in principle natural, and there is very little abstruse bidding theory to introduce in this section.

♠	A Q 7 5 2		
♡	K 10 8 3	1♣	1♠
◇	7 5	2NT	?
♣	10 3		

Bid 3♡, natural and forcing. It is possible that partner has a four-card heart suit in this auction. Even if he has not, he may still be able to show three-card spade support, in which case 4♠ will probably be the best game contract.

♠	A Q 7		
♡	K Q 10 7 5	1♣	1♡
◇	7 5 2	2NT	?
♣	A 3		

Bid 3♠. There is more than a sniff of a slam in the air after partner's strength-showing rebid, and 3♠ is the most descriptive bid available at this stage. It is quite safe to introduce a three-card suit in this situation, for the opener's 2NT rebid has virtually denied a four-card spade holding. 3♠ has the advantage of implying a five-card heart suit, and, if the opener is able to give preference to 4♡, 6♡ could easily prove to be the best slam contract.

WEST		EAST		WEST	EAST
♠	K 10 4	♠	A Q 7	1♣	1♡
♡	A J 6	♡	K Q 10 7 5	2NT	3♠
◇	A 10	◇	7 5 2	4♡	5♣
♣	K J 9 6 4	♣	A 3	5◇	6♡

♠ ♠

22. BIDDING THE FOURTH SUIT

'Fourth Suit Forcing' is a convention whose possibilities were completely ignored by Acol theorists for many years. They appeared to hope that, if they took no notice of it, it would eventually go away. In fact, the very opposite occurred and, despite the almost complete absence of guidance from above, the convention has grown in popularity to such an extent that a vast majority of rank-and-file Acol players attempt to use it – with varying degrees of success.

The basic idea behind the Fourth Suit Forcing principle is very simple and very logical. It is merely that, if the partnership has already bid three suits, it is most unlikely that you will want to bid the fourth one in a natural sense: with a good holding in the fourth suit, you will almost certainly be in a position to bid no trumps at the appropriate level and, with insufficient strength for that course of action, you will probably content yourself with expressing a preference between your partner's two suits. In view of this, a bid of the fourth suit is released as a semi-conventional, forcing bid, seeking further information about the opposite hand before deciding on the final contract. Without this aid, certain hands would become extremely difficult to bid:

♠ K 10 7 4 2		
♡ K 3	1♡	1♠
◇ J 8 3	2♣	?
♣ A Q 5		

You would clearly like to be in a game of some kind on this hand, but in which denomination? 4♠ could be correct if partner has some support which he has not yet revealed; 4♡ could be the best spot if he has a good heart suit and shortage in diamonds; and 3NT will probably be easy if partner can offer some assistance in the diamond department. But how do you investigate these various possibilities and leave all your options open? The answer is that you bid 2◇, the fourth suit, to show partner that you have good values but that you are unable to determine the final contract without a little more information from him.

THE FOURTH SUIT AT THE ONE LEVEL

1♣	1◇
1♡	*1♠*

This is the only sequence in which the fourth suit can be bid at the one level, but the principle behind it is exactly as normal. 1♠ here is forcing, not showing a spade suit prima facie, but announcing good values and asking the opener to describe his hand further.

♠	10 7 3		
♡	K 8 4	1♣	1♢
♢	A J 10 7 5	1♡	?
♣	K 3		

Bid 1♠. You are clearly still in the hunt for a game on this hand, but it is difficult to limit the hand accurately at this stage. If you were forced to make a limit bid, you would have to choose 3♡, but this would be a poor description of your holding. 1♠ leaves all the options open. If the opener has a spade guard, he will rebid the appropriate number of no trumps and you can raise accordingly; with a poor spade holding, he will rebid one of his suits or give preference to diamonds, and you might have to resign yourself to playing in a quiet part-score. In either case, the fourth suit bid will make your task much simpler on the next round.

THE FOURTH SUIT AT THE TWO LEVEL

♠	A Q 4		
♡	K J 7 5 3	1♢	1♡
♢	Q 8	1♠	?
♣	7 6 4		

Bid 2♣. It begins to sound as if all your high cards are working well and as if there is a good chance of reaching game on this hand, but your destination is still unknown. Partner's rebid over 2♣ should enable you to decide whether the hand belongs in no trumps, hearts or spades – or even diamonds.

This sequence is actually one of the weakest fourth suit sequences, in that it allows the opener to rebid his suit or give preference to your first suit without venturing beyond the two level. However, the 2♣ bid must guarantee a minimum of 10 or 11 points, for it may compel partner to bid 2NT if he has a minimum hand with a club guard.

It is sometimes correct to use the fourth suit even if you have a definite stop in the suit.

♠	A 7 3		
♡	K Q J 8 3	1♢	1♡
♢	9 2	2♣	?
♣	K 10 5		

3NT is a possible bid at this point, and it expresses the value of the hand quite well. However, the correct bid is 2♠, for two important reasons. In the first place, if partner is unable to bid no trumps and can give belated support to hearts, 4♡ will almost certainly prove to be the best contract. Secondly, if partner has something like Q–x in spades, it will be better for him to play the no trump contract; 2♠ invites him to do just that.

The fact that you are employing a bid of the fourth suit in a semi-conventional sense does not mean that you cannot also use it in a natural sense – provided that you clarify the situation for partner on the next round.

WEST	EAST	WEST	EAST
♠ J 8 3	♠ K Q 10 7 2	1◇	1♡
♡ 7	♡ A 8 6 5 4 2	2♣	2♠
◇ K Q J 9 7	◇ —	3◇	3♠
♣ A Q 7 4	♣ K 8	4♠	

When East introduces 2♠, the fourth suit, West interprets it as a conventional bid and makes his natural rebid of 3◇. When this is followed by 3♠, however, it becomes clear that the spade suit is a genuine five-card holding, and West can raise to the correct game contract.

THE FOURTH SUIT AT THE THREE LEVEL

♠ K Q 10 7 3			
♡ K 4		1♡	1♠
◇ A Q 7		2◇	?
♣ 10 7 5			

Bid 3♣, the fourth suit. It is impossible at this stage to predict what the final contract should be, but partner's reaction to 3♣ should clarify things considerably: if he rebids 3♡, there should be a good play for 4♡; if he gives preference to 3♠, you can raise to 4♠; and if he bids 3NT, that will do nicely.

It is important to remember that to bid the fourth suit at the three level should show a slightly stronger hand than if it is at the two level; since the opener will find himself in game if he has a good holding in the fourth suit and elects to bid no trumps, the responder should guarantee the values for an opening bid to embark on such a manoeuvre.

THE JUMP IN THE FOURTH SUIT

1♠	2♣
2◇	3♡

This kind of jump bid in the fourth suit can have little value in a natural sense, for it is most unlikely that you will be anxious to show a good holding in hearts in this way. If you have a good heart suit after the auction has started 1♠–2♣–2◇, it is clear that the hands must fit badly; you will therefore surely prefer to bid the appropriate number of no trumps or to make a simple bid of 2♡ in an effort to elicit more information about partner's hand and find the best playable spot.

The most useful interpretation of a jump in the fourth suit is to agree partner's second suit and to show a feature in the suit bid. Some authorities have suggested that the jump should not guarantee any particular holding in the suit and that it should merely invite partner to initiate a chain of cue bids if he feels so inclined, but this seems to me an unnecessary extravagance. After all, the sequence

    1♠   2♣
    2◇   4◇

is generally regarded as forcing, as is any jump raise to four of a minor. The responder will surely prefer to show his slam interest in this way if his hand contains losing hearts, reserving a jump to 3♡ over 2◇ for hands which not only contain excellent support for diamonds but also a key card in hearts.

The important point which remains to be determined is the nature of the feature in the fourth suit which is to be shown by the unnecessary jump. I would like to suggest the following simple rules:

(a) A jump to the three level in the fourth suit agrees the opener's last-named suit and shows the ace or king.

(b) A jump to the four level in the fourth suit agrees the opener's last-named suit and shows a void.

This differentiation between the kinds of control shown by a jump in the fourth suit follows our general philosophy of making use of little-known bids which have been gathering the dust in the cupboard for years, and of adding an element of precision to certain vague Acol sequences. What is more, it even makes some hands easier to bid.

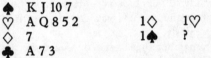

    ♠ K J 10 7
    ♡ A Q 8 5 2   1◇   1♡
    ◇ 7   1♠   ?
    ♣ A 7 3

The recommended test in this kind of situation is to ask yourself what you would have bid if partner had opened with 1♠. If, as in this case, your hand would have been too good for an immediate raise to 4♠, then it is too good for a direct raise to 4♠ now. The answer is to bid 3♣, agreeing spades, showing a high club honour, and expressing more than a passing interest in a slam – all in one bid.

    ♠ K J 9 3
    ♡ A J 10 5 4 3   1◇   1♡
    ◇ K 7 2   1♠   ?
    ♣ —

Bid 4♣, showing powerful support for spades, partner's last-named suit, and a void in clubs. The knowledge that all your high cards are concentrated in the three bid suits should enable partner to judge the slam prospects of the hand quite accurately.

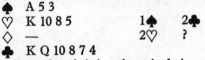

    ♠ A 5 3
    ♡ K 10 8 5   1♠   2♣
    ◇ —   2♡   ?
    ♣ K Q 10 8 7 4

Bid 4◇. Even though it is only a single jump now that partner has rebid 2♡, the leap to 4◇ means that you are agreeing partner's second suit, hearts, and showing a void in diamonds. The comparative lack of bidding space in this situation means that there is no straightforward way of agreeing hearts and showing the ace of diamonds; to do this, you may have to proceed via a simple bid in the fourth suit.

♠	9 7	
♡	K J 10 4	1♠ 2♣
◇	A 7	2♡ ?
♣	A Q 10 8 3	

Once again this hand is too strong for an immediate raise to 4♡. The best way of handling it is to bid 3◇, the fourth suit, and then return to 4♡ on the next round. An alert partner will realise that you are trying to tell him something, and it should not prove too difficult for him to unscramble the correct message.

RESPONDING TO THE FOURTH SUIT

We must now briefly consider the opener's action after the responder has bid the fourth suit at his second turn. His first duty is to bid no trumps if it is at all possible, remembering to jump to game if he has extra values.

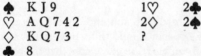

♠	K J 9	1♡ 2♣
♡	A Q 7 4 2	2◇ 2♠
◇	K Q 7 3	?
♣	8	

Bid 3NT. Partner's bid of 2♠ shows the values for 2NT, and you must jump to three to show that you have the values for game; a simple rebid of 2NT at this point would not be forcing.

If the opener has a poor holding in the fourth suit and cannot bid no trumps, he must make the most descriptive bid available. This will often take the form of preference to the responder's first suit.

♠	Q 7	1◇ 1♠
♡	10 3	2♣ 2♡
◇	A J 6 5 2	?
♣	K Q J 4	

Bid 2♠. Partner almost certainly has five spades for this sequence, and belated support may be just what he is waiting for.

Once again the opener must remember to give jump preference to the responder's first suit if he has extra values.

♠	7 3	1◇ 1♡
♡	K 9 4	2♣ 2♠
◇	A K 10 4	?
♣	A Q 7 5	

Bid 4♡. The responder has guaranteed the values for 2NT by bidding 2♠, but he has not promised to bid again after a minimum rebid by the opener. Since you clearly want to be in game now that partner has made an effort, you must jump to 4♡ at this point: even on those rare occasions on which partner has only four hearts, the hand should play quite well in the 4–3 fit.

Similarly:

♠	A Q J 3	1♣	1♡
♡	10 7 2	1♠	2◇
◇	8	?	
♣	A Q 9 6 4		

Bid 3♡. Although this hand only contains 13 high-card points, partner's failure to bid no trumps over 1♠ suggests that most of his points are working and that the two hands will fit well. Your three-card trump support and excellent distribution make this hand well worth a jump to 3♡.

If the opener can neither bid no trumps nor give belated support for his partner's original suit, he will have to rebid one of his own suits. This will often enable him to describe his hand admirably.

♠	7	1♡	1♠
♡	A Q 10 8 3	2♣	2◇
◇	J 4	?	
♣	K Q 9 6 4		

Bid 3♣, showing a five-card club suit and, by inference, a five-card heart suit. Here again the opener should think in terms of a jump rebid if he has extra values and can visualise game now that the responder has shown signs of life.

♠	7	1◇	1♠
♡	10 4	2♣	2♡
◇	A K J 9 3	?	
♣	A Q J 10 8		

Jump to 4♣. With two powerful minor suits, you are clearly anxious to play in game now that partner has shown extra values; a jump to 4♣ at this point shows two good five-card or longer minor suits.

♠	A K J 10 8	1♠	2♣
♡	9 2	2◇	2♡
◇	A Q 7 3	?	
♣	Q 3		

Bid 3♠. Partner's bid of 2♡ shows fair values and an interest in game, and you must tell him that, although you are unable to oblige in the no trump department, you still have ambitions for greater things.

RAISING THE FOURTH SUIT

Finally, there is one other possible course of action available to the opener: he can occasionally raise the fourth suit. This is an area of bidding which is rarely covered in text books and on which experts never seem to agree; let us therefore try to cast a guiding light through the murk.

The first important distinction to make is between 'possible' and 'impossible' raises.

This must rank as an 'impossible' raise, for, if the opener held a spade suit, he would have bid it over 1♡. By contrast:

$$1\spadesuit \quad 2\clubsuit$$
$$2\diamondsuit \quad 2\heartsuit$$
$$3\heartsuit$$

3♡ in this sequence is a 'possible' raise, in that the opener could have a 5–4–4–0 or 4–4–4–1 distribution and could therefore hold a four-card heart suit.

This distinction is fundamental in any attempt to analyse a single raise of the fourth suit. Since it is clearly possible on occasions for there to be a 4–4 fit in what happens to be the fourth suit, the primary meaning of a 'possible' raise in a major suit should be natural, showing a four-card holding.

♠	K 10 7 3	1♡	2♣
♡	A Q J 8 5	2♦	2♠
♦	K Q 9 4	?	
♣	—		

Bid 3♠, showing a four-card spade suit just in case there is a 4–4 spade fit between the two hands. Notice, however, that a raise of this kind will only be possible if the opener is strong enough to stand a conversion to 3NT by the responder if, as is likely, his bid of 2♠ was made on a non-existent suit.

♠	A J 7 4 2	1♠	2♣
♡	Q 10 8 5	2♦	2♡
♦	A 10 6 3	?	
♣	—		

Although it is quite possible that there is a 4–4 heart fit on this hand, it is not safe to make a natural raise to 3♡ at this point: after all, if partner's bid of 2♡ was not genuine, you cannot force him into 3NT when you have 11 points and he may only have 10 or 11. Your best rebid at this stage is probably 2NT, showing a good holding in the fourth suit. However, if your innate caution precludes a 2NT bid on 11 points and a void, you might prefer a simple rebid of 2♠.

The meaning of all 'impossible' raises and of a 'possible' raise in a minor suit is not quite so clear. My own view is that they should confirm a game-going hand with a definite stop in the fourth suit, suggesting that the no trump contract should be played from partner's hand.

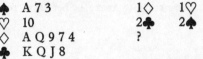

♠	A 7 3	1◇	1♡
♡	10	2♣	2♠
◇	A Q 9 7 4	?	
♣	K Q J 8		

Bid 3♠. This is clearly an 'impossible' raise, in view of your failure to rebid 1♠ over 1♡, and the suggested meaning is a definite spade guard, game-going values, and a desire for partner to play the hand. This last point is not merely a reflection of your natural modesty: it may be the key to a successful sequence if the full hands are something like:

WEST		EAST		WEST	EAST
♠	A 7 3	♠	Q 6	1◇	1♡
♡	10	♡	K J 8 4 2	2♣	2♠
◇	A Q 9 7 4	◇	J 8 3	3♠	3NT
♣	K Q J 8	♣	A 10 6		

Since his queen of spades will act as a second guard in the suit, East will probably have time to develop the diamonds and wrap up 3NT; if West is the declarer, on the other hand, a spade lead through the doubleton queen might easily prove fatal.

SUBSEQUENT BIDDING AFTER THE FOURTH SUIT

Everyone agrees that the fourth suit is forcing; what is seldom made clear is how far it is forcing, and even the very best text-books tend to evade this controversial issue. This is therefore yet another opportunity for us to add a little definition and precision to an extremely common Acol situation.

The first general point to make is that to raise the fourth suit or to make a jump bid in response thereto is forcing to game. The meaning of the subsequent bidding if there is a minimum response depends on the level at which the fourth suit was bid.

(a) *After the Fourth Suit at the One or Two Level*

When a player introduces the fourth suit at the one or two level, he does not guarantee to find another bid and he may pass a minimum response by his partner. For example:

(A)	1♡	1♠		(B)	1♣	1♠	
	2♣	2◇			2♣	2◇	
	2NT				2♠		
(C)	1♡	1♠		(D)	1♡	1♠	
	2♣	2◇			2♣	2◇	
	2♡				3♣		

None of these sequences is forcing. In each case, the opener has a minimum hand, and he is making the most descriptive rebid available; the responder is free to pass if he has no additional values and if he feels that a reasonable final contract has been reached.

Nothing difficult so far. However, the fog banks are beginning to gather, for we must now consider what it means if the responder bids on after one of these minimum sequences. Regular partnerships will probably prefer to place their own interpretation on certain fourth suit sequences, but the following simple rules should help any inexperienced navigators through the uncharted waters.

A simple return to the opener's first suit is forcing, still offering a choice of contract.

♠ K 4 3	1♠	2♣
♡ J 8	2◇	2♡
◇ A 10 7	2NT	?
♣ A J 10 7 2		

Bid 3♠. Partner's 2NT rebid promises an independent guard in hearts. However, it is still not certain whether he has five spades and four diamonds or a 4-3-4-2 distribution on which he was unable to open 1NT. 3♠, showing three-card support, will enable him to choose between 3NT and 4♠.

The only exception to this general rule occurs when the opener has already been able to describe his exact distribution in his two suits. For example, the sequence:

1♡	1♠
2♣	2◇
3♣	3♡

should not be construed as completely forcing. Since the responder already knows the exact distribution and the approximate strength of his partner's hand, he should be in a good position himself to decide whether to play in 3♡ or 4♡.

A simple return to the opener's second suit is not forcing, although it is clearly highly invitational.

♠ A Q 10 7 5	1♡	1♠
♡ J 6	2♣	2◇
◇ 10 4	2NT	?
♣ A 9 8 3		

Bid 3♣, showing four-card trump support and good values. This seven-loser hand was slightly too good for a raise to 3♣ on the previous round, bearing in mind that the responder often has to strain to raise the opener's second suit on inadequate values if he is reluctant to allow the bidding to die at the two level. Now that the fourth suit enquiry has elicited a depressing reaction from the opener, however, it looks as if you might have to settle for a part-score after all; partner will interpret your belated raise to 3♣ as extremely encouraging in this kind of sequence.

A simple rebid of the responder's major suit is forcing, showing a six-card suit and continuing the search for the correct game contract.

♠	A J 9 7 5 3	1♡	1♠
♡	8	2♣	2◇
◇	A 6 3	2♡	?
♣	K Q 4		

Bid 2♠. Partner's reply to your fourth suit enquiry was very disappointing, but you still have sufficient values for a game contract somewhere and you must continue the search for the best spot. 2♠ must logically be forcing in this auction, as must the 3♠ rebid in sequences of this kind:

(A)	1♡	1♠	(B)	1♡	1♠
	2♣	2◇		2♣	2◇
	2NT	3♠		3♣	3♠

In all these situations, the responder cannot be making a game try based on a good six-card suit: on such a hand, he would have rebid a non-forcing 3♠ over 2♣, without needing to resort to the fourth suit.

A simple rebid of the responder's minor suit is not forcing. The important distinction here is that, since the responder was not able to make an encouraging jump rebid on the previous round, he might have used the fourth suit as the only available game try.

♠	7	1♠	2♣
♡	J 6 3	2◇	2♡
◇	K 7 3	2♠	?
♣	A Q J 10 6 4		

Bid 3♣, not forcing. Since this hand was a little too strong for a simple rebid of 3♣ on the previous round, the 2♡ enquiry was undoubtedly correct. Now that partner has shown a minimum hand with a poor holding in hearts, however, you must be prepared to settle for a safe part-score in clubs.

(b) *After the Fourth Suit at the Three Level*

As we saw earlier, the responder needs the values for an opening bid in order to introduce the fourth suit at the three level. It is therefore sensible to agree that he also guarantees to find another bid if his partner's reply is below the game level; since the bidding is already at the three level, the opener may find it impractical to make a jump response in order to show extra values, and the knowledge that his partner will not pass a minimum rebid will often make the auction much easier to handle.

♠	A K 9 6 3	1♠	2♣
♡	A K 10 4	2♡	3◇
◇	J 8	?	
♣	10 5		

Bid 3♠. You clearly want to be in game now that partner has shown good values, but the correct denomination is still far from clear. The forcing rebid of 3♠ will give partner a chance to describe his hand further.

Similarly:

♠	A K 10 6	1♠	2◇
♡	A Q 5 2	2♡	3♣
◇	Q 7	?	
♣	7 5 3		

Bid 3◇. While you obviously have the values for game, it is difficult to limit your hand accurately at this point. The forcing rebid of 3◇ continues to describe your hand and keeps all the avenues open.

Having established that a minimum, below-game response to a fourth suit bid at the three level is forcing, we must consider in detail the various courses of action available to the responder.

A simple return to the opener's first suit below the game level is not forcing, although the tenor of the auction so far makes it extremely unlikely that the opener will pass.

♠	A K J 6 4	1♡	1♠
♡	Q 3	2◇	3♣
◇	J 7 2	3◇	?
♣	J 8 5		

Bid 3♡. It now appears that these hands fit very badly and that you may have to be content with a part-score. If partner can steel himself to pass 3♡, nine tricks could well prove to be the limit of the hand.

A simple return to the opener's second suit below the game level is forcing. There is only one sequence in which this can occur at the three level, and even in this case the bid is most unlikely to be made.

♠	6 3	1♠	2◇
♡	A Q 4	2♡	3♣
◇	A Q J 7 5 2	3◇	?
♣	7 2		

Since there might be three top losers in 5◇, there is a case for bidding 3♡ at this point. If partner has something like:

♠	K Q 10 7 4	◇	K 4
♡	K J 8 5	♣	9 5

4♡ could prove to be the only makeable game contract.

There are three sequences where the return to the opener's second suit is made at the four level and below game:

    A.   1♡–1♠–2◇–3♣–3♡–4◇
    B.   1♡–1♠–2◇–3♣–3♠–4◇
    C.   1♡–1♠–2◇–3♣–3NT–4◇

These are all clearly forcing; it would be difficult to construct a hand on which the responder would bid in this way and be anxious to stay in 4◇ at this point.

If the return to the opener's second suit is made at the game level, the inference is that the original fourth suit bid was really an advance cue bid.

    1♠   2♣
    2♡   3◇
    3NT 4♡

As we saw earlier, this sequence suggests that the responder has a top diamond and a hand which was a little too strong for a simple raise to 4♡ on the previous round.

A simple rebid of the responder's suit below the game level is forcing. This is fairly clear when it is made at the four level, but there are also two possible sequences where the rebid is made at the three level:

    A.   1♡–1♠–2◇–3♣–3◇–3♠
    B.   1♡–1♠–2◇–3♣–3♡–3♠

The responder is clearly continuing the search for the best game contract; he cannot really want to bid a non-forcing 3♠ at this point, for he could have bid 3♠ in that sense one round earlier.

Part Five

THE DEVELOPMENT OF THE AUCTION

♠♠

Generally speaking, the first two rounds of bidding will form a solid foundation for the entire auction. At least one of the partners will almost certainly have limited his hand by his first two bids, and any available suit fit will probably have come to light by this stage. The bidding on the third and later rounds will therefore tend to be more straightforward and less controversial than that on the second round; the development of the auction will often be a question more of judgement than of system, as the two partners decide whether to try for a game or a slam, or whether to be content with a part-score.

In view of this, it is not my intention in this final section to attempt to produce an exhaustive, but relatively unproductive, analysis of every possible bidding sequence consisting of five or more bids. It is simply proposed to take a general look at the way in which the auction might develop after an opening bid of one of a suit and a simple or limited response, omitting the case which has already been covered where the opener makes a reverse rebid. This general look will include a critical examination of one or two specific sequences which occur fairly frequently and which are often misinterpreted, with the usual fatal results.

For the sake of convenience, this section has been sub-divided into four chapters, depending on the nature of the responder's action on the second round.

CHAPTER 23. Responder shows a minimum hand.
CHAPTER 24. Responder tries for game.
CHAPTER 25. Responder shows strength.
CHAPTER 26. Responder makes a slam try. This chapter also acts as a convenient vehicle for a discussion of slam bidding in general.

23. RESPONDER SHOWS A MINIMUM HAND

There are a number of sequences in which the first two rounds of bidding reveal that the responder has a weakish hand. In these cases any effort towards game will have to emanate from the opener, and we shall consider in this chapter the various ways in which he can show extra strength on the third round.

RESPONDER REBIDS 1NT

A 1NT bid by the responder on the second round tends to show slightly better values than an initial 1NT response. The opener should therefore be more willing to make an invitational raise to two.

♠	A Q 9 4	1◊	1♡
♡	Q 2	1♠	1NT
◊	A K 8 5 4	?	
♣	J 6		

Bid 2NT. While you would not normally raise a 1NT response on a mere 16-count, partner's rebid of 1NT might conceal as many as 10 points. Furthermore, you can always be certain that 1NT on the second round is a completely natural bid, showing a good holding in the unbid suit; an initial 1NT is far less precise, for it might be little more than a 'courtesy' response on what is really a most unsuitable hand.

Belated support for the responder's suit on the third round is an encouraging move.

The opener's 2♡ bid in this sequence shows three-card heart support and a pronounced shortage in the unbid suit, clubs. Furthermore, the fact that the opener failed to raise to 2♡ on the previous round suggests that he has good values, and the responder is strongly encouraged to proceed further after this kind of sequence.

♠	J 7	1◊	1♡
♡	K J 9 6 4	1♠	1NT
◊	8 3	2♡	?
♣	A 10 4 2		

Bid 4♡. Now that the opener has shown heart support, short clubs and extra values, there must be an excellent play for ten tricks in 4♡.

For the opener to repeat one of his suits over the 1NT rebid does not show any extra values; he is simply showing the distribution of his hand and attempting to improve the final contract.

(A)	1◊	1♡		(B)	1◊	1♡
	1♠	1NT			1♠	1NT
	2◊				2♠	

Sequence A shows that the opener has six diamonds and four spades and an unwillingness to watch the hand being played in 1NT. Similarly, Sequence B indicates that the opener has five spades and therefore at least six diamonds. However, the responder will quite often push on after the latter sequence, for the knowledge that his partner has such a shapely hand might enable him to visualise game if his limited values appear to lie in the right place.

♠ K 7 2	1◇	1♡
♡ J 9 7 3	1♠	1NT
◇ J 5	2♣	?
♣ A 10 4 3		

Bid 3♣. Now that partner has shown 6–5 in his two suits, your top cards seem very suitable and you are well worth a try for game. There is an inference that the opener is not completely minimum for this sequence: since he would be unlikely to conceal a five-card spade suit, one can only assume that he intended to reverse into 2♠ if the bidding had started 1◇–2♣.

RESPONDER REBIDS TWO OF HIS SUIT

| 1♡ | 1♠ |
| 2◇ | 2♠ |

As we saw in an earlier chapter, a rebid of his original suit by the responder is always vaguely encouraging in this kind of sequence. If the opener still has an interest in a game contract, he will normally be in a position to raise the responder's suit – bearing in mind that two small cards would be adequate trump support in a sequence of this type.

However, there are occasions on which the opener is strong enough to visualise a game in no trumps.

♠ Q	1♡	1♠
♡ A K J 10 4	2◇	2♠
◇ K 8 6 3	?	
♣ A J 9		

Bid 2NT. A second-round bid of 2NT of this type will tend to show a full-value 18 points, for the fact that the hands obviously fit poorly means that the play in no trumps will not be too easy.

Similarly:

♠ Q	1♡	1♠
♡ A K J 8 3	2◇	2♠
◇ K J 7 4	?	
♣ A 5 2		

Bid 3♣. You are strong enough to make a try for game here, but the tenuous club holding means that 2NT would be a poor bid at this stage. The fourth suit bid of 3♣ is the best exploratory move available. It allows partner to play in 3NT if he can offer a little assistance in clubs, or to jump to 4♠ if he was close to a 3♠ rebid on the previous round; otherwise, he should be able to settle peacefully in 3♠. 3♣ is, of course, only a one-round force in this situation. Since the initial 2♦ rebid was not forcing and the responder has subsequently shown no great enthusiasm, it would be illogical to interpret 3♣ as more than a game try.

RESPONDER GIVES SIMPLE PREFERENCE

1♡   1♠
2♦   2♡

There are a number of ways in which the opener can make a try for game in this situation. If he has 4♡ in mind, he can raise to 3♡, suggesting a longish heart suit and a poor holding in the unbid suit; alternatively, he can bid 3♦ if he is 5–5 in his two suits, so that partner can judge whether or not his high cards are working well.

Apart from one exceptional case, belated support for the responder's suit is always encouraging.

♠ K 7 2   1♡   1♠
♡ A J 10 5 3   2♦   2♡
♦ A K 9 4   ?
♣ 5

Bid 2♠. Belated support of this kind shows three-card trump support, indicates a pronounced shortage in the unbid suit, and promises extra values; on a weaker holding, for example the above hand without the king of diamonds, the opener would have preferred to make an immediate raise to 2♠ on the previous round.

The only exception to this principle occurs where the opening bid may have been based on a three-card club suit.

1♣   1♦
1♠   2♣
2♦

If an opening bid of 1NT would be strong at the prevailing vulnerability, the opener's actions in this auction are consistent with a weak 4–3–3–3 hand; the belated return to 2♦ must not be assumed to show extra values.

It is occasionally possible to make a belated jump raise in the responder's suit.

♠ K Q 2   1♡   1♠
♡ A J 10 5 3   2♦   2♡
♦ A K 9 4   ?
♣ 5

Bid 3♠. While 2♠ would be encouraging in this situation, this hand is too strong for such action. The jump to 3♠ shows three-card trump support, a pronounced shortage in clubs, and a hand which was just below-strength for a game-forcing jump to 3◊ on the previous round.

Finally, the opener can make a try for game in no trumps after receiving simple preference.

♠	10	1♡	1♠
♡	A K 10 5 3	2◊	2♡
◊	K Q 7 5	?	
♣	A J 10		

Bid 2NT. This shows the usual 17–18 points, and the inference is that the 2NT bid was delayed because of a singleton spade. The responder should therefore be in a good position to judge the correct final contract.

Similarly:

♠	A 5 2	1♡	2♣
♡	A J 10 5 3	2◊	2♡
◊	K Q J 4	?	
♣	8		

Bid 2♠. This hand is worth a game try after partner's original two level response, but 2NT would be a poor bid in view of the fragile holding in spades. The bid of the fourth suit will allow partner to bid no trumps if he can offer any assistance in spades. If not, he should be able to judge whether to sign off in 3♡ or to jump to 4♡.

♠ ♠

24. RESPONDER TRIES FOR GAME

In the last chapter, we considered the various situations which arise when the opener takes up the running. In certain sequences, the second round of bidding shows that it˜is the responder who is interested in game.

RESPONDER RAISES TO 2NT

If the opener rebids 1NT and is raised to two, his reaction will depend on the nature of his 1NT rebid. If he has shown a three-point range, say 12–14, he is invited to push on to game if he has a maximum. If, on the other hand, he has studied the earlier chapters of this book and has adopted the 12–16 1NT rebid, the emphasis is rather different: the raise to 2NT in this case invites him to go on unless he has a minimum.

The other important point to make in this connection is that the opener should normally offer an alternative game contract if he has three-card support for his partner's major suit.

```
♠ K 8 3          1♣   1♠
♡ Q J 8          1NT* 2NT
◇ A 10 4         ?
♣ A J 7 3             *12–16
```

Bid 3♠. You are keen to go to game on this near-maximum hand, and you should take this opportunity to show your three-card spade support. Partner will know from your failure to raise to 2♠ immediately that your hand is completely balanced; he might nevertheless prefer to play in a 5–3 spade fit if he has, say, a singleton or small doubleton diamond.

RESPONDER BIDS 2NT

If the responder converts to 2NT over a suit rebid by the opener, the opener will raise to game in no trumps if he has a little to spare and is not anxious to suggest an alternative game contract.

If he is unwilling to play in no trumps, however, the opener's actions are far less straightforward. This is yet another area of bidding which is badly defined in Acol, and it will probably be helpful to analyse the various sequences in more detail.

Certain rebids by the opener over 2NT are patently weak and non-forcing.

```
(A) 1♡   1♠        (B) 1♡   1♠
    2♡   2NT           2♠   2NT
    3♡                 3♡

(C) 1♡   1♠        (D) 1♡   1♠
    2◇   2NT           2♠   2NT
    3♡                 3♠
```

In the first three sequences, the opener has a six-card heart suit and no ambitions. In Sequence D, he is suggesting a minimum hand with five hearts and four spades.

Similarly, there are other sequences in which the opener's rebid over 2NT is best played forcing.

```
(E) 1♡  1♠     (F) 1♡  1♠     (G) 1♡  2♣
    2♡  2NT        2◇  2NT        2♡  2NT
    3♣             3♣             3♠
```

In the first two of these sequences, the opener is accepting his partner's game try and showing three-card spade support. In Sequence G, he has a four-card spade suit and five or six hearts, and is offering the responder a choice of contract.

```
♠ A 10 7 2       1♡   2♣
♡ K Q J 5 4      2♡   2NT
◇ 6 4            ?
♣ A 3
```

Bid 3♠, which describes your hand well. It is not completely

impossible that partner has a four-card spade suit in this auction;
with a 4–1–3–5 or 4–2–2–5 distribution and a strong holding in diamonds,
he might well prefer 2NT to 2♠ on the second round.

The remaining sequences after a 2NT rebid by the responder are
much more obscure. For example:

The opener is at least 5–5 in the red suits, but is he expecting his
partner to bid again over 3◇? This is just the sort of point which arises
all too often at the table but which is rarely discussed in the reputable
text-books. The solution must be, I think, that a simple rebid of the
opener's second suit should not be forcing, in the same way as a simple
rebid of his first suit can be passed.

Bid 3◇, non-forcing. This sort of hand would be extremely difficult
to deal with if 3◇ is regarded as forcing in this situation. To play 3◇
as non-forcing means that you have to find an alternative bid if you have
a stronger hand with the same distribution; assuming that you are
unwilling to raise to 3NT, you must choose between a jump to 4◇
and an exploratory bid in the fourth suit – a manoeuvre which we shall
examine in more detail shortly.

Sequences in which the opener introduces a new suit on the third
round lead us into more uncharted waters.

(I) 1♠   2♡
     2♠   2NT
     3◇

This auction would undoubtedly cause a great deal of head-scratching
if it were to occur at the table, for the simple reason that you would
be most unlikely to find a discussion of this kind of sequence in any
authoritative treatise on bidding. Help is at last at hand, however, and it
can be shown by careful analysis that there is a logical meaning for the
3◇ bid. The first point to make is that the responder has already
painted an accurate picture of his hand: 10 or 11 points, a five-card
heart suit, indifferent support for spades, and a fairly balanced hand
with a reasonable holding in the minor suits. This means that the
opener is unlikely to have an urgent need for a further exploratory
bid in this situation, and there is therefore no practical reason why 3◇
should be regarded as forcing. Similarly, the opener will not be anxious
to introduce a four-card suit in this auction; while it would be splendid
for the opener to be able to settle in a diamond part-score if he held a

weak hand and managed to find a 4–4 fit, to introduce a four-card diamond suit on modest values cannot be a sound move – if the responder is unable to oblige by providing a four-card diamond holding opposite, he may have no safe haven to which to return.

This being the case, the most sensible interpretation of the 3◇ bid in this sequence is that it is non-forcing, showing a five-card suit which the opener was unable to introduce on the previous round.

♠ A Q 7 5 4	1♠	2♡
♡ 6	2♠	2NT
◇ Q J 10 6 3	?	
♣ Q 8		

Bid 3◇. The hand was not strong enough to bid 3◇ over the 2♡ response. Now that partner has shown a balanced hand with approximately 11 points, however, you cannot leave him to toil in no trumps: show the distribution and the strength of your hand by bidding 3◇.

(J)   1♡   1♠
     2♡   2NT
     3♣

This sequence is similar, but not identical. The important difference in this case is that the opener could have introduced his club suit on the second round with no embarrassment. While this sequence is still not forcing, therefore, the distribution of the opener's hand is not the same as in Sequence I: since he would have rebid 2♣ over 1♠ if he had either a five-card club suit or five hearts and four clubs, the clear inference is that the opener has a weakish hand with six hearts and four clubs.

♠ 7 2	1♡	1♠
♡ A J 9 8 5 3	2♡	2NT
◇ 6	?	
♣ K Q 7 4		

Bid 3♣. Partner would have a torrid time in 2NT. You must mount an urgent rescue operation and, while the final resting-place is probably 3♡, it costs nothing to offer partner a slight choice by showing your four-card club suit en route.

(K)   1♡   1♠
     2♠   2NT
     3◇

This situation is completely different. Now that the partnership has already found a playable fit, there is little need for the opener to introduce a new suit on a weak hand in an attempt to find a safer resting-place. The 3◇ bid in this sequence is therefore best used as a forcing, exploratory bid, ensuring that the best game contract is reached.

H

♠ A 8 2   1♡   1♠
♡ K J 10 5 3   2♠   2NT
◇ A Q 7 2   ?
♣ 5

Bid 3◇. You have just about enough to accept partner's game try, but it is by no means certain that 3NT is the correct contract. By bidding 3◇, drawing partner's attention to the gaping hole in your bucket, you can leave the way clear for a final contract of 4♠, 4♡ – or even 5◇.

The final category of sequences following a 2NT rebid by the responder finds the opener introducing the fourth suit.

(L) 1♡   1♠   (M) 1♡   1♠
     2♣   2NT   2◇   2NT
     3◇   3♣

These two sequences have one essential difference. Whereas the diamond suit in Sequence L could conceivably be genuine, the opener cannot possibly have four clubs in Sequence M: with a 0–5–4–4 or 1–4–4–4 distribution, the rebid over 1♠ would be 2♣, not 2◇.

This being so, there is a case for interpreting Sequence L as non-forcing and Sequence M as forcing, and this would be a perfectly playable method. However, it is recommended that a third round bid of the fourth suit by the opener should always be construed as forcing; this will frequently facilitate constructive bidding because, as well as obtaining vital information about the responder's hand, to bid the fourth suit often describes the opener's holding so well that he will make life extremely easy for his partner.

♠ K 10 3   1◇   1♡
♡ 3   2♣   2NT
◇ A K 10 8 4   ?
♣ A Q J 5

Bid 3♠. In this case, the spade suit cannot be genuine, for you neglected to rebid 1♠ over 1♡. 3♠ must therefore be an exploratory bid, showing the distribution of your hand and indicating that you are interested in greater things, particularly if partner has no wasted values in hearts.

WEST		EAST		WEST	EAST
♠ K 10 3		♠ A J 8		1◇	1♡
♡ 3		♡ J 9 6 5 2		2♣	2NT
◇ A K 10 8 4		◇ Q 9 7		3♠	4◇
♣ A Q J 5		♣ K 4		5♣	6◇

Notice how West's bid of the fourth suit enables East to judge that all his high cards are working and that there is no duplication of values in hearts. He is therefore able to accept West's slam try without further ado.

RESPONDER GIVES JUMP PREFERENCE

1♥ 2♣
2♦ 3♥

Nothing new to report here. The responder is showing the high-card values for an immediate raise to 3♥, but with only three-card trump support; the opener should be in a good position to judge the correct final contract.

There are just two important points to be made in connection with this situation. The first is that, after the opener has received jump preference, belated support for the responder's suit is forcing.

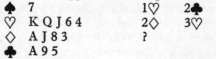

♠	7	1♥	2♣
♥	K Q J 6 4	2♦	3♥
♦	A J 8 3	?	
♣	A 9 5		

Bid 4♣. You are going to game after receiving jump preference, and it can cost nothing to make a mild slam try by completing an accurate description of your hand. The knowledge that you have extra values and that you are extremely short in spades may enable partner to co-operate in the search for a slam if all his high cards appear to be pulling their full weight.

The second point concerns a bid of the fourth suit by the opener.

(A) 1♥	2♣		(B) 1♥	1♠
2♦	3♥		2♦	3♥
3♠			4♣	

If the opener bids the fourth suit at the three level, as in Sequence A, he is probably suggesting a no trump contract and asking for a little assistance in the suit in question.

♠	A 7 3	1♥	2♣
♥	K Q 5 4	2♦	3♥
♦	K Q 9 8	?	
♣	10 7		

Bid 3♠. You are just about strong enough to accept partner's game try, and 3♠ suggests that 3NT will be the correct contract if partner is able to offer a little help in the spade department. Furthermore, if partner's holding in spades is something like Q–x, it will be important for him to play the no trump contract; 3♠ gives him the opportunity.

If the fourth suit is bid at the four level, as in Sequence B above, it can no longer be an attempt to find the correct game contract. The only sensible interpretation of the bid is that the opener is showing the ace of clubs and making a mild slam try.

♠	7	1♥	1♠
♥	A Q J 7 2	2♦	3♥
♦	K Q J 5	?	
♣	A 10 4		

Bid 4♣. If partner holds the right cards, there could be a slam opposite this very powerful hand. 4♣ indicates your slam interest, shows the ace of clubs, and invites partner to cue bid if he has a suitable holding.

RESPONDER GIVES BELATED SUPPORT

1♡	2♢
3♢	3♡

As we saw in an earlier section of the book, there are a limited number of auctions of this kind where belated support by the responder constitutes nothing more than a game try, showing three-card trump support and the high-card values for an immediate raise to three. Since the opener's hand is also limited by his earlier simple raise, he will not be tempted to take any dramatic action at this point: he simply has to choose between signing off, by passing or reverting to four of partner's minor, and pushing on to game, by raising to four in his own suit, by introducing a new suit at the three level as a probe for no trumps, or, more rarely, by having a shot at 3NT himself. All quite straightforward.

RESPONDER RAISES THE SECOND SUIT

(A)	1♠	2♣	(B)	1♡	1♠
	2♡	3♡		2♢	3♢

Once again the opener's third bid is merely a question of judgement. The responder promises four-card trump support, and suggests the same values as if he had raised an opening bid to three. However, since the responder will always be reluctant to pass a change of suit rebid, the opener should bear in mind that his partner might have strained a little to find the second-round raise, particularly in a major suit.

♠	10 4		
♡	K J 7 5	1♠	2♣
♢	8 6 4	2♡	?
♣	A J 8 3		

Bid 3♡, but only just. While you would be content with a gentle raise to two if partner had opened 1♡, you should give partner one last chance by scraping up a raise to three in this situation. The opener will realise that you might merely be doing him a favour by bidding again over 2♡.

If the opener can visualise game after his second suit has been raised, he can move forward in exactly the same way as if he had received jump preference; the points made in that connection above apply with equal force.

RESPONDER MAKES A CONSTRUCTIVE REBID IN HIS ORIGINAL SUIT

(A) 1♡ 2◇   (B) 1♡ 1♠   (C) 1♡ 1♠
    2♡ 3◇   2♠ 3♠   2◇ 3♠

As we found in the previous section, all these rebids by the responder are constructive, with Sequence A being the least encouraging and Sequence C the most encouraging of the three. Once again the opener has to judge whether or not to push on to game. If the responder's suit is a major, the choice is almost always between passing and raising to four. If the responder's rebid is three of a minor, however, the opener should bear in mind the possibility of playing in 3NT if he has extra values.

♠	A J 10	1♡	2◇
♡	A Q 9 7 5	2♡	3◇
◇	K 7	?	
♣	8 6 4		

Bid 3♠. This can only be a no trump probe in this situation, showing a good holding in spades and suggesting that the responder should convert to 3NT if he has a guard in clubs, the unbid suit.
Similarly:

♠	Q 5	1♡	2♣
♡	A K 10 9 4	2◇	3♣
◇	K J 5 2	?	
♣	Q 8		

Bid 3♠, the fourth suit. Partner's 3♣ bid is constructive in this sequence, and you are strong enough to try for game. 3♠ asks partner to bid 3NT if he can provide a little assistance in spades; if he is forced to sign off in 4♣, you can raise to game if you are in urgent need of points.

———————— ♠ ♠ ————————

25. RESPONDER SHOWS STRENGTH

Taking our consideration of the third round of the auction one stage further, we now consider the various situations which arise when the responder shows strength by making a forcing bid at his second turn.

RESPONDER BIDS THE FOURTH SUIT

The situation where the responder bids the fourth suit on the second round has been analysed exhaustively in the previous section of the book;

the opener's replies were also considered in some detail. Briefly, a bid of the fourth suit asks the opener to describe and limit his hand as best he can. His first duty is to bid no trumps if he has an independent guard in the fourth suit, remembering to jump to game if necessary in order to show extra values. If he is unable to bid no trumps, the opener can show belated support for the responder's first suit or rebid one of his own suits, once again remembering to jump if he has additional values and can visualise game after his partner's strength-showing rebid.

RESPONDER BIDS A THIRD SUIT IN A FORCING SITUATION

1◇   1♠
2♣   3♣

This type of sequence, which is a frequent source of disaster at the table, has already been discussed at length. As you will no doubt remember, the conclusion was that the 3♣ bid at this point should be a no trump probe, asking the opener to convert to 3NT if he has a suitable holding in hearts.

If the opener is unable to oblige with 3NT, he must remember that the sequence under discussion suggests that the responder only has a four-card spade suit. For the opener to jump to game in spades therefore suggests that he has four-card support.

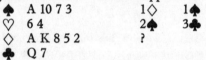

♠ A 10 7 3   1◇   1♠
♡ 6 4   2♣   3♣
◇ A K 8 5 2   ?
♣ Q 7

Bid 4♠. The responder must have good high-card strength to invite game in 3NT, and your four-card trump support and excellent top cards make this hand well worth a jump to game.

If the opener has raised his partner's suit on three-card support, he must consider his next move carefully if he is unable to bid 3NT. He may be able to offer an alternative contract by rebidding 3◇ on a five-card suit, or he may prefer to use a fourth suit bid of 3♡ if he has the values for game but needs to receive a little assistance in hearts before he can plump for 3NT. If neither of these two responses is practical, the opener will just have to settle for a part-score in the probable 4–3 spade fit. But there are also occasional hands on which it is correct to jump to 4♠ on three-card support.

♠ K 10 7   1◇   1♠
♡ 6 2   2♣   3♣
◇ A K J 8 3   ?
♣ K 10 4

Bid 4♠. Now that the responder has shown strength in clubs, this hand seems to be an excellent fit. Since partner will be able to ruff hearts with the three-card trump holding, the hand should play quite well in a reasonable 4–3 fit.

The other situations in which the responder makes a forcing bid in a third suit at his second turn occur when there is no known trump fit.

	(A) 1♣	1♡		(B) 1♠	2◇
	2♣	2♠		2♠	3♣

These sequences are both completely forcing, the first because the responder has reversed at the two level and the second because he has introduced a new suit at the three level. The responder's rebid is assumed to be natural, but it may occasionally be a no trump probe on a three-card suit – particularly in Sequence A where the opener's 2♣ rebid has already denied a four-card spade suit.

If the opener is unable to support his partner's second suit, he is invited to bid no trumps if he has a suitable holding in the unbid suit, remembering if necessary to jump to 3NT if he has extra values.

♠	10 5	1♣	1♡
♡	Q 7	2♣	2♠
◇	A J 9 5	?	
♣	A K J 7 2		

Bid 3NT. Partner's bid of 2♠ must guarantee at least the values for 2NT. Since you have 15 points and a good holding in diamonds, therefore, you must jump to 3NT; a simple bid of 2NT at this point would not be forcing.

Alternatively, if the opener has the values for game and an inadequate holding in the unbid suit, he may choose to bid the fourth suit to solicit partner's assistance.

♠	K 7 2	1♣	1♡
♡	J 3	2♣	2♠
◇	A 4	?	
♣	A Q 10 8 7 5		

Bid 3◇, the fourth suit. While you clearly have the values for game opposite the responder's reverse, your holding in diamonds may prove to be inadequate for the purposes of 3NT. 3◇ asks partner for a little assistance in the suit; if he is unable to oblige, you may have to settle for game in one of his suits, probably in 4♡.

RESPONDER JUMPS IN A THIRD SUIT

This situation was considered in detail in an earlier chapter. If he could have made a forcing bid in the same suit one level lower, a jump bid in a third suit by the responder is a semi-conventional bid, agreeing the opener's suit and showing a feature. The final denomination is therefore assured; the opener merely has to decide whether or not to accept his partner's invitation and try for a slam.

Other jumps in a third suit are natural and game-forcing.

(A)	1◇	1♠		(B)	1◇	1♠
	1NT	3♡			2◇	3♡

The responder promises five spades by both these sequences. As I was at pains to point out in an earlier chapter, he also promises precisely *four* hearts in Sequence A. Sequence B is not so clear-cut, for the responder could conceivably have two five-card major suits. However, the opener must not assume at this stage that there is more than a four-card heart suit opposite, and he should react in the same way in both these situations: raising to 4♡ with four-card support, bidding 3NT with a good holding in clubs, or giving jump preference to 4♠ with three-card support and a suitable hand; if he is unable to adopt any of these courses of action, he may have to give false preference to 3♠ on doubleton support.

♠	Q 7	1◇	1♠
♡	A 8 5	1NT	3♡
◇	A Q 6 5 3	?	
♣	J 6 4		

Bid 3♠. 3NT is out of the question in view of your weak club holding, and the hand will probably not play well in the 4–3 heart fit. The best available action is therefore to give false preference to 3♠; Q–x in adequate support opposite a known five-card suit.

RESPONDER GIVES BELATED SUPPORT

As we saw in an earlier chapter, there are a number of situations in which belated support by the responder is 100% forcing. The most common of these is the following:

1♡	1♠
2NT	3♡

The responder's 3♡ bid in this auction shows three-card support, and its primary meaning is to offer the opener a choice of game contract. Generally speaking, the opener will raise to 4♡ if he has a five-card suit and settle for 3NT if he only has four hearts. However, there are two other possible courses of action available to him:

(a) A bid of 3♠ in the above sequence would also be belated support, denying five hearts and showing three-card spade support just in case the responder has a five-card suit.

(b) A bid of 4♣ or 4◇ in the above sequence would show a five-card heart suit and a completely maximum hand on which a slam could be a distinct possibility if the responder also has extra values.

♠	K 2	1♡	1♠
♡	A Q J 6 4	2NT	3♡
◇	Q 9 3	?	
♣	A Q 8		

Bid 4♣, 'on the way' to 4♡. This advance cue bid can cost nothing; it shows a maximum hand containing five hearts and the ace of clubs, and it may encourage partner to co-operate in the search for a slam if he also has a little to spare.

26. RESPONDER MAKES A SLAM TRY

There are a number of sequences in which the responder's second bid is an obvious slam try. The following are among the most common of these:

(a) Where the opener rebids in no trumps and the responder makes a quantitative raise to 4NT.

(b) Where the responder effects a delayed game raise sequence: for example, 1♡–1♠–2♠–4♡ or 1♡–1♠–2♡–4◇.

(c) Where the responder makes a forcing jump to four of a minor; for example:

(A)	1◇	1♠	(B)	1♠	2♣
	1NT	4◇		2◇	4◇
(C)	1♠	2♣	(D)	1♠	2♣
	2NT	4♣		2♡	4♣

(d) Where the responder makes an obvious cue bid at his second turn. This may take the form of an ace-showing bid, as in the sequence 1♠–2♣–2◇–3♡, or of a void-showing bid, as in the following sequences:

| (A) | 1◇ | 2♣ | (B) | 1♣ | 1♡ | (C) | 1◇ | 1♡ |
| | 2◇ | 4♡ | | 2♡ | 3♠ | | 1♠ | 4♣ |

There would be little point in considering the development of auctions of this type in any greater detail. In each case, the responder has shown the nature of his holding fairly exactly. Any subsequent move must come from the opener, who will have to use his judgement as to whether his hand warrants co-operation in the quest for a slam; the factors he will take into account are the nature of his top controls, the extent to which the two hands appear to fit, the quality of his trump suit, the strength of his hand in relation to the previous bidding, and so on.

Instead of attempting a further analysis of specific bidding sequences, therefore, it is proposed in this chapter to take a critical look at the principal conventional aids to slam bidding. The assumption is that either the opener or the responder judges from the auction to date that there are distinct chances of a slam. If this is the case, he will often need some kind of mechanism with which to check that there are sufficient controls between the two hands: twelve absolutely certain tricks will be of little use to the declarer if the opponents are able to cash the first two tricks.

CUE BIDDING

The observant reader will no doubt have noticed that the vast majority of successful slam sequences presented in the earlier pages of this book include a cue bid or two at the vital stage of the auction. This is quite deliberate. Although the various 4NT control-asking conventions are regrettably just as popular as ever, my view is that cue bidding is an infinitely more valuable aid to good slam bidding.

Let us consider once again one or two hands which have already made an appearance in previous chapters.

♠	K J 8 5 2		
♡	J 9 4	1♣	1♠
◇	A 7 5	4♣	?
♣	Q 3		

As you will remember, the opener's 4♣ rebid in this sequence is semi-conventional, agreeing spades and showing a good six-card club suit. You are clearly interested in a slam, particularly now that your queen of clubs is destined to fulfil a significant role, and the important task is to check on the top controls between the two hands. Inexperienced players might blast into some kind of 4NT convention at this point, but a little foresight will reveal that this cannot possibly be the correct answer: while it would be extremely gratifying to find partner with three aces, what do you intend to do if he shows two? Are you going to have a shot at 6♣ and watch the opponents cash two top hearts? Or are you going to linger in 5♠ and find when dummy goes down that partner has second-round control of hearts? There is clearly no satisfactory answer to these rhetorical questions, and the solution is to avoid the problem altogether by cue bidding 4◇ over 4♣; to consult partner in this way and to draw his attention to your weakness in hearts is the only accurate way of bidding the hand.

Similarly:

♠	K 3		
♡	J 9 5	1♠	2♣
◇	A Q 4	4♣	?
♣	Q 10 8 7 2		

Partner's raise to 4♣ is forcing, showing four-card trump support and interest in greater things. Your high cards are clearly good enough to justify your co-operation in the search for a slam, but once again an uncouth 4NT enquiry would be an extremely ill-judged bid: if partner replies 5♡ to show two aces, you would be committed to playing in

6♣, or conceivably in 5NT, with no means of knowing whether or not the opponents can cash the first two heart tricks. Once again cue bidding provides the answer. Bid 4◇ over 4♣. If partner can oblige with a return cue bid of 4♡, you can show your key card in spades by bidding 4♠, and leave the rest to partner. And if the opener is unable to bid 4♡ over 4◇, you will just have to settle for 5♣; this will tell partner that, although you entertained great hopes of a slam, the absence of a heart control in your hand has precluded any further action; he should then be able to decide what to do.

This last example raises a point of considerable importance in the field of cue bidding: it concerns the occasions on which it is both prudent and advisable to cue bid a second-round control, that is, a king or a singleton. This is an aspect of slam bidding which has been developed significantly in recent years. Briefly, it is possible to cue bid a second-round control in the following situations:

(a) Where the partnership has already cue bid first-round control of the suit.

♠	K 9 6 3	1♡	2♠
♡	K J 10 7 5	3♠	4♣
◇	A Q 4	4◇	4♡
♣	3	?	

Bid 5♣. Partner has already shown the ace of clubs by his 4♣ cue bid. Since the bidding to date suggests that a small slam is almost certain and that a grand slam is a distinct possibility, it can cost nothing to continue to describe your hand by showing your second-round control in clubs.

(b) Where you have already denied first-round control of the suit by a previous cue bid.

♠	10 4	1♣	1♡
♡	K 10 7 4 2	3♡	4◇
◇	A Q 3	4♠	?
♣	K 4 2		

Bid 5♣. Since it is normal to cue bid first-round controls in ascending order, your 4◇ bid denied the ace of clubs. Now that partner has co-operated in the search for a slam by cue bidding the ace of spades, there can be no ambiguity if you take the opportunity to show the king of clubs, which is a vital card in this auction.

(c) Where you are anxious to show strength by cue bidding but have no first-round control to show; this will normally occur when you are the weaker hand in the auction.

♠	7 3		
♡	A K J 8 5	1♣	1♡
◇	K 9 5 2	4♡	?
♣	6 4		

Bid 5◇. You are clearly strong enough to investigate slam possibilities here, and there is no better way of showing your interest than by cue bidding your feature in diamonds. It is perfectly true that this may cause your partner to place you with the ace of diamonds. However, this is most unlikely to prove fatal: since your trump holding is so good, partner will not be able to jump too high without consulting you further.

(d) Where the earlier auction makes it clear that your second-round control will be of vital interest to partner and will simplify the subsequent bidding.

♠ K 8 6		
♡ K J 7 5 2	1◇	2♡
◇ A K	4♡	?
♣ Q 7 4		

Bid 4♠. Partner's jump raise in the forcing situation shows exceptionally good trump support and a limited hand; he is therefore likely to have A–Q–x–x of hearts and Q–J–x–x–x of diamonds. The critical situation arises where he has a 2–4–5–2 distribution with one of the black aces. If this is the ace of spades, he will be unable to proceed over 4♠; since he cannot have the king of clubs as well as the ace of spades for his limited raise to 4♡, this is just what you want. And if his ace is the ace of clubs, he will be able to bid it over 4♠ and enable you to jump to 6♡ with complete confidence. Notice how the slightly unusual 4♠ cue bid is markedly superior to a 5◇ cue bid or a 4NT enquiry: the former will embarrass partner if he has the ace of clubs and two spade losers, and the latter will embarrass you if he has the ace of spades and two club losers. Notice, too, that while partner may think that your 4♠ bid shows the ace, this cannot possibly mislead him fatally: your honour holdings in hearts and diamonds ensure that he will never be able to jump too high.

BLACKWOOD 4NT

The Blackwood 4NT enquiry for aces is one of the most popular conventions of all. Regrettably, it is probably *too* popular. As was hinted in the previous paragraph, many of the hands on which the inexperienced player swings into action with a 4NT bid can be developed far more accurately by means of a chain of cue bids. Generally speaking, Blackwood should be employed to check on aces only when you have established by other means that a slam is a distinct possibility. In other words, Blackwood should only be used to keep you out of bad slams – not to get you into good ones.

Having said all this, it must be admitted that there are certain hands on which Blackwood is the ideal tool.

♠ A
♡ K Q 7 5 2   1♡   4♡
◇ K Q J 7 4   ?
♣ K 5

Bid 4NT, Blackwood. It looks as if you can underwrite a slam of some kind after partner's jump to game; a check on aces should tell you exactly how high to go.

Everyone knows the simple replies to the Blackwood 4NT and 5NT enquiries. However, there are one or two important points which may have escaped the notice of even the most experienced Blackwoodsman.

(a) *The 5NT Rebid.* If the 4NT bidder subsequently bids 5NT, he is not only asking for kings: he is also announcing that the partnership holds all the aces, and this information may be all the responder wants to know.

♠ 7   1◇   1♡
♡ K Q 6 4   4♡   4NT
◇ K Q 9 8 6 5   5◇   5NT
♣ A 3   ?

Bid 7♡. Now that partner's 5NT bid has confirmed that your side holds all the aces, your excellent diamond suit and vital trump honours make the grand slam a near-certainty. Moreover, you are in a much better position to bid it than partner will ever be.

(b) *The Sign-Off in 5NT.* If the response to 4NT is so disappointing that the Blackwood bidder is anxious to sign off in no trumps below the slam level, it is generally agreed that he should introduce an unbid suit at the five level; this asks partner to convert to 5NT. Thus, in the following sequence:

1♣   2♡
3♣   4♣
4NT   5◇
5♠

the implication is that the opener regrets that he ever succumbed to the temptation of Blackwood; 5♠ asks the responder to convert to 5NT, which the opener will presumably pass, hoping that he can make exactly eleven tricks.

Now, let us take this one stage further. Suppose that the opener does not pass his partner's compulsory conversion to 5NT:

1♣   2♡
3♣   4♣
4NT   5◇
5♠   5NT
6♣

Regular partnerships might like to allot a specific meaning to this type of sequence, wherein the Blackwood bidder elects to bid six of the agreed suit after first suggesting that his partner should sign off in 5NT. One extremely valuable use for this sequence is to ask the responder to bid seven of the agreed suit if he has the queen of trumps. Consider the following hands:

WEST	EAST	WEST	EAST
♠ 7	♠ A 4	2♡*	3♣
♡ A K Q 10 2	♡ 9 5	3◇	4◇
◇ A K 6 4 3	◇ Q 8 7 2	4NT	5♡
♣ K 4	♣ A 10 7 5 3	5♠	5NT
		6◇	7◇

*Acol Two.

Once West finds two aces and four diamonds in the opposite hand, he is perfectly justified in thinking in terms of a grand slam. However, 7◇ will only be a good contract if partner has the queen of diamonds, and normal bidding methods make it difficult to locate the vital queen with any degree of certainty. The suggested 4NT–5♡–5♠–5NT–6◇ sequence specifically asks the responder to bid the grand slam if he has the queen of trumps, and East is happy to oblige.

(c) *The Cue Bid after 4NT.* As we saw in paragraph (b) above, a bid of a new suit at the five level after the initial response to Blackwood is normally used as a braking mechanism. We must now move on to consider a bid of a new suit one level higher.

1♡   4♡
4NT   5♡
6♣

The opener's 6♣ bid in this auction is a grand slam try. The point to decide is whether it is a kind of asking bid, seeking second-round control in clubs, or whether it is an invitation for partner to cue bid his second-round controls in ascending order. Either method is perfectly playable; one of the main purposes of this book is to draw your attention to these little-used sequences, so that you will be able to bring some of them into action with complete confidence at the table.

(d) *Key-Card Blackwood.* An alternative form of Blackwood which was first suggested more than thirty years ago has been gaining popularity in recent years. This is generally known as Key-Card or Five Ace Blackwood, and the principle is that the king of trumps is included as an additional ace in the responses to 4NT, which are as follows:

5♣	0 or 4 'aces'
5◇	1 or 5 'aces'
5♡	2 'aces'
5♠	3 'aces'

This method is almost certainly more efficient than ordinary Black-wood, its principal advantage being that it enables a player to use Blackwood even when he has a weakish trump suit. For example:

WEST	EAST	WEST	EAST
♠ 7	♠ A K Q 9 4	1♡	2♠
♡ A Q 8 6 4	♡ J 7 5 3	3◇	3♡
◇ K Q J 7	◇ A 2	4NT	5♡
♣ K Q 4	♣ 8 5	No	

Once East's 5♡ response reveals that two key cards are missing, West is perfectly content to settle in game. Without the aid of Key-Card Blackwood, East-West would find it much more difficult to stay out of the indifferent heart slam.

(e) *Roman Blackwood.* Another variation of the Blackwood convention which has attracted rather more attention than it really deserves is Roman Blackwood. This method attempts to identify the actual aces held by means of the following responses to 4NT:

5♣	0 or 3 aces
5◇	1 or 4 aces
5♡	2 aces of the same colour
5♠	2 aces of the same rank
5NT	2 other aces.

A more economical alternative method is to use 5♡ to show 2 aces of the same colour or rank (♣◇, ♣♠, ◇♡, ♡♠) and 5♠ to show 2 other aces (♣♡, ◇♠).

While the greater definition of these responses is superficially attractive, I regret to report that Roman Blackwood is not as accurate as its supporters like to believe. Consider the following points:

(i) While it is intellectually satisfying to be able to identify from time to time which two aces partner has, it is most unlikely that this know-ledge will be of any real use to you. It might at first sight seem as if Roman Blackwood enables you to ask for precise aces when you have a void, but this is not so. Suppose, for example, that you bid 4NT on a slam-going hand including the ace of hearts and a void in spades: if partner replies 5♠, showing two aces of the same rank, all will be well; but what if he bids 5◇, showing one ace? You now have no way of telling whether he has a useful ace or the wasted ace of spades, and the conclusion must be that a hand containing a void and one ace must be developed by cue bidding and not be resorting to any kind of 4NT convention. The fact of the matter is that knowing which two aces partner holds will only help you in one extremely rare situation: when there is one ace missing and you are able to judge to play the hand in 6NT rather than in six of a suit.

(ii) In order to identify the precise ace holding, it is necessary to make the two-ace responses to 4NT range from 5♡ to 5NT. This means that you will no longer be able to bid 4NT when you need *three* aces in partner's hand, in case he has only two aces and is forced to make a response higher than five of the agreed trump suit.

(iii) Similarly, the need to make the 5♣ and 5◇ responses show either of two possible ace holdings increases the danger that the 4NT bidder will misunderstand the reply. This is clearly only a small point, but it helps to make the overall case against Roman Blackwood almost overwhelming.

CULBERTSON 4/5 NO TRUMP

Although the convention does not figure among my personal favourites, it would be disloyal in a book on Acol not to mention the Culbertson 4/5 No Trump, which has always been the recommended slam convention for Acol players. The important difference between Culbertson and the various forms of Blackwood is that, in addition to asking partner about his controls, the 4NT bid conveys some valuable information about your own hand. Instead of one of the partners being in control and making the final decision, Culbertson 4/5 enables either player to exercise his judgement at the crucial stage.

The conventional requirements for the 4NT bidder are either three aces or two aces and the king of a bid suit. The responses are:

(a) With two aces, or with one ace and the kings of all bid suits, bid 5NT.

(b) With an ace of a bid suit, or with the kings of all bid suits, either bid six of the agreed trump suit or five of a suit which is not the sign-off suit.

(c) With an ace or void in an unbid suit, bid five in that suit.

(d) With neither an ace nor all the bid kings, sign off in five of the lowest genuine suit bid by the partnership.

An important point to make in connection with these responses is that they are always left to the responder's discretion. He is not compelled to show an ace just because he has one; neither is he compelled to sign off because he has no ace. Let us look at just one example of the way in which the responder is free to exercise his judgement.

♠ A 7	1♡	3♣
♡ K J 8 5 2	3◇	3♡
◇ K J 10 3	4♡	4NT*
♣ 9 4	?	*Culbertson.

Bid 5♡. You are not quite strong enough to commit your side to a slam by bidding 5♠ to show the ace. On the other hand, you are a little too good to sign off in 5♣, bearing in mind that you have already limited your hand with your simple raise to 4♡ on the previous round. The solution is to make the encouraging response of 5♡. If partner has the ace of hearts, he will be able to draw the obvious inference that you have the spade control – and therefore a minimum hand.

On hands on which it can be employed, the Culbertson 4/5 is undoubtedly an extremely effective convention: 'an adult weapon, whereas Blackwood is merely a nice toy', as the late S. J. Simon once commented.* My one complaint about the convention is that the opportunities for its use are too rare: the desire to investigate a slam and the requirements for a 4NT bid rarely seem to occur simultaneously. But maybe I am just unlucky.

BYZANTINE BLACKWOOD

My own favourite 4NT convention is Byzantine Blackwood, which has been developed in recent years by a regular team-mate of mine, Jack Marx, and which was first introduced in tournament play by the Sharples twins. Briefly, the idea is that the responses to 4NT should not only show aces; they should also incorporate other key features of the hand.

The responses to 4NT are set out below, assuming that:

A=any ace.
K=king of agreed suit.
Q=queen of agreed suit.
k=the king of a half-key suit; that is, an unsupported suit introduced by the 4NT bidder or, if no such suit exists, a suit bid by the responder to 4NT.

5♣ shows	(a)	No ace
	(b)	A A A
	(c)	A A K
5◇ shows	(a)	A
	(b)	A A A A
	(c)	A A A K
5♡ shows	(a)	A A
	(b)	A KQ
	(c)	A K K
	(d)	A K k
5♠ shows 4 key cards	(a)	A A KQ
	(b)	A K KQ
	(c)	A A K K
	(d)	A A A k
5NT shows 5 key cards	(a)	A A A KQ
	(b)	A A K KQ
	(c)	A A A K K
	(d)	A KQ KQ

* *Design For Bidding*, by S. J. Simon.

(e) A A A A K
(f) A A A A k
(g) A A k (Where the previous bidding shows that 5NT cannot mean 5 key cards)

Just two simple examples, taken from Jack Marx's own summary of the system,* should be enough to show its potential.

WEST	EAST	WEST	EAST
♠ K 9	♠ A Q 8 7 3	1♣	1♠
♡ A 8 3 2	♡ 4	2♡	3◇
◇ 7 4	◇ A K 8 6	3♠	4♣
♣ A K Q 9 8	♣ J 10 4	4♡	4NT
		5NT	7♣

The five key cards shown by the 5NT response can only be ♠K, ♡A and ♣AKQ; East can therefore bid the grand slam with complete confidence.

WEST	EAST	WEST	EAST
♠ 6 5	♠ A K 7	1♡	3♣
♡ K Q 10 8 6	♡ A 7 3 2	3◇	3♡
◇ A K 5 4	◇ Q J	4♣	4NT
♣ K 5	♣ A Q 10 6	5♠	5NT
		6◇	7NT

Following a Byzantine 4NT enquiry, 5NT confirms the joint possession of all the aces and asks partner to show how many more features he holds: a king not previously shown or an overlooked key-suit queen is one feature, and a king-queen ranks as two. Once East has located ♡KQ ◇A and ♣K by the 5♠ response, he can investigate the grand slam by asking for any other features; the one feature shown by the 6◇ response can only be ◇K.

THE GRAND SLAM FORCE

Whatever kind of 4NT convention you favour, a direct jump to 5NT is generally agreed to be a grand slam try, enquiring about the quality of partner's trump suit. This convention is sometimes known as 'Josephine', its invention being attributed to Josephine Culbertson; in fact, history shows that the entire credit belongs to her husband, Ely Culbertson.

In its original form, a free bid of 5NT asks partner to bid seven if he has two of the top three honours in the agreed trump suit; otherwise he signs off in six. Many extensions to the Grand Slam Force have since been proposed, and it is certainly desirable to make good use of any idle responses. One attractive structure of six-level responses to

* *Byzantine Blackwood*, by Jack Marx; *Bridge Magazine*, April 1972.

5NT is as follows, the proviso being that the response must never be higher than six of the agreed suit.

6♣ — Neither ace nor king of the agreed suit. (And, if clubs are trumps, any other holding not including two of the top three honours).

6◇ — Either the ace or king of the agreed suit.

6♡ — Either the ace or king of the agreed suit plus one more trump than partner could reasonably expect from the previous bidding.

6♠ — Q–x–x–x–x of the agreed suit, which can clearly only be spades.

One simple example of this system in action.

WEST	EAST	WEST	EAST
♠ A 10 7 6 4	♠ K 8 5 3 2	1♣	1♠
♡ 9 5	♡ A J 7	4◇	4♡
◇ —	◇ J 6 4	5NT	6♡
♣ A K Q 7 5 3	♣ J 2	7♠	

West's double jump to 4◇ agrees spades and shows a void in diamonds. When East is able to cue bid the ace of hearts, West can visualise a grand slam if his partner's trumps are adequate for the purpose. He therefore asks specifically about spades by jumping to 5NT, and he is delighted to learn that, while East cannot oblige with both the king and queen, he has either the ace or king and one more trump than he has already promised. That will do nicely, thank you.

THE BARON GRAND SLAM TRY

As we have just seen, the revised responses to the 5NT Grand Slam Force make the bid both more flexible and more practical. Another method of expressing interest in the quality of partner's trump suit for similar purposes is the Baron Grand Slam Try, whereby a bid of six in the suit immediately below the agreed trump suit asks him to bid seven if his trumps are reasonably good in relation to the bidding so far.

WEST	EAST	WEST	EAST
♠ A K 9 7 5 3	♠ Q 8 4	2♣	2◇
♡ A	♡ 10 7 5 3	2♠	3♠
◇ K Q 4	◇ A 8 6 3	4♣	4◇
♣ A K Q	♣ 7 5	4NT	5◇
		6♡	7♠

West's jump to 6♡, which cannot possibly be natural in view of the preceding bidding, asks partner to bid seven of the agreed suit if his trumps are relatively good. Since Q–x–x is more than the opener could reasonably expect to find in the weak hand, East should have no qualms about bidding the grand slam.

FIVE OF A MAJOR

One form of slam try which has acquired a semi-conventional meaning in recent years is the unforced bid of five of a major, and it is time that this valuable aid to better slam bidding was officially incorporated into the Acol framework. The meaning of the five level bid varies slightly depending on the nature of the previous bidding.

(a) *If the partnership has bid three suits*, to bid five of an agreed major suit shows two top losers in the unbid suit. If partner also has two top losers, he simply passes; if he has a control in the crucial suit, he can proceed as follows:

(i) With a losing singleton, he bids six in the agreed suit.

(ii) With first-round control, he makes a cue bid in the unbid suit.

(iii) With the guarded king, he bids six in the agreed suit if he is scheduled to play the hand; if he would not be the declarer in the agreed major, he bids 5NT to give partner a choice of contract.

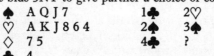

Bid 5♠. Now that partner has been able to cue bid the ace of clubs, the future of this hand depends entirely on his holding in diamonds. If he has two top losers, he will pass 5♠ and that will be quite high enough; if he has the king of diamonds or a losing singleton, he will push on to 6♠; and if he has the ace of diamonds, he will cue bid 6◇ over 5♠ and you will be able to think in terms of the grand slam.

(b) *If the opponents have overcalled*, to bid five of an agreed major suit shows two losers in the enemy suit; if partner has a control in the crucial suit, he can proceed in the same way as in paragraph (a) above.

(c) *If there are two or more unbid suits*, the meaning of five of a major depends on who bids it. Five of a major by the stronger hand shows all the missing first-round controls and asks partner to go on if he has good trumps.

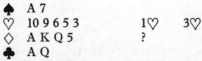

Bid 5♡. There is little point in initiating a cue bidding sequence when you have all the first-round controls. All you really need from partner is a good trump suit, and the jump to 5♡ will convey this precise message.

Conversely, five of a major by the weaker hand denies the missing
first-round controls and shows strong trumps.

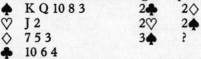

♠ K Q 10 8 3	2♣	2◇
♡ J 2	2♡	2♠
◇ 7 5 3	3♠	?
♣ 10 6 4		

Bid 5♠. While you have no side-suit features to cue bid, your trump
suit is so good that you must express an interest in a slam; 5♠, showing
good trumps and very little else, describes the hand admirably.

INDEX TO BIDDING SEQUENCES

Precision Bidding in Acol claims to analyse in detail almost every sequence of bidding which is likely to occur in an uncontested auction. In order that the book can be used as a reference work to settle problems and queries, the following index has been compiled to show where each sequence is discussed in the preceding text. The order in which the sequences are listed below follows the natural order of the bids; that is to say, sequences commencing with 1♣ appear before those commencing with 1♡, and sequences commencing 1♣–1◇–1♡ are listed before those commencing 1♣–1◇–1NT.

Sequences which would have a similar meaning if one or more of the bids contained therein were to be made in a different suit are included in the index under the lowest-ranking combination of suits. For example, a jump rebid of 2NT by the opener has the same meaning no matter which one of the six possible combinations of suit opening bid and suit response has preceded it; the sequence will therefore be referred to below under 1♣–1◇–2NT rather than under, say, 1◇–1♠–2NT. On the other hand, the exact meaning of jump preference to the opener's first suit after a 1NT rebid depends on whether it is made in a minor suit or in a major suit; the two references below will therefore be found under 1♣–1◇–1NT–3♣ and 1♡–1♠–1NT–3♡.

Bids marked * have a generally-accepted conventional meaning. OP1, RE1, OP2, RE2 refer to the opening bid, the first response, the opener's rebid, the responder's rebid, and so on.

ALPHABETICAL INDEX